Japan

PAST AND PRESENT

BY

EDWIN O. REISCHAUER

Foreword by Sir George Sansom

THIRD EDITION, REVISED

1964

ALFRED A. KNOPF · *NEW YORK*

L. C. CATALOG CARD NUMBER: 64-12896

THIS IS A BORZOI BOOK,
PUBLISHED BY ALFRED A. KNOPF, INC.

ORIGINALLY PUBLISHED *in 1946. Reprinted three times.*
SECOND EDITION, *Revised and Enlarged, January, 1953. Reprinted seven times.*
THIRD EDITION, *Revised, February, 1964.*
Reprinted, October 1964.

To *my brother, Bob*

FOREWORD

Few countries have been more copiously described than Japan, and perhaps few have been less thoroughly understood. In the last century there were a number of works dealing with the picturesque or the exotic aspects of that country, most of which, though sometimes a trifle deceptive, were passable books of travel. During the same period there were written a few important studies of Japanese political and social history which are still standard works, though they are used only by a few specialists. But it is a remarkable fact, which I think will be accepted by any teacher who has been responsible for instruction in schools or colleges, that before the outbreak of the war in the Far East there was no single short book which gave a lucid and tolerably complete picture of Japan's early history and her development in modern times. There were plenty of learned treatises on this or that, but nothing to give the average educated reader what he needed.

After the outbreak of war, there appeared in profusion a flood, or at least a considerable stream, of books about Japan, chiefly of topical interest. Some of these were interesting and useful. Others, however, were of a different type. Understandably, but regrettably, they belonged to that class of historical work, all too common in the last few decades, of which the purpose is not to discover or expound truth but to promote one of those perversions of systematic thought which are known by the suitably ill-sounding name of 'ideologies.' Now that the war is over, the average reader has a right to expect something more rational, more readable and more reliable.

I think that Dr. Reischauer's book fulfils these requirements. He has excellent qualifications for his task — familiarity with the country he describes, a first-class linguistic equipment, a good training as an historian, and most important of all an approach to his subject which is neither prejudiced nor sentimental. He narrates the leading facts of Japanese history from early times, with just and interesting comment. He explains easily and competently the evolution of modern Japan to the conditions described in his concluding chapters. I can truthfully say that I do not know of any short book on Japanese history which gives so much useful information in so brief and simple a form.

G. B. SANSOM

PREFACE

During the war and early postwar period I spent four years in Washington, at which time I forgot much of the detailed information about Japanese history I had once known, but to my surprise I discovered that the fading of unessential detail had helped to clarify for me the main outlines of Japanese history as a whole. On two or three occasions while in Washington, I was requested to give four or five hours of lectures covering the whole historical development of Japan. These requests seemed unreasonable to one accustomed to the more leisurely pace of university lectures, but again to my surprise I found that a meaningful account of this vastly complex story could be made in a few hours' time, if confined to essentials and presented in general and broadly interpretive terms. This experience suggested the possibility of a similar presentation of Japanese history in print. The result was the original edition of this book, which I wrote for the most part during the autumn of 1945 while still in Washington.

Since then much has happened in Japan which is worth adding and which also affects the interpretation of preceding decades. In the second revised edition of 1953 I made only an occasional emendation of the account of the earlier history of Japan, but I expanded the story of the 1920's and 1930's and added a long section covering the first seven postwar years. I also appended a chronological table of the major events in Japanese history, as a means of providing the reader with the most important names and dates in easily accessible form, without burdening the text with names and incidents not necessary to an understanding of the story as a whole.

The chief addition I made in the portion of the text treating the prewar period was to include an analysis of Japanese politics in terms of the power groups within Japanese society during the 1920's and 1930's. My principal change in interpretation was to stress those forces *opposed* to the growth of democracy rather than the democratic tendencies themselves. I did this not so much because of a change of my own views as because of the need to adjust the argument to the reader. At the time I drafted the original manuscript there was a marked tendency among Americans, and perhaps others as well, to overlook the spontaneous growth of democracy in prewar Japan, whereas at the time I first revised the text many people seemed instead to overestimate its strength.

The 1953 revision took the postwar history of Japan only through the occupation period. Since then more than a decade has elapsed, and Japan today is a very different country from what it was when the American occupation ended. Thus, the book as revised at that time no longer lived up to the latter part of its title.

Another revision, therefore, seemed in order. While it could be argued that it is diplomatically inappropriate for me, in my present position as Ambassador of the United States to Japan, to write on recent Japanese history, and particularly on the years I have been in this post, it has seemed to me that, since this book is still widely read by persons seeking to learn about Japan, there would be even less scholarly propriety in my leaving it with such a misleading description of the "present." Consequently, I have taken advantage of a few days of vacation from my duties in Tokyo to make the changes embodied in this revision.

With the exception of this Preface and the Table of Contents, I have made no change whatsoever before page 211. The remainder of Chapter XIII, "Occupation," is a slight rewriting and condensation of the rest of that chapter together with certain sections taken from the original Chapter XIV, "The New Japan." The present Chapter XIV is almost entirely new. The Chronology has been slightly emended from 1945 on and is entirely new after late 1952. The Bibliographical Note has been redone throughout.

In the first edition, under the heading of Acknowledgments, I expressed my great indebtedness and thanks to Sir George Sansom, Professor Serge Elisséeff, Professor Hugh Borton, Professor Edward A. Kracke, Professor Richard McKinnon, Dr. and Mrs. G. H. Danton, and to my sister-in-law, Jean Reischauer for preparing the maps. In the second revised edition I added my thanks to Mrs. Susan Guttman, Dr. Allan B. Cole, Dr. Toshio Tsukahira, Dr. Howard Hibbett, and Miss Tamako Niwa for their many extremely helpful and valuable suggestions. I should like to take this opportunity to express my appreciation for help on this third revised edition to Miss Marie Comeau and Dr. H. Peter Ch'en. The latter, who has been in a better position than I during the last few years to take note of the flood of good books appearing on Japan, has given me great assistance in the compilation of the Bibliographical Note and has been kind enough to check the accuracy of some of my statements and give me valuable advice on correcting them.

EDWIN O. REISCHAUER

Belmont, Massachusetts

CONTENTS

LIST OF MAPS

Japan
Past and Present

Chapter I

GEOGRAPHIC BACKGROUND

In the islands of Japan nature fashioned a favored spot where civilization could prosper and a people could develop into a strong and great nation. A happy combination of temperate climate, plentiful rainfall, fairly fertile soil, and reasonable proximity to other great homes of civilized man predestined the ultimate rise of the inhabitants of these islands to a place among the leading peoples of the world.

The four main islands of Japan, strung out in a great arc along the coast of East Asia, cover the same spread of latitude and the same general range of climate as the east coast of the United States. The northern island of Hokkaido parallels New England; the heart of the country from Tokyo west to the Inland Sea corresponds to North Carolina; and the southern island of Kyushu parallels Georgia.

Americans have often tended to overemphasize the smallness of Japan, contrasting it with the vast stretches of our own country, or to other geographic giants like Russia and China. A more reasonable comparison would be with the countries of western Europe. Japan is smaller than France or pre-war Germany but slightly

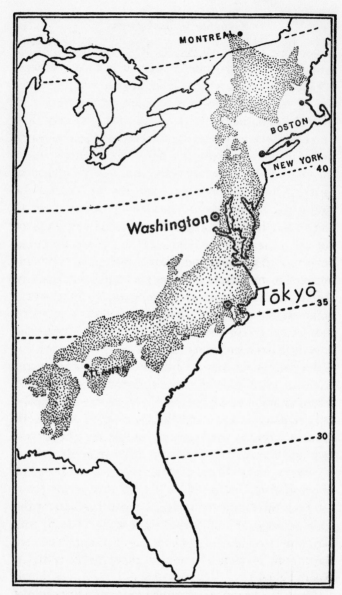

JAPAN SUPERIMPOSED AT THE SAME LATITUDE
ON THE EAST COAST OF THE UNITED STATES

larger than the British Isles or Italy, the homes of the two greatest empires our Western world has ever seen.

Like Italy, Japan is a mountainous country. Throughout all four of the main islands are great stretches of towering mountains and jumbled hills. The combination of rugged coast line and precipitous mountainsides makes of the whole country one of the beauty spots of the world, but it leaves little land for the Japanese farmer, who finds only about twenty per cent of the land surface of his islands level enough for cultivation.

The mountains of Japan have pushed the Japanese out upon the seas, making them the greatest seafaring people of Asia. Sea lanes have been great highways within Japan; sea routes have beckoned the Japanese abroad; and the cold and warm sea currents which bathe the shores of the islands have always provided rich fishing grounds for the hardy Japanese fishermen.

Nature has been rather niggardly with Japan in mineral resources. Coal the islands have in some abundance, but few other sub-soil riches in significant quantities. The mountains of Japan, together with the heavy rainfall, have, however, given Japan one great asset in the modern world — water power, all the more important in a land comparatively poor in other respects.

Next to its favorable climate, the geographic factor of greatest importance in shaping the history of Japan has been the factor of isolation. Japan is a part of the Chinese zone of civilization, that zone in East Asia centering around China which has been dominated by the culture developed in ancient times on the plains of North China.

The Chinese sphere of civilization is itself the most

isolated of the great spheres of early civilization, cut off from the centers of early culture in India, the Near East, and the Mediterranean world by the great land barrier of the mountain ranges and vast deserts of Central Asia, and the jungles and rugged terrain of Southeast Asia and the Malay Peninsula.

In this relatively isolated zone of Chinese civilization, Japan was in the past the most isolated area of all. Like England, Japan is an island country, but the straits between western Japan and Korea, the nearest continental land, are well over 100 miles wide, many times the width of the Straits of Dover; and some 500 miles of open sea stretch between Japan and China, the home of civilization in East Asia. In days of primitive navigation these water barriers were very broad, and made of Japan the most isolated of all the older countries of the world.

Culturally Japan is a daughter of Chinese civilization, much as the countries of northern Europe are daughters of Mediterranean culture. The story of the spread of Chinese civilization to the alien peoples of Japan during the first millennium after Christ is much like the story of the spread of Mediterranean civilization to the alien peoples of northern Europe during the same period. But the greater isolation of the Japanese from the home of their civilization and from all other peoples meant that in Japan the borrowed culture had more chance to develop along new and often unique lines, and to grow into distinctive patterns of civilization.

One popular concept is that the Japanese have never been anything more than a race of borrowers and imitators. The truth is quite the contrary. Although

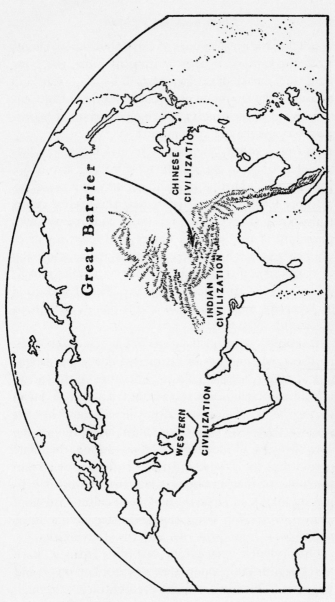

Great Barrier

CHINESE CIVILIZATION

INDIAN CIVILIZATION

WESTERN CIVILIZATION

ANCIENT CENTERS OF CIVILIZATION IN ASIA AND EUROPE

geographic isolation has made them very conscious of borrowings from abroad, it has also led them to develop one of the most distinctive cultures to be found in any civilized area of comparable size.

Take, for example, things as basic as domestic architecture and the manner in which the Japanese live at home. The thick straw floor mats, the sliding paper panels in place of interior walls, the open, airy structure of the whole house, the recess for art objects, the charcoal heating braziers, the peculiar wooden and iron bathtubs, and the place of bathing in daily life as a means of relaxation at the end of a day's work and, in winter, as a way of restoring a sense of warmth and well-being — all these and many other simple but fundamental features of home and daily life are unique to Japan and attest to an extremely distinctive culture rather than one of simple imitation.

Isolation has also made of the Japanese a highly self-conscious people, unaccustomed to dealing with foreigners individually or as a nation. The Japanese are always strongly conscious that they are Japanese and that all other peoples are foreigners. Isolation has made them painfully aware of their differences from other peoples and has filled them with an entirely irrational sense of superiority, which they are anxious to prove to themselves and to others. Isolation has made it difficult for them to understand the attitudes and actions of other peoples. In short, the factor of geographic isolation during the past two thousand years helps explain the national traits which led Japan to political isolation and to crushing defeat in the Second World War.

❖❖❖❖❖❖❖❖❖❖❖❖❖❖❖❖❖❖❖❖❖❖❖❖❖❖❖❖❖❖❖

Chapter II

THE EARLY JAPANESE

Although the Japanese, like all other modern peoples, are the result of racial mixtures, they are essentially a Mongoloid people, closely related to their neighbors on the continent in Korea and China. According to popular theories the early Japanese came to their islands from the south by way of Formosa and the Ryukyu Islands, but archaeological evidence indicates clearly that most of the early Japanese came to Japan by way of Korea. Some originally may have come from more distant regions in northeastern Asia, and others may have come originally from the coastal areas of South China. There they may have been in contact with the peoples of Southeast Asia and the adjacent islands, which might explain the many close parallels between primitive Japanese institutions and those of the southern areas of the Far East.

Despite the basically Mongoloid origins of the Japanese, the first inhabitants of the islands seem to have been the ancestors of the modern Ainu, a people probably in part of proto-white stock; that is, a group which split off from the white race at such an early time that

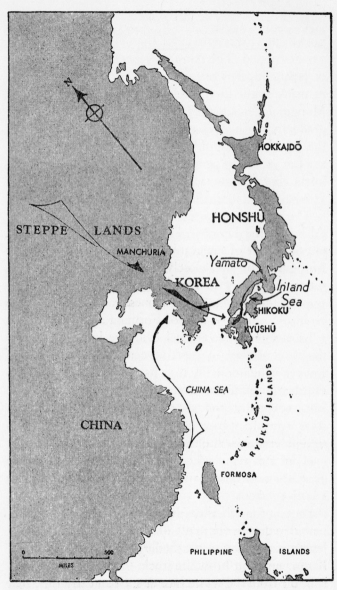

MIGRATIONS TO JAPAN IN EARLY TIMES

not all the characteristics of the Caucasian type had as yet developed. The Ainu may once have inhabited all of Japan, but they possessed a neolithic culture inferior in many ways to the neolithic cultures of the early Mongoloid invaders of Japan. As a result they were gradually pushed eastward and northward through the Japanese chain of islands until they now exist only as a fast vanishing people living in primitive settlements in the more remote sections of the northern island of Hokkaido and in smaller islands even farther north.

The Ainu contributed little to Japanese culture, but they may have contributed considerably to Japanese physical characteristics, one of which is the relative hairiness of the Japanese when compared to other Mongoloid peoples. The bristling moustaches of the Japanese officers and business men may well be their Ainu legacy.

Bronze and iron probably first reached Japan about the first century of the Christian era, brought by a wave of Mongoloid invaders from Korea. These invaders clearly had close contacts with the semi-nomadic culture of the steppe lands of northeastern Asia. They were fighting men on horseback, carrying the long straight iron sword of northern Asia, and like the nomads of this region they buried their dead leaders in great mounds. One of their most common symbols was a semi-precious stone curved in the shape of a huge comma, and another was a round bronze mirror, usually considered to be the symbol of the sun. Similar curved jewels are common archaeological finds throughout Korea, and the bronze mirrors obviously were borrowed from the Chinese, showing that these people had

already had some contact with the higher civilization
of China before coming to Japan.

These invaders, with their superior bronze and iron
civilization, soon became the dominant group among
the varied peoples of early Japan. They were the
founders of the historical Japanese state. Three of their
most important possessions, the sword, the curved
jewel, and the mirror, in time became the "Three Imperial Regalia," which even today are the symbols of
imperial authority.

The invaders from Korea were organized into petty
clans. Chinese traders who visited western Japan
around the year A.D. 200 found the country divided
into scores of small clan states, each ruled by a high
priestess or a high priest. At about that time feminine
rule, strongly implied in Japanese mythology, seems to
have been giving way to masculine rule.

A feeling of clan solidarity and a belief in the importance of hereditary rights and authority were undoubtedly strong among these people, for these forces
have been dominant throughout Japanese history and
are still much alive in modern Japan. Probably the figure of the aristocrat soldier, the man on horseback, was
already important in Japanese society, for this shadowy
figure of early Japan survived the deluge of borrowed
Chinese civilization, to emerge at a later day as the
backbone of a feudal Japan.

The religion of the early Japanese was primarily a
naïve nature worship which, probably under Chinese
influence, later came to include a certain amount of
ancestor worship. Nameless at first, it was later given
the Chinese-sounding name of Shinto, "the way of the

gods," to distinguish it from the continental religion
of Buddhism. Shinto was based on a simple feeling of
awe in the presence of any surprising or awesome phenomenon of nature — a waterfall, a mountain crag, a
large tree, a peculiarly shaped stone, or even some
lowly thing awesome only in its capacity for irritation,
such as an insect. Anything awe inspiring was called
kami, a word usually translated as "god" but basically
meaning "above," and by extension "superior." This
simple Shinto concept of deity should be borne in mind
in trying to understand the deification in modern
Japan of living emperors and of all Japanese soldiers
who have died for their country.

Places where people often felt a sense of awe became
cult places and eventually shrines. Today tens of thousands of such shrines dot the landscape of Japan. Some
are now great institutions dating back to shadowy antiquity, others merely miniature edifices of stone or
wood recently erected in front of an old oak tree or in
a deep recess of a cave.

The underlying stream of Shinto today remains little
changed since prehistoric times. Much has been done
during the past 1,500 years to make an organized religion of this simple nature worship, and, more recently,
by emphasizing the early mythology connected with
Shinto, to employ it as a force for national solidarity
and an inspiration for fanatical patriotism. But despite
these imposed superstructures, the true basis of Shinto
remains unchanged, a simple and naïve nature worship.

The possessors of the iron and bronze culture first
crossed from Korea to northern Kyushu and western
Honshu about the first century of the Christian era,

but these migrations from Korea to Japan continued for several centuries longer. As their numbers in Japan increased, they pushed their way up the broad highway of the Inland Sea to the central portion of Japan, conquering and absorbing the earlier inhabitants as they went.

One of the clans which, according to its own misty traditions, moved up the Inland Sea from an earlier home in Kyushu, finally settled in the small Yamato Plain not far from the eastern end of the Inland Sea. There it grew and prospered, establishing offshoots in new areas and absorbing other clans, until it had won a vague suzerainty over all of central and western Japan and even over parts of southern Korea.

Japanese control over southern Korea is represented in traditional Japanese history as the result of a semimiraculous conquest by a warrior empress. A more plausible explanation would be that clans in southern Korea, feeling themselves more akin to related clans which had earlier crossed to Japan, sought aid from the peoples of western Japan against new invaders from northern Korea. In any case, Japanese power in southern Korea was apparently at its height in the second half of the fourth century and gradually waned thereafter, coming to an end in the year 562.

The suzerainty of the Yamato clan within Japan did not extinguish the autonomous rights of the other clans, but the priest-chief of the Yamato group became the chief among clan chiefs, and the special cults of this clan became the principal cults of the whole land. In this way worship of the Sun Goddess, the mythological progenitress of the chiefs of the Yamato clan, became the supreme cult of Japanese Shinto.

From the priest-chiefs of the Yamato clan, who gained supremacy over their fellow priest-chiefs during the third or fourth century, stemmed the Japanese imperial family. This was not so spectacular an origin as the direct descent from a Sun Goddess claimed in Japanese tradition. Nevertheless it was an origin of great antiquity when compared with the origins of other ruling families of the world. And the suzerainty of the Yamato clan was the start of the Japanese state itself, a loose association of clans under one supreme clan — scarcely the empire described in traditional Japanese history, but unmistakably the beginning of a new nation.

Chapter III

THE COMING OF CHINESE CIVILIZATION

The peoples of northern Europe have always been conscious of their double heritage—their primitive Teutonic ancestry and the cultural legacy of ancient Greece and Rome. Similarly, the Japanese have a double historical heritage — the primitive stock of early Japan and the civilization of China. As in northern Europe, true history only started for Japan when the broad stream of a highly developed civilization reached its shores and, in a new geographic setting, combined with the simple native traditions of a primitive people to form a new culture, derived directly from the old civilization but differentiated from it by new geographic and racial ingredients.

The people who formed the early Yamato state in Japan had long had some contact with Chinese civilization, as may be seen from their early use of the Chinese bronze mirror. Fresh immigrants from Korea continued to bring to Japan the arts and sciences of the continent, and some knowledge of writing probably penetrated to the Japanese from China at a relatively early date. However, the first borrowings from China were made unconsciously and very slowly. Not until the second half of the sixth century did the Japanese become fully conscious of the advantages of the superior continental civilization and the desirability of learning more about it. The result was a sudden acceleration in the rate at which elements of Chinese culture were imported into the islands and absorbed by the Japanese.

Why this spurt in the long process of learning from China should have come at just this moment in Japanese history is not easy to determine. The Japanese people may have reached a level of cultural attainment and political organization then, which for the first time permitted more rapid and more conscious learning from abroad. And the renewed vigor displayed by Chinese culture at that time may have facilitated the process.

China's history as a highly civilized part of the world reaches back to the second millennium before Christ. Its first great period as a colossal military empire came during the period of Rome's greatness, roughly from about 250 B.C. to 200 A.D. An era of political disunion and disruption followed, and came to an end only in the second half of the sixth century, when a new and greater Chinese empire emerged from the chaos of three centuries of civil wars and barbarian invasions. The new Chinese empire was far richer and stronger than the first. In fact, during the seventh and eighth centuries China was, with little doubt, the richest and most powerful land in the whole world. This period was known by the dynastic name of T'ang, a period of unprecedented grandeur and might, and of brilliant cultural attainments. It is small wonder that the primitive Japanese in their isolated island country felt the reflected glory of the new Chinese empire and awoke to a new awareness of the great land across the sea.

The start of the heavy flow of Chinese influence to Japan is usually dated about 552, the year when the Buddhist religion is said to have been officially introduced to the Yamato clan by a missionary from a kingdom in southern Korea. Actually, Buddhism had probably entered Japan even earlier, but this incident affords a convenient date to mark the time when the Japanese first started consciously to learn from the Chinese.

During the next few centuries Buddhism served as an important vehicle for the transmission of Chinese culture to Japan. Buddhism is by origin an Indian religion. It had slowly spread to China and had won a place of importance in Chinese culture during the troubled era between the two great empires. It was a vigorous missionary religion at that time, and missionary zeal carried it beyond China to Korea and from there to Japan. Korean, Chinese, and even occasional Indian priests came to Japan from the sixth to eighth centuries. In turn, scores of Japanese converts went to China to learn more of the new faith. Returning from the continent, these Japanese student priests, even more than foreign missionary teachers, took the lead in transmitting to Japan the new religion and many other aspects of Chinese civilization. They were the true pioneers in planting and nurturing in Japan the borrowed culture of China.

In the second half of the sixth century Buddhism and other new influences from abroad so affected the Yamato clan that clashes broke out between factions

Students who had returned from China formed an important element in a clique at the Yamato court which seized power through a carefully engineered coup in 645. From that time on the Yamato state was definitely committed to a policy of trying to create in Japan a small replica of China, a miniature T'ang in the forested islands on the eastern fringes of the civilized world.

With the glory of China before their eyes, it was little wonder that the Japanese made this attempt. Other petty states in Korea, Manchuria, and on the southwestern borders of China, dazzled by the grandeur and might of T'ang, were making the same attempt. Truly amazing, however, were the zeal and energy with which the Japanese approached the problem, displaying an enthusiasm for learning which promised great things for their remote and backward land.

Under the influence of Chinese ideas, the Japanese for the first time conceived the idea of the Yamato state as an empire, and at that, an empire on an equal footing with China. Prince Shotoku even dared to phrase a letter to the Chinese emperor as coming from the Emperor of the Rising Sun to the Emperor of the Setting Sun. With the new imperial concept, the ruler of the Yamato state for the first time assumed the dignity and majesty of an emperor. The priest-chief of the clan became in theory all-powerful, an autocratic monarch in the Chinese tradition. But he did not lose his original role as high priest. He retained a dual position. Even today the Japanese emperor is in theory the Shinto high priest of ancient Yamato tradition, and at the same time the all-powerful secular ruler of Chinese tradition.

Possibly also under the influence of Chinese social concepts and of the Chinese prejudice against ruling empresses, the ancient custom of rule by women came to a definite end in Japan in the second half of the eighth century, after an unfortunate incident between a ruling empress and a Buddhist priest. Only many centuries later, long after the imperial line had become politically insignificant, did women again appear on the throne. Japanese women, who in the earliest times had enjoyed a position of social and political dominance over men, gradually sank to a status of complete subservience to them. Their rights and influence in early feudal society seem still to have been considerable, but in time even these rights were lost, as the women of Japan became socially and intellectually mere handmaids of the dominant male population.

Below the emperor the Japanese created a complex central government patterned after the tremendous centralized administration of T'ang China, one of the most highly developed and complex governments the world has ever seen. Under a Supreme Council of State, with its Prime Minister and Ministers of the Left and Right, were eight ministries, in concept not unlike the departments of our own government. Under the ministries in turn came scores of bureaus and other offices.

This organization was fantastically over developed for the needs of a small and loosely organized state, still close to a primitive clan society. Naturally much of the central government was little more than a paper organization which functioned, if at all, far differently from the Chinese prototypes. But the wonder is not that the Japanese fell short of complete success in creating a Chinese type of central government in Yamato. The surprising thing is that they had the ambition and energy to undertake such a gigantic and grandiose task, and that they already had sufficient understanding of the principles and mastery of the mechanism of Chinese government to create a fair semblance of its complex central administration.

One gains some idea of the scope of the undertaking and the degree of success achieved by considering the capital cities founded by the Japanese as part of their attempt to transform Japan into a little T'ang. In earlier ages there had been no cities, towns, nor even any semi-permanent buildings. Now the Japanese attempted to build a capital city comparable to Ch'ang-an, the great capital of T'ang, a metropolis of close to one million population and very probably the greatest city in the world at that time.

Ch'ang-an was a great rectangle in shape, some five miles by six miles, surrounded by massive walls. A magnificent palace stood at the northern end of the city and broad straight thoroughfares divided it neatly in checkerboard fashion. The first Japanese imitation of Ch'ang-an was undertaken in the year 710 near the modern town of Nara in the Yamato plain. The Japanese naturally reduced the scale, allowing the new capital an area of some two and a half by three miles. They failed to build the customary Chinese city wall, and the population of the capital was so far short of the goal that the western half of the city was never built up at all; but broad thoroughfares were laid out, and

stately tile-roofed Buddhist temples and probably imposing palaces and residences were constructed. Even
today several of these Buddhist temples still stand, the
oldest wooden structures in the world and the finest
remaining examples of Far Eastern architecture of the
T'ang epoch.

Toward the end of the eighth century, the Japanese
court, possibly with a view to escaping the increasing
influence of the great Buddhist temples which ringed
the Nara capital, decided to abandon this first city and

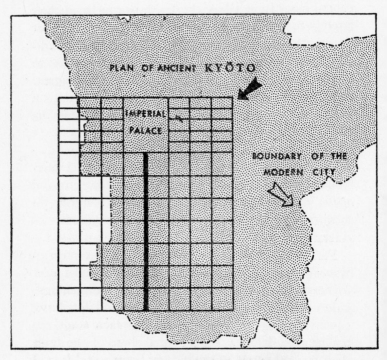

PLAN OF ANCIENT KYOTO

build a new capital. In 794 this second city was laid out at Kyoto, a few miles north of Nara. Again the scale was grandiose, a rectangle some three by three and a half miles, and again the Chinese city wall and the western half of the city never materialized. But this second capital never disappeared, as did the first. It survived the vicissitudes of the ages, remaining the imperial capital of Japan until 1868, and the checkerboard pattern of the principal streets of Kyoto today still reflects accurately the Chinese-style city laid out over 1,000 years ago.

The creation of a central government in Japan based on Chinese models was an easier task than the creation of the Chinese type of provincial administration. Clan spirit and clan autonomy were still too strong to tolerate the direct rule of all parts of the land by a bureaucracy dispatched to the provincial centers from the court. But the Japanese at least created the outward forms of the Chinese provincial system. The land was divided into prefectures and sub-prefectures, and over these were placed officials with high-sounding titles. Since most of these provincial posts, however, were given to local aristocrats, control from the central government remained vague and probably subject to the tolerance of local leaders.

Perhaps the most daring step taken by the Japanese was an attempt to adopt the Chinese system of land-ownership and taxation. In early T'ang China, agricultural land was in theory nationalized and distributed equally among the peasants, so that each adult tax-paying male could carry an equal share of the taxes. This he paid partly in produce and partly in labor, or in military service, which was considered a form of labor for the state.

Even in well-organized China, with its highly trained bureaucracy, this cumbersome system worked imperfectly, tending to break down completely every few decades. The Japanese wrote the system into elaborate law codes drawn up on Chinese models. To put it into practice in clan-ridden Japan was a different matter. For a century or so, the system did operate after a fashion in the capital area and in localities held directly by the Yamato clan, but in more remote parts of the country it was a dead letter from the start.

Closely connected with the Chinese tax system was the huge peasant conscript army it provided. China, with its long frontiers and warlike nomad neighbors to the north, needed such large levies, but they were quite meaningless in isolated Japan. A so-called army was created from peasant conscripts of the capital areas where the tax system was in force, but these peasant soldiers never constituted anything more than labor gangs. Despite the creation on paper of a foot-soldier army, the aristocrat on horseback remained the true Japanese fighting man.

The process of learning and borrowing from China was of course not limited to the political field. In fact, what the Japanese were learning at this time in cultural and intellectual fields had much more prolonged influence in Japan than did the borrowed political institutions. The latter for the most part decayed rapidly, and eventually disappeared in all but name, but many of the religious concepts, artistic skills, and literary forms learned during these centuries, far from losing their original vigor, developed and helped form the basic cultural patterns of later ages.

After the triumph of the pro-Buddhist faction at the Yamato court in the second half of the sixth century, this continental religion enjoyed the uninterrupted favor of the central government. Splendid temples were erected at government expense; impressive Buddhist ceremonies were sponsored by the court and the noble families. Many a Japanese emperor retired from the heavy burdens of his dual secular and religious role to the more peaceful life of the Buddhist monk. As was the case with so much else in the newly imported continental culture, the influence of Buddhism was still weak in the provinces, but in the capital district the new religion was supreme, and enjoyed official favor far greater than that afforded even the native cults of Shinto.

With Buddhism came many of the arts and crafts of China. The Buddhist temples were themselves great architectural achievements, and housed beautiful and deeply spiritual bronze and wooden statues of Buddhist divinities, exquisite religious paintings, and other magnificent works of art. Some had been brought from the continent. Others of equal beauty and artistic merit were produced in Japan, showing how readily the Japanese acquired the artistic skills developed during the centuries by the Chinese.

Several temple halls and store rooms dating from the seventh and eighth centuries still stand, filled with the artistic achievements of that age. They attest to the amazing success with which the Japanese transplanted much of the best in Chinese artistic tradition and indicate the early development of a happy combination of artistic taste and superb craftsmanship which ever since has characterized the Japanese.

In art, the Japanese could have had no better teachers than the Chinese, but in the field of writing Chinese influence was less happy. Japanese is a language of simple phonetic structure and highly inflected words. Hence it can be easily written by phonetic symbols, and these are necessary to represent the language properly. The Chinese writing system, on the other hand, leaves little possibility for phonetic transcription or for the representation of inflections. Since Chinese lacks inflection and since in ancient Chinese the words tended to be monosyllabic, the Chinese found it possible to use a writing system in which each monosyllabic word or word-root is represented by a special symbol, called a character or ideograph. These characters range from a simple line, 一 to represent "one," to more complex characters, such as the monstrosity in twenty-five strokes 灣 representing the word "bay."

The Chinese student has always been faced with the grim necessity of mastering several thousand of these characters before he could be considered literate. The ancient Japanese were faced with this and with the added difficulty that the Chinese writing system was not suitable to the writing of Japanese. Had Japan been the neighbor of some Western country using a phonetic script, such as our own alphabet, the Japanese would have quickly learned to write their native tongue with efficiency and ease. Unfortunately geographic accident decreed otherwise, and the Japanese were burdened with the crushing weight of the most cumbersome of writing systems. Like the youth of China, the youth of Japan was sentenced generation after generation to years of mentally numbing memory work, simply in order to learn the rudiments of writing.

Because of the difficulties involved and also because of the tremendous prestige of all things Chinese, the ancient Japanese made little effort to write their own language. Proper names and brief poems in Japanese were spelled out laboriously with one Chinese character used phonetically for each syllable, but little else was attempted. Instead the Japanese wrote in pure and often reasonably good classical Chinese. Using Chinese much as medieval Europeans used Latin, they wrote their histories, geographies, law books, and official documents of all sorts. They even attempted to imitate Chinese literary forms, and men of education prided themselves on their ability to compose poems in Chinese.

The most interesting and significant form of literary endeavor at this time was history writing. This was to be expected in a cultural daughter of China, for the Chinese have always been historically minded, prone to take the historical approach to any subject or situation. The writing of history was always an important function of government in China, and as a result the Chinese were inveterate and extremely good historians.

Since Japan was in its own eyes an empire on the Chinese model, obviously she too needed an official history. Several early efforts to write one resulted in two extant works, the *Nihon Shoki*, a great official history compiled in 720, and a smaller work called the *Kojiki*, which is said to have appeared in 712, and may have been one of the preliminary drafts on which the *Nihon Shoki* was based. Both are extremely important works, for they are fairly reliable historical accounts for the period from about A.D. 400 on, and they contain much naïve mythology and historical tradition from earlier eras which throw a great deal of light on primitive Japanese beliefs and social institutions before they were submerged under the flood of more advanced ideas and institutions from China.

However, the statesmen and historians of the time were not satisfied with a simple, uncolored presentation of the mythology and historical traditions of the Yamato clan as transmitted orally by professional court reciters. They were determined to prove by their work that the rulers of Yamato were and always had been true emperors, unique rulers of Japan, and that Japan was a great and old country, worthy of standing beside China. Strengthening their mythology and scanty historical traditions with elements from Chinese philosophy and history, they wove the whole into an impressive pseudo-history. The Sun Goddess, one of the chief objects of worship by the ancient Yamato clan, was considered to be the progenitress of the imperial line, and her grandson was described as descending to Japan from heaven and the latter's grandson, in turn, as becoming the first emperor, ascending the throne in 660 B.C. This date, like so much else of this pseudo-history, is of course pure fantasy, possibly arrived at in the early seventh century simply by counting back 1,260 years, a major time cycle according to Chinese reckoning.

The place of the *Nihon Shoki* and *Kojiki* in the historiography of Japan is fundamental, but unfortunately that is not their only claim to fame. They were to be lifted from comparative obscurity many centuries later by narrow-minded patriots and ultra-nationalists seeking in the primitive pre-Chinese periods of Japanese history native virtues which would justify their own belief in the superiority of Japan. Despite the extraordinary naïveté and occasional indecency, according to Western standards, of the early mythology preserved in the *Kojiki* and *Nihon Shoki*, the modern Japanese in a sense made these two books into bibles of ultra-nationalism; and at times official policy even forced upon the Japanese people the acceptance of their historical absurdities as sober facts.

Chapter IV

THE GROWTH OF A NATIVE CULTURE

The period of greatest learning from China lasted from the late sixth century until the early ninth century, when a subtle change began to take place in the attitude of the Japanese toward China. The prestige of all things Chinese remained great, but the ninth century Japanese were no longer so anxious to learn from China or so ready to admit the superiority of all phases of Chinese civilization over their own.

One reason for this slowly changing attitude toward Chinese culture was the political decay of T'ang, which became marked as the ninth century progressed. Perhaps even more fundamental was the intellectual growth of the Japanese themselves, resulting in a gradual reassertion of a spirit of cultural independence. Three centuries of assiduous learning from the Chinese had created, at least in the capital district, a cultured society with its own political and social institutions, patterned of course after Chinese models but changed and adapted to fit Japanese needs by over two centuries of conscious experimentation and slow unconscious modification. The Japanese were no longer a primitive people, overawed by the vastly superior continental civilization and eager to imitate blindly anything Chinese. Japan was reaching a state of intellectual maturity and was ready to develop a culture of its own.

One sign of the changing attitude in Japan was the ending of official contacts with China. The last of the great embassies left Japan for T'ang in 838 and returned the next year. Later embassies were proposed but were argued down by courtiers who felt their value no longer warranted the decided risks of the trip across the East China Sea. Some private traders and student monks continued to travel between the two lands, but for the most part Japan lapsed into its earlier state of virtual isolation from the continent, and this isolation in turn made the Japanizing of imported Chinese civilization all the more inevitable and rapid.

The slow rise of native Japanese culture is perhaps best observed in the development of an adequate means of writing the native tongue. This writing system was developed slowly during the ninth and tenth centuries by the process of using certain Chinese characters in greatly abbreviated form as simple phonetic symbols devoid of any specific meaning in themselves. Since the Chinese characters each represented one monosyllabic word or word-root, the phonetic symbols derived from them normally stood for a whole syllable, such as *ka*, *se*, or *mo*. The result was a syllabary and not an alphabet, such as our own system of writing.

The Japanese syllabary, or *kana* as it is called, was at first a confused affair. For one thing, the Chinese characters used were abbreviated in two different ways. In one system, called *hiragana*, the whole character was written in a very stylized or cursive form. Thus, the Chinese character 奴 meaning "slave" became the *hiragana* symbol ぬ standing for the sound *nu*. In the other system, called *katakana*, some element of the character was chosen to represent the phonetic value of the whole. Thus, this same Chinese character for "slave" became the *katakana* symbol ヌ also standing for *nu*. Another complexity was that the choice of characters for abbreviation as *kana* was at first quite haphazard, and usually several were used for any one syllable. In fact, both *hiragana* and *katakana* have only been standardized in recent decades, and variant *kana* forms are still commonly used in every day correspondence.

The Japanese syllabaries formed more clumsy systems of writing than alphabets, but they were, nevertheless, reasonably efficient systems for writing Japanese, and with their development appeared a growing literature in the native tongue. As stated previously, poems had been composed in Japanese even at the height of the Chinese period, and had been laboriously written down by the use of unabbreviated Chinese characters to represent each syllable phonetically; but these poems were usually extremely brief, following a strict pattern of thirty-one syllables, merely enough to suggest a scene or an emotion. The classical Japanese poem was delicate and beautiful within its narrow bounds, but it was distinctly limited as a literary form.

The *kana* syllabaries made possible more extensive literary work in Japanese, and in the tenth century stories, travel diaries, and essays appeared, written in Japanese which sometimes achieved considerable literary distinction. For the most part educated men, much like their counterparts in medieval Europe, scorned the use of their own tongue for any serious literary purpose and continued to write histories, essays, and various official documents in Chinese; but the women of the imperial court, who usually had insufficient education to write in Chinese, had no other medium for literary expression than their own language. As a result, while the men of the period were pompously writing bad Chinese, their ladies consoled themselves for their lack of education by writing good Japanese, and created, incidentally, Japan's first great prose literature.

The golden period of the first flowering of Japanese prose was in the late tenth and early eleventh centuries. Most of the writers were court ladies living in ease and indolence, and their commonest form of literary expression was the diary, liberally sprinkled with poems of thirty-one syllables to commemorate moments of deep emotional feeling. Some of the diaries told of travels, but more often they concerned the luxurious life and constant flirtation and love-making which characterized the court at this time.

The outstanding work of the period, however, was not a diary but a lengthy novel — the *Tale of Genji*, written by Lady Murasaki early in the eleventh century. This is an account of the love adventures of an imaginary Prince Genji, made slightly tedious to a modern reader by the similarity of his many experiences, but unquestionably a distinguished piece of writing and one of Japan's outstanding contributions to world literature.

The diaries and novels by court ladies were clear evidence of the existence of a true native Japanese culture. They had no clear prototypes in Chinese literature. Everything about them was distinctly Japanese. The transplanted Chinese civilization had flowered into a new culture, and the Japanese, a people but recently introduced to the art of writing, had produced a great literature of their own.

One may wonder why Japanese writing is still burdened with Chinese characters, if a thousand years ago the Japanese had already developed a phonetic script which was satisfactory for writing their language. The only explanation is the continued prestige of the Chinese language, and still more of the Chinese characters themselves. Learned writers inevitably tended to slip Chinese characters standing for individual uninflected words, such as nouns, into a Japanese text written in *kana*. From the twelfth and thirteenth centuries on, this became standard procedure, and eventually it became customary to write as many uninflected words and the roots of as many inflected words as possible with characters, leaving for *kana* only the tag ends of words, such as inflections which could not be represented conveniently by characters.

The natural complexities of such a mixed system of writing were increased by two other factors. Since thousands of Chinese words were gradually incorporated into the Japanese language, most of the characters stood not only for the Japanese version of the original Chinese word, but also for the corresponding Japanese word. It is as if the Chinese character for "water," 水, were to be used in English to represent the word "water" in "water wheel" and also to represent the element *aqua* in "aquatic."

The second factor was that many Chinese characters stood for Chinese words which corresponded in meaning to several different Japanese words. For example, the Chinese word *shang*, written by the character 上, has Japanese equivalents variously read as *ue*, *kami*, *agaru*, *ageru*, and *noboru*, to list the commonest, just as it has such English equivalents as "on," "above," "upper," "to mount," and "to present." This multiplicity of Japanese readings for many characters and the coexistence of both Japanese and Chinese readings for most of them means that every line of modern Japanese presents a series of little problems in reading and interpretation. The result is a writing system of almost unparalleled difficulty and cumbersomeness, which has been a serious impediment to the intellectual and technical development of modern Japan.

The obvious cure for this situation would be to abandon the use of Chinese characters and to return to the pure phonetic writing as it existed around the year 1,000 — or, still better, to adopt the Latin alphabet. But this would be no easy task. In modern times tens of thousands of technical and scientific words have been borrowed from Chinese or coined in Japan by joining two or more Chinese characters and pronouncing the resulting compound in the Chinese way. Unfortunately, Chinese type words in the Japanese vocabulary run very strongly to homophones. A standard dictionary lists no less than twenty distinct words, mostly of Chinese type, pronounced *kōkō*, and an exhaustive list of more specialized scientific terminology would probably add several dozen more. Because of these homophones, many, if not most, modern scientific terms, to be understood, must be seen as they are written in characters. Consequently, the dropping of Chinese characters from modern written Japanese would entail a wholesale modification of the technical and scientific vocabulary. Thousands of Chinese type words would have to be dropped, and new ones based on native Japanese roots or on words from Western languages would have to be substituted for them. It would be a tremendous undertaking, but in the long run probably well worth the attempt.

Although the appearance by the tenth and eleventh centuries of a new and distinctive Japanese culture was perhaps best seen in the literature of the time, it was evident in other fields also. The arts of painting, sculpture, and architecture all showed definite and sometimes marked signs of Japanese characteristics quite distinct from the original Chinese patterns, and political and social institutions changed so radically as to bear little resemblance to the Chinese prototypes.

The key figure of the Chinese political system was the bureaucrat, the scholar-civil servant who operated the complicated central government and went out to the provinces to collect taxes and maintain order. Thousands of these bureaucrats were required, and the recruiting of wise and capable men for the higher posts was a matter of crucial importance to the whole state. For this purpose, the Chinese had developed a system of civil service examinations. It centered around the great central university at Ch'ang-an where periodic examinations were given on classical subjects. Candidates who succeeded best in the examinations went directly to high government posts. In this way, men of scholarly talents from all walks of life could reach positions of responsibility, and among the educated classes a vital tradition of public service was built up.

The Japanese borrowed only the outward forms of this system. With their strong traditions of clan loyalty and hereditary rights, they could not bring themselves to accept its spirit. They created a central university where the Chinese classics were studied and examinations were held, but only in rare cases did scholars with little family backing attain positions of much responsibility. In the provinces, political authority remained in the hands of local aristocrats masquerading as civil servants appointed by the central administration, while at the capital courtiers of noble lineage held most posts of importance, leaving to the scholar bureaucrats the humbler clerical jobs.

In China, the central government was constantly kept busy fighting the natural tendency for the taxpaying peasants and their lands to gravitate into the hands of powerful families with sufficient influence at court to protect their holdings from the encroachments of tax collectors. In Japan, this tendency was even stronger, for there was no powerful civil servant class to protect the interests of the state, and local aristocrats, in key positions as provincial officers, joined with court nobles in despoiling the public domain.

The nationalized land system had probably been a dead letter from the start in more remote parts of the country. During the late eighth and ninth centuries it decayed rapidly even in the capital district. Local men of influence slowly built up tax-free estates, usually by illegal means, and court aristocrats acquired in their own names large tracts of land as rewards for their services or through political manipulations of a less honorable nature.

On the one hand, the local gentry needed protection for their holdings from the tax collectors of the central government. On the other hand, powerful court families and great monasteries were acquiring large tax-free estates, and needed local men to represent their interests on these lands. From these reciprocal needs a pattern of land-holding gradually developed in which provincial manors and estates were controlled and operated by local aristocrats but were owned, at least in theory, by influential court families or monasteries. The peasant, who came to have definite proprietary rights to his own little tract of land, gave to the local aristocrat, acting as estate manager, a generous portion of his produce; and the estate manager, in turn, passed on to the noble court family or great monastery a share of his income in payment for protection from the central government.

Tax-free manors grew and expanded during the eighth and ninth centuries until, by the tenth, the national domain had virtually disappeared. With its disappearance, the income of the state from taxes, the economic basis for the Chinese form of centralized government, dwindled to almost nothing. As a result, provincial governmental agencies, which had never been strong, withered away almost completely, leaving behind imposing but meaningless administrative titles, such as Governor or Vice-Governor. Even the central administration became largely an empty shell, a great paper organization with court nobles sporting high titles but with little working personnel, scanty funds, and greatly reduced functions of government. The complex system of rule through eight ministries was for all practical purposes abandoned, and new and simplified organs of government were developed to handle what few political duties the central government still had.

The net result of all this was that centralized government ceased to exist for most parts of Japan. Each estate, freed from encroachment by tax collectors and other state agents, became a small autonomous domain, a semi-independent economic and political unit. The contacts it had with the outside world were not with any government agency but with the great court family or monastery which exercised a loose and distant control over it.

The noble court families and monasteries became, in a sense, multiple successors of the old centralized state. Any centralizing forces in the economic and political life of Japan were represented largely by them and not by the bureaus of the central government. These families and monasteries became to a certain degree states within the hollow framework of the old imperial government, each supported by the income from its own estates and, through family government or monastery administration, exercising many of the functions of government in its widely scattered manors throughout the land.

The imperial family, though retaining great prestige because of its past political role and its continuing position as leader in the Shinto cults, became in fact simply one among these central economic and political units. It exercised a theoretical rule over a shadow government, but in reality it controlled only its own estates and lived on the income from them, and not from government taxes. In time, even control over its own private affairs was lost, as one of the court families, the Fujiwara, gradually won complete mastery over the imperial family by intrigue and skillful political manipulations.

The Fujiwara were a prolific family of many branches, descended from a courtier who had taken the lead in the pro-Chinese *coup d'état* of 645. The family had come to control many estates throughout the land and thus enjoyed an income probably greater than that of any other family, not excluding the imperial family itself. Its method of winning unchallenged dominance at the capital was to gain direct control over the imperial family through intermarriage. A daughter of the head of the family would be married to a young emperor, and the emperor, bored with the endless ceremonies required by his double role as secular and religious leader, would be easily persuaded to abdicate and retire to a simpler, freer life as soon as the son the Fujiwara girl had borne him was old enough to sit through these ceremonies in his place. This would leave a Fujiwara girl as empress dowager, and her father, the powerful head of a large and rich court family, as the grandfather of the new child emperor.

By such tactics the Fujiwara gained complete control over the imperial family during the middle decades of the ninth century. From that time on, it became customary for the head of the Fujiwara family, instead of an imperial prince, to act as regent for a child emperor or to occupy the new post of Civil Dictator when an adult was on the throne. During the course of the ninth and tenth centuries, appointment to these two alternating posts, as well as to that of Prime Minister and to most of the other high offices in the central administration, became the hereditary right of members of the Fujiwara family, and the successive family heads completely overshadowed the emperors not only as the real holders of the reins of government but also as the openly recognized arbiters of taste and fashion at court.

In later centuries, the dominant role in the dwindling court aristocracy was from time to time regained by strong emperors, and the various official posts of the Fujiwara in time became almost meaningless, as all political power slipped away from the imperial court. However, the Fujiwara and offshoots of this great family retained their virtual monopoly of all high court posts almost without interruption from the late ninth century until the early nineteenth century.

In another country such a long and almost complete dominance exercised by one family over the imperial family would probably have resulted in a usurpation of the throne. Not so in Japan. Hereditary authority was so strong a force that outright usurpation was not to be contemplated. Instead, the Fujiwara set the time honored Japanese pattern of control from behind the scenes through a figurehead. Throughout most of Japanese history, it has probably been the rule rather than the exception for the man or group in nominal political control to be in reality the pawn of some other man or group. This factor has in recent times tended to conceal the realities of Japanese politics, and has often confused and baffled the casual observer of the Japanese scene.

Major Points:

1. Japanese leave China to develop own culture - due to: a) political decay of T'ang
b) intellectual growth of Nips

2. As a result Japs dvp adequate means of writing - syllabary
   a. extensive literary work in Japanese
   b. 10-11th cent - golden period for Jap. prose
      * women create first prose literature
   c. Chinese characters in written language - makes system of writing difficult and cumbersome

3. Japanese borrow outward forms of civil service examination system
   - nationalized land system fails
   - local men gain tax-free estates
   - local aristocrats operated ? control manors & estates which were owned by civt families & monasteries
   - peasant works land for protection from central government

4. Establishment of Fujiwara Family
   a. through intermarriage gain control over imperial f
   b. set up system of control from behind the scenes (figureheads)

Chapter V

THE DEVELOPMENT OF A
FEUDAL SOCIETY

During the tenth and eleventh centuries, the Fujiwara held the spotlight on the stage of Japanese history, but, despite the brilliance of the literary and artistic accomplishments of the court they dominated, others off stage were preparing the next acts in the drama. The capital aristocrats had transformed the borrowed civilization of China into a native culture, but they had lost control over the political and economic life of the country.

While the courtiers were going through the forms and ceremonies of little more than a sham government, and devoting their energies more to the arts of poetry-writing and love-making than to governing, the provincial aristocrats were gaining practical experience, managing their estates and ruling the peasants on these estates with hardly any control or direction from the capital. The decadent, effeminate courtiers at Kyoto were producing a literature and an art that future generations were to look back to with pride, but their less sophisticated and hardier country cousins were laying the foundations for an entirely new Japan.

The gradual decline of Chinese political institutions at the capital and the weakening of the central government's control over the provinces have made the period of Fujiwara supremacy appear to be one of unmitigated political decline. In reality the political decay at court was more than offset by the rapid growth of the once backward provincials in political experience and in general sophistication. During the height of the Chinese period they had participated but little in the brilliant culture transplanted from T'ang to the capital district, and they had been completely overshadowed by the noble families at court, but at the same time they were slowly absorbing much of the basic knowledge and many of the essential skills of the continental civilization. By the tenth and eleventh centuries they had reached a stage of cultural development which permitted them to start laying the broad foundations of a new society and a new political structure, entirely independent of the old patterns established by the court.

The central figure in this new society, as in the earlier clan society of the provinces, was the aristocratic fighting man on horseback. In ancient times he had been the soldier leader of the clan. Now he was the manager of a tax-free estate, defending his lands from marauders by his skill as a horseman and his prowess with the bow and sword. He had become a knight, resembling to a surprising degree his counterpart in the early feudal society of Europe.

Individual knights usually owed allegiance to court families or central monasteries which were the nominal owners of their estates, but this relationship, which had been the outgrowth of an early need for protection from the tax collectors of the central government, afforded them no protection from their local enemies. For this, they needed the aid of other fighting men, the knights on other local estates. Quite naturally these warrior aristocrats began to form small local cliques for their mutual protection.

These cliques were held together by common interest, ties of marriage and of old friendships, and sometimes the qualities of leadership displayed by a local warrior hero. Particularly in the eastland did such associations of knights flourish, possibly because the greatest concentration of estates in the whole land was to be found on the Kanto Plain around the modern city of Tokyo, and also because the continuing campaigns against the retreating Ainu in northern Honshu made the need for such associations all the more evident.

The tenth and eleventh centuries saw many clashes and small wars between different groups of knights in the provinces. These contests are often described in histories as revolts against imperial authority, for one faction would resist domination by another faction which enjoyed the backing of the central government. The provincial knights, however, for the most part showed little desire to assume the governmental prerogatives of the Kyoto court. They were content to leave the central government undisturbed as long as they themselves could continue to rule the peasants on their own estates and to organize their cliques for local defense without interference from the capital.

The court aristocrats, rather than the knights themselves, eventually brought these provincial warriors onto the capital stage. The courtiers, lacking all knowledge of the arts of war themselves, would from time to time bring knights from their provincial estates to the capital to help protect their interests or to overawe their enemies. Sometimes the knights were used to defend the court from the great local monasteries, which often attempted to force their will upon the effete courtiers by a joint display of Buddhist relics and armed might drawn from the warriors of the monastery estates. At other times, the knights were brought in to settle, by a show of force or by actual conflict, factional disputes over the imperial succession and the headship of the Fujiwara family.

In the middle of the twelfth century disputes of the latter type led to fairly large scale clashes between the two strongest warrior cliques of the time in support of two quarreling court factions. The warrior cliques centered around two great provincial families, the Taira and the Minamoto, both of whom claimed descent from cadet branches of the imperial family which, because of declining income, had been forced to seek their fortunes in the provinces. There they had merged with the local aristocrats and had risen to leadership among them because of their prestige as descendants of emperors.

As a result of two small wars in 1156 and 1160, one of the court factions won out over the other. A far more significant outcome was the sudden realization on the part of Taira Kiyomori, leader of the victorious Taira clique of warriors, that he and his band now formed the paramount military force in the land and that the emperor and his court were powerless in his hands. To the consternation of the courtiers, Kiyomori and his leading knights settled down in Kyoto and took over control of the court, Kiyomori taking for himself the title of Prime Minister and adopting the old Fujiwara trick of marrying his own daughter to the emperor and putting her son on the throne.

By settling in Kyoto and becoming in effect a new group of courtiers, Kiyomori and his henchmen weakened their hold over the knights of their clique who remained on their estates in the provinces and who tended to resent the position and pretensions of the court aristocracy. Meanwhile the remnants of the Minamoto family slowly recouped their fortune in their old family stronghold in eastern Japan. Eventually the Minamoto felt themselves strong enough again to challenge Taira supremacy, and in a bitterly fought war between 1180 and 1185 they completely crushed the Taira faction. The Taira leaders either were killed or committed suicide, and the new boy emperor who was the grandson of Kiyomori perished with his Taira relatives in the final battle of the war.

Minamoto Yoritomo, the leader of the triumphant Minamoto faction, profiting from the mistakes of the Taira, left Kyoto and the court alone and settled down at the small seaside town of Kamakura, near the estates of his relatives and his partisans in the Kanto region of eastern Japan. In typically Japanese fashion, he decided to permit the emperors and Fujiwara to continue their sham civil government unmolested. He took for himself only the title of Shogun, a term perhaps best translated as "Generalissimo," and he rewarded his men not with government posts but with the more lucrative positions of estate managers in manors formerly con-

JAPAN IN THE FEUDAL PERIOD

trolled by members of the Taira faction. Although personally commanding the only strong military force in
all Japan, Yoritomo was content to permit the continuation of the fiction that an emperor and his civil government ruled the land and that he himself was merely
the commander of the emperor's army. Yoritomo and
his band, however, constituted the only effective central government Japan possessed, and Kamakura became the true political capital of the land. Thus Japan's
first military dictatorship was established.

The administration which Yoritomo and his successors set up at Kamakura was not in theory or in outward form a national government. It was merely a
simple but efficient organization designed to control
the relatively small band of knights that owed personal
allegiance to the Minamoto. It was, in fact, nothing
more than a "family" government, not of a single clan
as had been customary in ancient times, but of a loose
association of knights held together by bonds of family
relationship or by long-standing ties of friendship and
traditions of mutual support.

Under the Shogun, three small offices were created
as the chief organs of this "family" government — an
office to watch over and control the affairs of the individual knight members of the clique, an administrative
board, and a final court of appeal, making legal decisions based upon the customary law which had gradually developed among the provincial warrior aristocrats
during the preceding two centuries and which the Kamakura administration issued in codified form. The
provincial organization of this government was even
simpler than its central administration. It consisted only

of the individual knights themselves, free to manage their individual estates as each saw best, but organized for mutual defense under a constable in each province.

The whole "family" government of the Minamoto may have been designed simply to control the private affairs of the clique and not to administer the nation as a whole, but by controlling the members of this group, who had now been spread throughout the whole land as the key class of estate managers and local knights, the government at Kamakura effectively controlled all classes of society throughout Japan. Its member knights ruled the peasants, who were serfs on their estates, and they also controlled the purse strings of the court aristocracy, which derived its income from these same estates. Although it maintained the fiction of being a private organization, the Kamakura regime had become the most effective central government Japan had yet known; and the people of all classes, realizing that Kamakura alone had the power to enforce its decisions, went there rather than to Kyoto for justice and looked to the Shogun's administration rather than to the emperor's court for leadership.

An ambitious retired emperor in 1221 dared challenge this indirect and unannounced control of national life by Kamakura, but found himself overwhelmed by the Minamoto cohorts. The incident revealed conclusively that imperial rule was at an end. The imperial family and the noble families around it continued to receive their income from the estates they nominally owned, but as far as political realities were concerned, the emperor and his court had become anachronistic survivals of an earlier age, with no valid place in the political order of feudalism. Yet the prestige of the imperial line and its continuing religious functions kept alive the fiction of imperial rule during the following six centuries of feudalism, until new conditions made possible its reappearance as a significant element in the political life of the nation.

The Kamakura system centered around the Shogun, the leader of the clique, and in theory the only unifying force was the personal loyalty of each individual knight to the Shogun. In practice, however, the person of the Shogun soon became an unimportant factor, and the system proved to have amazing strength of itself.

Yoritomo, the first Shogun, jealously rid himself of his hero brother and other leading members of his family. After the death of Yoritomo, factional strife among his descendants, fostered by his wife's relatives, who had the family name of Hojo, soon led to the elimination of his heirs. In 1219 an assassination ended the Minamoto line, and thereafter the Hojo, who in typical Japanese fashion contented themselves with the title of "Regent," ruled through a puppet Shogun, first chosen from the Fujiwara family and then from the imperial family.

Thus, one finds in thirteenth century Japan an emperor who was a mere puppet in the hands of a retired emperor and of a great court family, the Fujiwara, who together controlled a government which was in fact merely a sham government, completely dominated by the private government of the Shogun — who in turn was a puppet in the hands of a Hojo regent. The man behind the throne had become a series of men, each one in turn controlled by the man behind himself.

The rise of the provincial warrior class to a position of dominance produced a new culture as well as a new political system. The literature and art of the tenth and eleventh centuries had been an expression of the culture of the narrow court society under Fujiwara leadership. The new culture naturally inherited much from this glorious period, but the most significant and, in time, dominant elements in it came from the warrior class of the provinces.

The knight brought with him his own concepts and attitudes, which were in some respect similar to those of his counterpart in medieval Europe. In contrast to the effete courtier at Kyoto, he gloried in a life of warfare, in the Spartan virtues, and in the ascetic practices of self-discipline and physical and mental toughening. He made a cult of his sword, and this cult, revived in recent years, accounts for the extraordinary pride of the modern Japanese officer in his old-fashioned, long, curved sword. The warrior reemphasized personal loyalties and the importance of family ties, and his two outstanding virtues, Spartan indifference to suffering or death and a great capacity for unswerving personal loyalty, became characteristics of the Japanese people as a whole.

The warrior's tastes in literature produced a whole new type of prose writing — the heroic tale of warfare, quite different from the diaries and novels of the court ladies. These martial tales usually centered around the conflicts between the Taira and Minamoto factions, which became the central themes of much of later Japanese literature.

The successive triumphs of the Taira and Minamoto

marked the commencement of 700 years of unbroken rule by warrior aristocrats. Small wonder that the impress of feudalism lies so heavily upon the nation and that the attitudes and ideals of the feudal warriors have sunk so deeply into the consciousness of the Japanese people. Accustomed for so long to rule by wearers of the sword, even in recent times the Japanese have looked instinctively to their military men for leadership and have been prone to assume that military men *per se* were always honest and sincere. Seven centuries of domination by the feudal military class has left patterns of thought and behavior which have not been easy to discard in recent times and which will not be easily erased even today.

Accompanying the political transformation of the twelfth and thirteenth centuries was a great religious awakening. Significant new currents appeared in Japanese Buddhism, and these currents became the main flow of Buddhism as it has existed in Japan ever since. The appearance of new trends in religion at this time was unquestionably connected with the increasing spread of culture and knowledge to classes outside of the old court aristocracy — to the provincial gentry, the townspeople, and even to the peasantry; and the rapid triumph of the new Buddhism over older forms of the religion was certainly in part the result of the rise of new classes to prominence in national life.

The Buddhist awakening of early feudal times was also partly the outgrowth of new influences from China, as contacts with the continent, fostered by a growing international trade in Far Eastern waters, became more frequent and increasingly significant. Buddhist monasteries themselves led in establishing these new contacts with China, sponsoring trading ventures overseas with a view to obtaining funds for the erection of new buildings. Many fine thirteenth and fourteenth century temples were to some extent paid for by such trading ventures, as was also the beautiful "Great Buddha" at Kamakura, erected in the second half of the thirteenth century and said still to be the largest bronze statue in the world.

Buddhism came to China as a highly intellectualized philosophy with rich and colorful religious ceremonials that appealed to the upper classes, but during the T'ang and post-T'ang periods a growing emphasis on the less austere and more popular philosophic concepts of Buddhism led to a general philosophic reorientation and popularization which made it increasingly a religion of the people.

Early Indian Buddhism stressed the evil and vanity of human existence. It held out little hope for improving man's lot in this world but centered its interest primarily on what it called "release from the cycle of rebirth." The Buddhists accepted the common Indian belief that the individual is born again and again into this world. He may be born into a better state or a worse one, depending on the sort of life he lives in each successive rebirth. This process goes on endlessly unless the individual realizes that his own desire for things that cannot really satisfy him brings about his repeated rebirth into an incurably evil world: the only way to escape "the cycle of rebirth" is to overcome all desire. One who has done this has attained *nirvana,* a state of mind in which one is indifferent to life's trials and the individual ego loses its identity in the cosmos, much as a single drop of water loses its identity in the vastness of the ocean.

Such a pessimistic attitude toward life had little appeal for the Chinese and other East Asiatic peoples, who have always tended to regard human life as essentially good. When Buddhism first came to China, the beautiful art, sacred literature, colorful ceremonies, broad learning, and peaceful monastic life, which had all become integral parts of the Buddhist religion, recommended it to the Chinese as much, if not more, than the type of philosophy embodied in original Buddhism. In fact, Buddhism could have had no broad philosophic appeal to the masses in China and Japan until a philosophic reemphasis and reorientation had taken place.

Perhaps the most startling development in this reorientation was the change in the concept of *nirvana* itself. For the common believer it became a Paradise where the individual soul went for an after-life of bliss, while innumerable hells, rivaling Dante's creations, became the deserts of the wicked. Arguing that the degenerate age in which they lived made enlightenment and salvation by one's own efforts impossible, popular preachers of the time put forth the doctrine that salvation now was possible by the grace of another — through the intervention of one of the host of gods and demi-gods with which the Buddhist pantheon had become peopled. Belief, not philosophic enlightenment or exemplary conduct, became the chief emphasis, and calling on the name of Buddha became the most meaningful act of faith.

These doctrines found vigorous expression in Japan

in the tenth and eleventh centuries and eventually resulted in the development of new sects of Japanese
Buddhism, quite different from the earlier sects established in Japan in the eighth and ninth centuries, which
had emphasized for the most part fine points of meta-
physics and theology. The first of the new popular
sects in Japan was founded by the monk Honen in
1175. It quite understandably took the name of Pure
Land Sect, for the Pure Land was a term for Paradise.
In true reforming fashion, Shinran, one of the disciples
of Honen, split away from his teacher, and in 1224
founded the True Pure Land Sect. This sect in time
outstripped in popularity all other Japanese Buddhist
sects. Even today it is the largest and strongest Buddhist group within Japan and the only one with a significant missionary movement abroad.

Both of these Pure Land Sects were definitely expressions of the religious feelings of the lower classes,
which were assuming importance for the first time in
the intellectual life of the nation. These sects taught a
simpler way to salvation for less sophisticated minds,
and from the start they won much of their strength
by direct street-corner preaching to the poor.

Shinran showed his opposition to the intellectual aristocracy of the earlier monastic sects by at first for-
bidding the founding of monasteries, and he preached
the "equality of all in Buddhism." In an effort to bring
the clergy closer to the people and nearer every day
life, he permitted his priests to marry, a custom which
gradually spread to most types of the clergy in all
sects. One of Shinran's successors started a movement
to translate into Japanese certain of the Buddhist

scriptures, which had been transmitted to Japan in classical and often very difficult Chinese. This same priest also founded discussion groups among the lay believers, which in time evolved into large, influential lay congregations.

These congregations were perhaps the chief organs of intellectual life for the lower classes during the feudal period. In time some even became the agencies through which the people asserted themslves in politics. Congregations of the True Pure Land Sect killed their feudal leaders in two west coast provinces of Japan in 1488 and thereafter controlled this area themselves. During the sixteenth century the great temple-castle of the sect, located in a town which later became the commercial city of Osaka, was able to defy siege by the strongest feudal faction in Japan for a period of ten years.

Side by side with the two Pure Land Sects, there soon developed a third popular sect, founded in 1253 by the priest Nichiren and usually known by his name. Basically much like the other two, it relied even more on street-corner preaching, but differed radically from them in its religious fanaticism, which was the legacy of its dynamic but bellicose founder. Nichiren, in sharp contrast to the pacifistic, tolerant, and all-embracing spirit which Buddhism had always shown, was an intolerant fighting man of religion, who openly attacked other Buddhist sects as leading men only to damnation. His sect became a fighting church, often engaging in acts of open warfare with the members of other sects during the turbulent feudal period. Nichiren, again in contrast to the dominant international spirit of Buddhism, was himself a narrow nationalist, a forerunner of the nationalistic movement of modern times. To him Japan was the land of the gods and the center of the universe, and Japanese Buddhism was the only true Buddhism.

It is, indeed, a curious fact that the popular Buddhism of feudal Japan had in many ways come to resemble Christianity more than historic Buddhism. Reversing the basic pessimism of the early faith, it had come to stress a real after-life and salvation through faith. And the early feudal religious reformers, in their translations of the scriptures, their creation of lay congregations, their marriage of the clergy, their militant sectarianism, and their nascent nationalism, resembled to a surprising degree the Protestant reformers of Europe. These religious trends, coupled with the development of a feudal system which found much closer parallels in medieval Europe than in East Asia, make the early feudal period in Japan a time for startling comparisons with Europe and strong contrasts with other countries in the Far East.

While the lower classes were turning to the popular Buddhist sects for religious and intellectual expression, the warrior caste found a different answer to its religious and philosophic needs in still another Buddhist sect brought to Japan in the late twelfth and early thirteenth centuries by Japanese monks returning to their homeland from study in China. This sect was known as Zen, a word meaning "meditation," and it derived perhaps as much from native Chinese schools of mysticism as from the early Buddhist emphasis on meditation.

In Zen the emphasis was on being in harmony with

Fr.

the cosmos — on achieving oneness with nature. Zen was anti-scholastic and anti-rational. Its adherents sought sudden intuitive insight as a result of extreme physical discipline and mental concentration, rather than wisdom through book learning or through logical thought. As a means of training in Zen, the master would pose a seemingly trivial or irrational problem, such as the nature of the sound caused by a clapping motion made with only one hand instead of with two. The student would meditate upon this problem for days, but any answer describing the nature of sound or the reasons for the absence of sound would not be tolerated by the master. The train of meditation started by this problem was intended to result in a flash of sudden enlightenment regarding the nature of the Buddha, the oneness of the universe, or other problems equally profound.

The anti-scholasticism, the mental discipline — still more the strict physical discipline of the adherents of Zen, which kept their lives very close to nature — all appealed to the warrior caste, with its predilection for the Spartan life. Zen rapidly became the philosophy of the military men of feudal Japan, giving them a philo-sophical foundation on which to base their lives. With their support, it rose to a position of wide influence and great prestige. Zen contributed much to the devel-opment of a toughness of inner fiber and a strength of character which typified the warrior of feudal Japan; and Zen has continued to play its role in recent years by giving spiritual strength and firmness to many mem-bers of the officer caste.

Chapter VI

GROWTH AND CHANGE IN THE FEUDAL SYSTEM

The Kamakura system, however well it worked at its inception, was peculiarly susceptible to the ravages of time and change. It was effective as long as its member knights remained a small and well-knit group, loyal to each other, but as the generations passed, loyalties based on family friendships and comradeship in half-forgotten campaigns wore thin. Scattered as they now were through the estates of the whole land, the descendants of the old band of knights from the Kanto region, who had won control of Japan in 1185, felt less and less the oneness of spirit of the original clique or the old sense of personal loyalty to Kamakura.

Another factor in the dissolution of the clique was its growth in numbers. The class of knights grew rapidly with each generation, but the number of positions as estate managers could not increase correspondingly. The natural tendency was for each knight to divide his feudal income from the estate he managed among all his sons. As a result of this process, many a knight in the latter part of the thirteenth century received so small an income that he had difficulty in maintaining his status as a mounted warrior, able to answer the call of his lord fully equipped with horse, armor, and weapons.

Despite these weakening factors, the Kamakura system lasted a century and a half. During this time it withstood the most dangerous threat of aggression from abroad that Japan was to experience prior to recent years. This threat was the attempted Mongol invasions of 1274 and 1281.

The Mongols, a nomadic people of the steppe lands north of China, in the first half of the thirteenth century conquered all of Central Asia, southern Russia, and much of the Near East, and their armies penetrated to Silesia and through Hungary to the Adriatic Sea. At the eastern end of this vast empire, they completed the subjugation of Korea in 1259 and crushed the last organized resistance in China itself in 1276.

In the east only Japan remained free of their rule, and the Mongol emperor, Kublai Khan, probably looking for more worlds to conquer, sent emissaries to Japan, demanding the capitulation of the island kingdom. The terrified courtiers of Kyoto were ready to accede, but the staunch warriors of Kamakura refused, making their stand unmistakably clear by beheading some of the emissaries.

Such a direct affront could not go unpunished, and in 1274 a strong Mongol force set out on Korean ships to subdue Japan. Certain small islands were seized and a landing was made at Hakata Bay in northern Kyushu, but before any decisive engagement had been fought, the Mongols decided to withdraw to the continent because of the threat to their fleet of inclement weather. That they would return was a foregone conclusion. For the next several years Kamakura kept many of its knights from the western part of the country on guard in northern Kyushu, busy constructing a wall around Hakata Bay to contain the vaunted Mongol cavalry in the event of a second landing there.

The Mongols came again in 1281, this time on a great joint armada of Korean and Chinese ships, and again a landing was made at Hakata Bay. The invasion forces numbered some 150,000 men, the greatest overseas expedition the world had as yet seen. The Mongols were accustomed to large scale cavalry tactics which had met no match anywhere in the world, and they had superior weapons at their disposal, such as the gunpowder bomb hurled by a catapult.

Against this overwhelming force, the Japanese had a mere handful of knights, accustomed only to single combat. But the Mongols were slowed by the wall the Japanese had built and by the attacks of smaller, more mobile Japanese boats in the narrow waters of the bay. Before they could deploy their full forces ashore, a typhoon descended upon the fleet and destroyed it, bringing the invasion to a spectacular and disastrous conclusion. To the Japanese the typhoon was the *kamikaze*, the "Divine Wind," protecting the land of the gods from foreign invaders. The incident has of course loomed large in Japanese historical tradition and has contributed much to the irrational conviction of most Japanese that their land was sacred and inviolate.

The danger to Japan was past, but dissatisfaction and unrest on the part of the warrior class of western Japan remained as an aftermath of the invasions. Many knights had become impoverished during the long months and years away from home in the service of Kamakura, and there were no spoils to divide among the victors. The wavering loyalty of the knights had suffered a serious blow; yet the Kamakura system was strong enough to survive another fifty years.

The final blow came from a new and surprising source, a retired emperor who is known by his post-humous name of Daigo II. This ex-emperor was an historical misfit who had the antiquated idea that the imperial line should really rule. Gathering a force of discontented warriors from the capital district and soldiers from local monastery estates, he led a revolt against Kamakura in the year 1331. The revolt in itself would have meant little if the whole Kamakura system had not been ripe for dissolution. The warriors of western Japan for the most part declared for the imperial cause, and Ashikaga Takauji, the general sent from eastern Japan to subdue the uprising, suddenly switched sides in 1333. A second force was raised in the Kanto region, but this time the general in command did not even march on Kyoto. Instead he seized Kamakura itself, destroyed the Hojo family, and thus brought to an end a century and a half of centralized rule.

Daigo II, who naïvely assumed that the way was now open for the resumption of imperial rule as it had existed five or six centuries earlier, was in for a rude awakening. Ashikaga Takauji was a realist who knew where power lay, and he soon deserted Daigo II, driving the unhappy monarch from Kyoto in 1336 and putting a member of a collateral line of the imperial family on the throne. Daigo II and his followers withdrew to the mountain fastnesses south of the Nara Plain and there set up a rival imperial court. From this vantage point they and their successors continued the hopeless struggle against the Ashikaga family for almost sixty years. In the year 1392, they were induced to give up and were lured back to Kyoto by the promise that the line of Daigo II would alternate on the throne with the line set up by Takauji. No one who had observed the Ashikaga family's past record of treachery could have been surprised that they did not live up to their agreement. No member of the line of Daigo II ever sat on the throne again.

Daigo II had failed completely in his fantastic attempt to restore imperial rule in feudal Japan, but Ashikaga Takauji, who had had himself appointed Shogun in 1338, was little more successful in his attempt to recreate the unity of Kamakura. He set up a line of Ashikaga Shogun at Kyoto who managed to retain the title until 1573, but no Ashikaga Shogun ever exercised effective control over all the military leaders and powerful Buddhist monasteries of the land. During a large part of these two and a half centuries, the government of the Shogun was almost as much of a political sham as the imperial court itself. The third Ashikaga Shogun came as close as any member of his family to ruling the whole country for a brief period after the surrender of the imperial faction of Daigo II in 1392, but Ashikaga power declined rapidly thereafter. From 1467 on, civil wars were chronic throughout Japan. Strong feudal lords drove Ashikaga Shogun out of Kyoto and set up puppet Shogun in much the same way that the earlier Shogun had done these same things to the imperial family.

The fourteenth and fifteenth centuries presented a picture of increasing political disruption and confusion, as all central control slowly disappeared. The basic cause for the growing political disunity was that the warrior class had grown so fast during the Kamakura period that a united government based simply on ties of personal loyalty was no longer possible. New forms of political organization were necessary before unity could be restored.

The restoration of unity proved to be a slow process. The first step actually was the creation of new feudal units smaller than the old nation–wide warrior clique. Certain constables or other warriors who for one reason or another had won a strong local following gradually assumed the role of feudal lords in the late Kamakura period. In the wars that marked the end of the Kamakura regime it became evident that the individual knight felt a primary sense of loyalty to his local lord and not to the Hojo and their puppet Shogun. During the fourteenth and fifteenth centuries the dominant figure in the political system was more and more the feudal lord, not the individual knight, as the land became divided into a large number of virtually independent feudal domains.

As the feudal lord, or Daimyo rose to power, the knight began to sink into insignificance and finally disappeared from the scene. One reason for this was that the old estates gradually lost their identity in the domains of the various Daimyo, and the position of estate manager became a thing of the past. Also, large bodies of foot soldiers began to replace the individual knight as the backbone of the fighting forces of Japan. Thus the knight lost his favored place both as a military man and as a key figure in the political and economic order.

Some descendants of the old warrior families became themselves Daimyo. Others became part of a new petty aristocracy of military and administrative officials serving in the domains of the Daimyo and supported by fixed salaries or by the income from small tracts of land assigned to them by the Daimyo. But there was no longer a clear-cut line between these knights as fighting men and the peasantry, who were as capable of serving as foot soldiers as the best of the warrior class. For this reason the congregations of the True Pure Land Sect could challenge the supremacy of the feudal leaders. Peasants in time of war were now soldiers, and in the fifteenth and sixteenth centuries many men of very humble origin unquestionably pushed their way into the upper ranks of the new feudal aristocracy, while many members of the old warrior class sank to the status of peasants.

The gradual disappearance of the estates into the domains of the Daimyo was an unfortunate development for the imperial family and the old court aristocracy at Kyoto, which had for centuries derived their income from these estates. Revenues from this source had been dwindling, and finally they ceased altogether. During the fifteenth and sixteenth centuries the imperial line, various branches of the Fujiwara, and other old court families eked out a miserable and precarious existence; but they managed to survive, earning their living by serving as patrons of trade and manufacturing guilds in Kyoto and by exploiting the few arts and aptitudes permitted them by aristocratic tradition.

One emperor was even reduced to selling his calligraphy on the streets of the city, writing out in his beautiful hand a poem or motto requested by some patron and receiving in exchange a small gift. Lack of funds to pay for proper funeral services or coronation ceremonies forced the imperial family to get along without a properly invested emperor during three different periods in the sixteenth century. At one time there was no duly enthroned emperor for a period of twenty-one years. The fortunes of the imperial line had indeed sunk low. Only the force of historical tradition kept it and its satellite court aristocracy from disappearing entirely.

The political chaos of the Ashikaga period and the sad state of the imperial court have left behind a traditional picture of these two and a half centuries as a dark age in Japanese history. This picture is far from accurate, for the political confusion was but a sign of rapid growth, and in the turmoil the Japanese as a whole were making great strides forward culturally and economically.

With the financial eclipse of the court aristocracy, cultural leadership in the capital city of Kyoto naturally passed to the Shogun's court. In fact, some of the Ashikaga Shogun are far better known to history as patrons of art than as political leaders. Gathering about them some of the finest artists and literary men of the day, they at times presided over a culturally brilliant if politically ineffective court.

As was to be expected in this turbulent age, the artists and men of letters usually were Buddhist priests and monks, and the great monasteries more than ever became the repositories of learning and the centers of creative art. The Zen monks in particular dominated the cultural life of the time. This was not so much because they received official patronage as because they were in much closer contact with China than any other group and were consequently the first to learn of new cultural trends on the continent. Actually, the predominantly Zen culture of the Ashikaga period was a rich blending of the native culture with many new cultural elements from the continent.

Despite their traditional anti-scholasticism, the Zen monks reintroduced the use of pure Chinese as an important literary medium, and at the same time they led in the development of Japan's first true dramatic form, the so-called *Nō* drama. A major purpose of *Nō* was to teach concepts of Buddhism. Since it had evolved originally from early religious dances, symbolic dances quite naturally remained one of its most important features. But perhaps the greatest merit of the *Nō* was the fine poetic recitations chanted by the actors and an accompanying chorus. The texts of the *Nō* drama still remain one of the great literary expressions of the Japanese people, and a small band of devotees even today keep the *Nō* alive as a highly formalized and completely outmoded dramatic form.

In the field of architecture, fresh influences from China made for significant new forms, but the Zen culture of the Ashikaga period found its fullest expression in painting. Zen monks, living simple lives close to nature, took with enthusiasm to the Chinese style of monochrome landscape painting, often rivaling the skill and depth of feeling of the Chinese masters. The richness of the artistic work of the time is seen in the fact that side by side with this Chinese school of painting existed a vigorous native school specializing in picture scrolls portraying the history of some temple or the incidents of a famous campaign, such as that against the Mongols.

The medieval Zen monks also brought from China three other arts which became so characteristic of Japanese culture that they are now considered to be typically Japanese. One was landscape gardening, which the Japanese developed to a perfection unexcelled in any other land. The second was flower arrangement, which started with the placing of floral offerings before representations of Buddhist deities but eventually became a fine art which is now part of the training of every well-bred Japanese girl. The third was the tea ceremony, an aesthetic spiritual ritual in which a beautiful but simple setting, a few fine pieces of old pottery, a slow, formalized, extremely graceful ritual for preparing and serving the tea, and a spirit of complete tranquillity all combine to express the love of beauty, the devotion to simplicity, and the search for spiritual calm which characterize the best in Zen.

Increased trade contacts with the continent, which had brought many new cultural impulses from China, also served as an impetus to an unprecedented and rapid expansion of Japanese trade and industry. Another impetus may have been the decline and disappearance of the estates. As long as these had existed, they tended to

be self-contained economic units, but their going allowed a wider exchange of goods and greater specialization in production by localities or by groups within
each locality. Because of the need for protection from
the many restrictions and fees in a feudal society, this
new economic specialization usually resulted in the formation of guilds of merchants dealing in certain
commodities and guilds of manufacturers producing
various types of wares.

Under the guilds, trade and manufacture expanded
steadily, and centers of paper-making, metal-working,
weaving, and the like grew up all over the land. Small
market places developed into little trading towns.
Kyoto remained the largest city of Japan, but gradually a rival city of purely commercial and industrial
origin grew up at the eastern end of the Inland Sea.
This town, later to be called Osaka, was until the late
sixteenth century a type of free city outside the domains of the feudal lords, dominated only by the local
merchants and the great temple-castle of the True Pure
Land Sect.

The true measure of the economic growth of Japan
during the feudal period is perhaps best seen in foreign
trade. There had been some trade with the continent
ever since Prince Shotoku sent the first official embassy
to China, but overseas trade began to assume significant
proportions only in the late twelfth century. From that
time on, it grew steadily until by the fifteenth and sixteenth centuries it was a tremendous factor in the economic life of Japan.

The Japanese imported from the continent tropical
products, which had originally come from Southeast

Asia or even from India, and manufactured goods from China, such as silks, porcelains, books, manuscripts, paintings, and copper cash. The last loomed largest in bulk and value, because from the thirteenth century on, money increasingly replaced rice and cloth as the chief medium for exchange in Japan, and the Japanese depended almost entirely on China as the source for their currency.

In the early feudal period, Japanese exports were limited for the most part to raw goods, such as sulphur, lumber, gold, pearls, mercury, and mother of pearl. However, by the fifteenth and sixteenth centuries Japan itself was exporting large quantities of manufactured goods to China and the continent. Chief among these were swords and painted folding fans and screens. Folding fans and screens apparently were inventions of either the Koreans or the Japanese and were highly prized in China. The curved swords of medieval Japan, made of the finest laminated steel and unexcelled even by the famous blades of Damascus or Toledo, were in great demand throughout East Asia and were exported by the thousands.

In the early days, the Koreans were the chief mariners and traders in the waters between Japan and the continent, but slowly the Japanese themselves took to the sea. In the late eleventh century, Japanese traders were crossing to Korea; in the twelfth, some were venturing as far as China; and by the fourteenth and fifteenth centuries, they were beginning to dominate the shipping and commerce of the whole East China Sea.

Various groups in Japan participated in this lucrative trade with the continent. As mentioned previously,

many Buddhist monasteries sponsored trading ventures
in order to raise funds, as did various families of feudal
lords, including the Ashikaga themselves. In fact, the
Ashikaga, in order to secure some of the profits of this
trade for their shaky regime, accepted the Chinese
theory that international trade was simply the bringing
of tribute to the Chinese court by barbarian peoples
and the beneficent bestowal of gifts upon the barbarians
by the court in return. To fit this pattern, some of the
Ashikaga Shogun, with complete disregard of the theory of imperial rule, permitted themselves to be invested as "Kings of Japan" by the emperors of the
Ming dynasty of China and then sold credentials to
private Japanese traders, to give them legal and official
status in their trading ventures in China.

Despite the interest in foreign trade on the part of
the monasteries and the Shogun in central Japan, leadership in overseas trading was taken primarily by the
small feudal lords, the ordinary warriors, and the merchants of western Japan, who merged to form a class
of adventurous and hardy mariners. Like their counterparts in Europe, these men of the sea were primarily
traders, but they were not averse to piracy when opportunity offered. Credentials from the Ashikaga or
trading permits from the Chinese court meant little to
them. Already in the thirteenth century piratical acts
by Japanese warrior-merchants had become frequent
in Korean waters, and during the fourteenth century,
Japanese pirates became a menace to the very existence
of the kingdom of Korea. Emboldened by their successes in Korean waters, they shifted their activities
more and more to the coast of China. As the Ming dy-

nasty declined in the sixteenth and early seventeenth centuries, Japanese pirates ravaged the great coastal cities of China almost at will, contributing greatly to the final collapse of the dynasty during the middle decades of the seventeenth century.

The so-called Japanese pirates of the sixteenth century were not always pirates, however, nor were they always Japanese. Many Chinese joined them in preying on the coastal trade and cities of China. One of the most important elements in this mixed group of Chinese and Japanese, who were both traders and pirates, was furnished by the natives of the Ryukyu Islands. Closely related to the Japanese and speaking a variant form of the language, they owed a dual allegiance in the seventeenth century to China and to the great Daimyo domain of Satsuma in southern Kyushu.

When the European merchant-adventurers rounded the Malay Peninsula and entered Far Eastern waters early in the sixteenth century, they found the seas dominated more by Japanese than by Chinese. In the course of the century, thousands of Japanese established themselves as traders and adventurers in the towns and colonies of Southeast Asia; and the Spanish and Portuguese, recognizing the martial traditions and fine fighting qualities of the Japanese, frequently employed them as mercenaries in their campaigns and wars in the Far East. In a typical colonial city like Manila, the Japanese community grew large and strong, and in the early seventeenth century, Japanese adventurers were influential enough at the Siamese capital to engineer a successful revolution there and to put a friendly faction in power.

During the "dark ages" of political confusion in
Japan, the people had developed industrially to a point
where they equalled or even excelled their Chinese
teachers in many fields of manufacturing. Despite the
feudal political framework, they had built up a far
stronger commercial system than they had achieved in
previous ages; and in a burst of new physical power and
vitality, their warrior-traders had come to dominate the
waters of East Asia. Japan entered the feudal period
in the twelfth century, a small, weak, economically
backward land on the fringes of the civilized world.
It emerged in the sixteenth century from a prolonged
period of feudal anarchy, an economically advanced
nation, able in many ways to compete on terms of
equality with the newly encountered peoples of Europe and even with the Chinese.

Chapter VII

THE REESTABLISHMENT OF
NATIONAL UNITY

The vigorous Japan of the early sixteenth century still showed no signs of recreating an effective central government, but the foundation of a new form of political unity had been laid. This foundation consisted of the Daimyo domains, into which almost all of Japan was now divided. Since each domain was an effective political unit in itself, national unity could be achieved simply by establishing some form of association or accepted leadership among the Daimyo.

The realms of the Daimyo varied greatly in size, but they tended to be compact, well-defined political units, perhaps subordinate to some other feudal domain, but in any case entirely independent of the emperor or Shogun. The Daimyo himself was a paternalistic but absolute monarch within his own realm. Aiding him in his rule over the soldiers, peasants, and merchants of the principality was a class of officials and military officers, who formed the little court at the central castle of the Daimyo and lived on the hereditary salaries he assigned them and their families.

With their military heritage, most of the Daimyo were intent upon developing the military strength of their domains. Some of the more powerful Daimyo, who ruled over several provinces, built up efficient fighting machines, with the peasantry as the backbone of the economic life of the realm and as the reservoir for military manpower, with the feudal aristocracy furnishing administrators and officers for the army, and with the merchants providing a transport corps in time of war.

The natural tendency was for the larger and stronger realms to swallow up or win dominance over weaker neighbors. In the second half of the sixteenth century, this process resulted in the creation of a single paramount power in Japan. The first great figure in the reunification of the country was Oda Nobunaga, a Daimyo who ruled over three provinces around the modern city of Nagoya east of Kyoto. By seizing the capital in 1568, he became the virtual dictator of central Japan, and he proceeded to consolidate his power by breaking the military might of the powerful central monasteries and by capturing the great temple-castle of the True Pure Land Sect in Osaka after a ten-year siege. But Nobunaga never achieved his goal of winning hegemony over all Japan. His career was cut short when a treacherous vassal murdered him in 1582.

Nobunaga's place as undisputed ruler of central Japan was soon assumed by his ablest general, Hideyoshi, a man of lowly birth who had risen to power by sheer ability. Within a few years of Nobunaga's death, Hideyoshi had eliminated the remnants of the Oda family and had established his supremacy over the remaining vassals of Nobunaga. He reconstructed the great castle at Osaka as the seat of his military government, but he gave evidence of a reviving interest in the imperial court at Kyoto by taking for himself the old Fujiwara posts of Prime Minister and Civil Dictator.

In 1587 Hideyoshi crushed the power of the great Satsuma realm of southern Kyushu and thereby won control over all western Japan. Three years later, all of eastern and northern Japan submitted to him after he had eliminated the chief Daimyo realm in the Kanto area. The restoration of political unity in Japan had at last been completed, and peace came to the land suddenly after more than a hundred years of incessant civil war.

Hideyoshi found himself in control of a superabundance of professional warriors who knew nothing but warfare. Possibly in order to drain off some of their excess fighting spirit, and probably because he himself, like many successful generals before him, fell victim to the world conqueror complex, Hideyoshi decided to embark on a program of world conquest, which for him meant the conquest of China. To do this he needed passage through Korea, and when the Koreans refused, he invaded the peninsula from the south in 1592. The Japanese armies rapidly overran almost all of Korea, but were eventually checked when they over-extended their lines of communication and met the armies of China, which had come to the aid of its Korean satellite. The Japanese were forced back to southern Korea, where they held on for several years despite a gradually deteriorating situation and difficulties in maintaining their communications by sea. The death of Hideyoshi

in 1598 gave them a welcome excuse for abandoning
the whole venture, and their armies streamed home.
Japan's first organized attempt at overseas conquest had
ended in complete failure.

The political vacuum created by the death of Hideyoshi was soon filled by one of his foremost vassals,
Tokugawa Ieyasu, who had been Hideyoshi's chief
deputy in eastern Japan, where he had built himself a
castle headquarters at the small village of Edo, the
future Tokyo. In 1600, Ieyasu decisively defeated a
coalition of rivals, and fifteen years later he destroyed
the remnants of Hideyoshi's family when he captured
the great Osaka castle by trickery and overwhelming
might.

Ieyasu, impressed by the inability of the heirs of
Nobunaga and Hideyoshi to keep the reins of government in their own hands, was obsessed with the idea
of building up a political system strong enough to survive his death. Political stability became his primary
goal, and it was equally sought and maintained by his
successors. There is no doubt that the Tokugawa created political stability. During the first half of the
seventeenth century they created a political system
which was to endure almost unchanged for two and a
half centuries, and which was to establish a state of domestic peace as complete as that enjoyed by any people
at any time. Unfortunately, they secured peace and
stability by a series of rigid controls over society, by
ruthless suppression of many of the most creative tendencies in the Japan of that day, and by a return to
many of the outmoded forms of feudalism — in short,
by resorting to what was essentially a reactionary

policy even in the early decades of the seventeenth century.

The Tokugawa, like the Minamoto before them, rejected the idea of rule from the old central district around Kyoto and established their new military capital at their castle in Edo, which they expanded into one of the greatest fortresses man has ever created. It was protected by wide moats, high embankments, and massive castle walls, arranged in a series of concentric circles with an overall diameter of slightly more than two miles. Today, the inner circles of the great castle form the beautiful imperial palace grounds in the heart of Tokyo.

The central part of Japan, including the Kanto Plain on the east and the old capital district in the west, was held directly by the Tokugawa themselves, by various branches of the family, and by the feudal lords and warriors who had backed Ieyasu in the great battle for supremacy in 1600. This central area was strategically the heart of the country. It contained most of the larger plains and much of the best agricultural land of Japan, and also a large proportion of the commercial towns and cities. Three great cadet families of the Tokugawa were established at three key points, the town of Mito, east of Edo; Nagoya, near the geographic center of the Tokugawa domains; and Wakayama, a few miles south of Osaka in the west. Most of the remainder of the central area was divided into fiefs held by other members of the family and by old and loyal allies of the Tokugawa. Holders of large fiefs were called "hereditary Daimyo," signifying their early support of Ieyasu, and the lesser vassals were

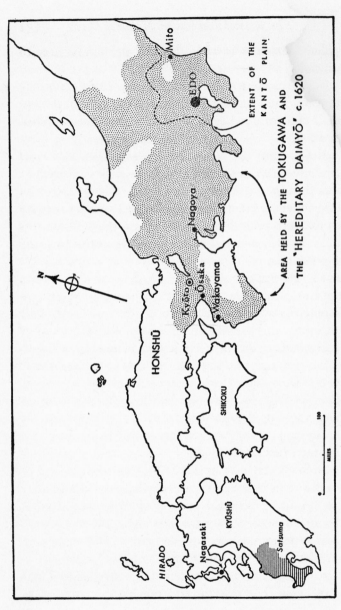

JAPAN IN THE TOKUGAWA PERIOD

EXTENT OF THE
KANTŌ PLAIN

AREA HELD BY THE TOKUGAWA AND
THE "HEREDITARY DAIMYŌ" c.1620

Mito

EDO

Nagoya

Kyōto
Ōsaka
Wakayama

N

HONSHŪ

SHIKOKU

0   100
MILES

KYŌSHŪ

HIRADO

Nagasaki
Satsuma

called "standard bearers." Beyond the central area to
the north and west stretched the realms of the Daimyo
who had recognized Ieyasu's rule only after his victory
in 1600. These lords were called "outer Daimyo," and
their control was the most difficult problem of Tokugawa rule.

Both categories of Daimyo were allowed virtual
autonomy within their realms, but the Tokugawa
worked out a careful system of checks and controls to
prevent any of them from becoming a military menace
to the new central authority. Severe restrictions were
placed on the construction or repair of castles, marking
the end of a century of castle building which has left
many picturesque old fortifications scattered around
Japan. Each Daimyo was forced to leave in Edo, as
hostages, members of his own family, such as his wife
and sons, and he himself was compelled to maintain a
permanent residence there and to spend alternate periods in residence at Edo and at his fief. A close watch
was kept at important barriers on the highways of the
land to look for "women leaving Edo and firearms
entering Edo," for the departure of hostages or the
smuggling in of weapons would have indicated a
planned revolt.

Perhaps the most interesting measure taken by Edo
to insure its control over the Daimyo was the creation
of a group of officials known as *metsuke*, who acted on
the one hand as censors in ferreting out cases of misrule
and maladministration on the part of Tokugawa officials, and on the other hand as secret police spying
on all men or groups who could be a menace to Tokugawa rule. The Edo government has the dubious dis-

tinction of being one of the first governments in the world to develop an extensive and efficient secret police system and to make of it an important organ of state. With three centuries of experience in such practices, it is not surprising that the secret police should have loomed so large in the political make-up of Japan in recent years.

The Tokugawa left the age-old fiction of imperial rule undisturbed. They actually helped reenforce it by fairly generous economic treatment of the emperors and their courtiers, while keeping them under close surveillance and strict control. Ieyasu in 1603 took for himself the old title of Shogun, indicating that in theory he was merely the generalissimo of the emperor's armies. To insure that his death would not upset the supremacy of his family, he abdicated two years later in favor of one of his less gifted but more dependable sons. As a result of this move, Ieyasu's death in 1616 produced no political repercussions.

The early Edo leaders were determined to do everything they could to insure that the ineptness or stupidity of some future Shogun should not bring disaster to the regime. They created a strong, complicated central administration quite capable of ruling the land with or without the Shogun, many of whom proved to be little more than figureheads. This central administration consisted of a Prime Minister — a post often left vacant — a council of state made up of four or five "elders," a group of "junior elders" who controlled the affairs of the petty vassals of Edo, a large body of civil administrators, and the *metsuke*.

The membership of the administration was recruited

on a basis of natural selection from among the members of the rapidly expanding Tokugawa family, the "hereditary Daimyo," the "standard bearers," and all the petty gentry of the central area. When first Japan had needed a large bureaucracy in the seventh and eighth centuries, it was lacking, but by the seventeenth century, education and learning had become so widespread that there was no dearth of educated men or capable administrators for the Edo government.

In support of the prime objective of political stability, the early Tokugawa adopted a policy of social stability. Nobunaga, by crushing the military power of the True Pure Land Sect and by taking over control of the commercial city of Osaka, had struck a severe blow at the rising political power of the middle and lower classes. Hideyoshi, the common foot-soldier, lacking even a family name, who had risen to become the virtual ruler of all Japan, had typified in himself the complete breakdown of the clear class cleavages of early feudalism, but it was he who struck the second great blow against the political aspirations of the lower classes. Wishing to reduce the overly large military establishments of Japan, which were unnecessary in a unified land, he drew a sharp line between the peasants and the aristocratic warrior class of officers and demanded that all peasants surrender their swords and other weapons to the government and forsake their past role of peasant-soldiers.

The Tokugawa simply followed and developed this policy. Adopting the social theories of Confucianism, which had developed some 2,000 years earlier in China, they created a hierarchy of four social classes — the warrior-administrator, the peasant, the artisan, and the merchant. The top class of warrior-administrators was to a large degree an artificial creation in imitation of the true warrior class of early feudalism. The members of this new fixed aristocracy were known as *samurai*, meaning "feudal retainers," and their badge was the long and the short sword each *samurai* wore at his side. The merchants, despite their real intellectual and cultural status in society and in complete disregard of their high economic position, were placed last in the social order because, according to Confucian theory, they were an unproductive class. This unnatural stratification of social classes was reactionary even in seventeenth-century Japan, but the Tokugawa and the favored *samurai* class as a whole enforced it rigidly and blindly for two and a half centuries.

The early Tokugawa not only borrowed the antiquated social theories of early Confucianism; they encouraged the study of the whole philosophy of Confucianism, perhaps in the hope that it would be a stabilizing factor in the intellectual life of the land. Confucianism, with its emphasis on proper relationships between the ruler and the ruled, seemed admirably suited to be a state philosophy fostering a deep sense of loyalty to the regime.

As early as 1608 Ieyasu appointed a prominent Confucian philosopher to be "attendant scholar" at his court. From this small beginning grew a strong school of Confucianism at Edo, teaching the orthodox interpretation as it had been formulated in China in the twelfth century by a group of philosophers, who had added to the ethical doctrines of the early Confucian-

ists a ponderous superstructure of metaphysical speculation. Soon groups of thinkers grew up in opposition
to the orthodox Edo school, representing various un-
orthodox schools of Confucianism which rejected the
rigid interpretations of the twelfth century masters.
One of the best results of this scholarly interest in Confucianism in Tokugawa Japan was the development
within the *samurai* class of a body of trained students
and thinkers who as statesmen contributed greatly to
the efficient administration of the Tokugawa and as
teachers helped keep Japan intellectually alive, despite
the stultifying effects of the basically reactionary political and social system.

The long period of interest in Confucianism also
served to imbue the people as a whole with many of
the high ethical and moral standards of this Chinese
philosophy. Buddhism remained the dominant religion
of the masses and enjoyed a status of official patronage,
but Confucianism slowly became the strongest intellectual and ethical force in Japan. Buddhism began to
show signs of slow inner decay, which has in modern
times robbed it of much of the vigor it possessed in the
Ashikaga period, but Confucianism grew in influence
and strength. It became perhaps the dominant philosophy in Japan and a major source for the unwritten ethical code of the *samurai*, which recent scholars have
described in romantic terms as *Bushido*, the "way of
the warrior."

Perhaps the most drastic measures taken by the Edo
government in order to insure political stability were
in the field of foreign relations, which, with the coming
of Europeans to Far Eastern waters, assumed more

significance than ever before in Japanese history. The first Europeans to reach Japan were Portuguese mariners who landed on an island off the southern tip of Kyushu in 1542 or 1543. Trade relations soon sprang up between the Portuguese and the feudal lords of western Kyushu, who learned the use of firearms from the European traders.

Contacts with the Portuguese took on a new aspect when St. Francis Xavier, the famous Jesuit missionary, introduced Christianity to Japan during a two year stay there from 1549 to 1551. He and many other Jesuits who followed in his footsteps met with considerable success in their proselytizing. The Buddhist churches soon recognized Christianity as a dangerous rival and opposed it bitterly, but several of the petty lords of Kyushu favored the missionaries, realizing that Portuguese traders tended to bring their ships to ports where the Jesuits had been welcomed. A minor Daimyo, who himself had earlier embraced Christianity, managed with the aid of the Portuguese to build the fishing village of Nagasaki in western Kyushu into the chief port for foreign trade in all Japan. Many small lords had already become Christians, when in 1578 one of the great Daimyo of Kyushu was converted. Japanese of all classes in western Japan and particularly in Kyushu were beginning to embrace the new faith. It is estimated that there were some 150,000 Christians in Japan around the year 1580 and twice that number in the early seventeenth century.

Hideyoshi and the Tokugawa who followed him had no particular objection to Christianity on religious grounds, but they looked upon it with deep suspicion as a political menace to their rule. The Christians, as a sizable group of Japanese owing some sort of vague allegiance to a remote European "ruler," the Pope, were in their eyes a group which could not be trusted and a possible threat to the reestablished unity of Japan. Furthermore, Hideyoshi and the early Tokugawa were fully aware of the colonial expansion of the European powers in Southeast Asia, where the Christian missionaries had seemed to serve as forerunners of military penetration and conquest. The Japanese leaders were desirous of retaining profitable trade relations with the Europeans, but they gradually came to the conclusion that for reasons of national safety and political stability, Christianity must go.

In 1587, the very year Hideyoshi completed the subjugation of western Japan, he issued a decree ordering all Christian missionaries banned from Japan. However, he made little effort to enforce this decree until ten years later, when irritated by the bickering between the Portuguese Jesuits and the Spanish Franciscans, who had started missionary activities in Japan in 1593, he executed nine European priests and seventeen native Christians.

Ieyasu at first reversed this stern policy, befriending Spanish missionaries in an unsuccessful attempt to persuade Spanish merchants to establish direct trade contacts in the Edo region. The arrival at this time of Protestant Dutch and English traders, who had no interest in proselytizing, convinced Ieyasu that it was not necessary to tolerate Christianity in order to retain trade relations with European countries. The Dutch established a trading post at Hirado, an island off the northwest coast of Kyushu in 1609, and the English, too, set up a trading post there in 1613. At about the same time Ieyasu reverted to Hideyoshi's policy of persecuting Christianity, and his successor in 1617 returned to the extreme measure of executing European missionaries and native believers. In the next few years all the missionaries were either killed or forced to leave Japan, and thousands of Japanese Christians either apostatized or else suffered the death of martyrs. A common practice of the time was to order people suspected of being Christians to tread upon a cross or some other sacred symbol, and to kill those who refused to comply.

The persecution of Christianity came to a dramatic conclusion in the years 1637 and 1638, when the long Christianized peasantry of a region near Nagasaki rebelled in desperation over economic and religious oppression. Some 37,000, basing themselves on an old dilapidated castle, withstood for almost three months the assault of the assembled might of the central government, supported by the fire power of certain Dutch vessels. The Christian rebels were eventually slaughtered almost to a man, and with this final catastrophe Christianity ceased to exist as an organized religion in Japan.

Meanwhile, the successors of Ieyasu, with increasing suspicion of all foreigners and a growing zeal to preserve the *status quo* at all costs, had started to close the doors of Japan to virtually all foreign intercourse. The English had already given up their trading post at Hirado as an unprofitable venture, and all Spaniards were expelled from Japan in 1624. The Portuguese in turn were expelled in 1638 for suspected complicity in the Christian rebellion, and when they sent an embassy to Japan two years later to seek the reopening of trade relations, the Japanese answered emphatically in the negative by executing the envoys.

The Tokugawa treatment of its own overseas traders and adventurers was just as severe as its treatment of foreign traders and missionaries in Japan. Fearing that overseas Japanese and traders traveling to foreign ports might bring back to Japan the Christian religion or dangerous foreign ideas, Edo decreed in 1636 that henceforth no Japanese was to go abroad and no Japanese resident abroad was to return to Japan. Two years later this decree was followed by another prohibiting the construction of large ships suitable for overseas trade, and as a result the native merchant marine was limited to small vessels for coastal commerce among the Japanese islands. The overseas expansion of the Japanese merchants was thus brought to an abrupt end, and thousands of Japanese abroad were permanently cut off from their homeland and left to lose their racial identity in the native population of the towns of Southeast Asia.

Despite this extremely reactionary policy of national isolation, the Tokugawa were wise enough not to cut off all contact with other nations. They preserved Nagasaki as a window looking out on the rest of the world. Chinese merchants were allowed to visit and trade there under careful supervision, and the Dutch trading post at Hirado was moved to a small island in Nagasaki harbor, where the Dutch merchants were kept in virtual year-round imprisonment.

The measures the early Tokugawa took to insure the continuance of their regime were indeed drastic. They stifled the normal social and economic development of the land, laid a heavy hand upon the initiative of the people, and so isolated Japan from the rest of the world that she dropped far behind Europe in scientific and industrial achievements. Even Japan's population stopped growing after about 1700 and remained relatively static at about 30,000,000 during the remaining century and a half of Tokugawa rule. And yet, it must be admitted that the Tokugawa were supremely successful in establishing the political stability they sought. Between the middle of the seventeenth century and the middle of the nineteenth, no revolution, disturbance, or incident in any way threatened the rule of the Tokugawa. The peace of the land was broken only by occasional and sporadic outbursts of man and nature — a great fire at Edo, a destructive earthquake, the last great eruption of the now extinct volcano of Fuji, an occasional rice riot by impoverished city-dwellers, scattered riots by still more impoverished peasants demanding a greater share of their own produce — but nothing on a national scale and nothing which could shake the existing political or social order.

Perhaps the best idea of the carefully guarded political tranquillity of this time can be gained from the story of the only political incident that at least emotionally shook the nation during these two hundred years. It has become the favorite literary and dramatic theme in modern Japan. This was the incident of the "Forty-Seven *Ronin*," which took place between 1701 and 1703.

A minor feudal lord was so grievously insulted by a more important lord that in rage he drew his sword and wounded his tormenter. To have drawn his sword within the castle grounds of Edo was an offence punishable by death, and the Edo authorities ordered the unlucky man to commit suicide and confiscated his fief. His feudal retainers lost their status as full-fledged *samurai* and became *ronin,* which was a term for a masterless *samurai* who had lost his normal place in society.

Forty-seven of these *ronin* vowed to take vengeance upon the lord who had caused their master's downfall, but realizing that the police would be watching for just such a move on their part, they decided first to lull the suspicions of the authorities. They bided their time for two years, while their leader took up a life of debauchery and degradation to prove that nothing was to be feared from him. Then, on a snowy winter night, they assembled at Edo, broke into the residence of their lord's old enemy, and avenged themselves fully by taking his head and the heads of several of his *samurai.* By this act they of course flouted the authority of Edo, but their self-sacrificing loyalty to their master made them at once national heroes, living up to the best traditions of personal loyalty of the warrior class. After much debate the government finally permitted them to atone for their crime by the honorable death of *seppuku,* commonly called *harakiri,* which is suicide by the painful method of cutting open one's abdomen. This they did, and today the simple graves of the forty-seven *ronin* stand side by side in a quiet little temple compound in Tokyo.

The two centuries of strictly enforced peace under

the watchful eye and firm hand of the Edo government
have left an indelible mark upon the people. The bellicose, adventurous Japanese of the sixteenth century
became by the nineteenth century a docile people looking meekly to their rulers for all leadership and following without question all orders from above. They grew
accustomed to firmly established patterns of conduct.
A thousand rules of etiquette, supplementing instruc-
tions from their rulers, governed all their actions.

As a result of this rigid regimentation of society, the
Japanese have become a people who live together in
their cramped islands with relatively few outward signs
of friction. Nowhere in the world is proper decorum
more rigorously observed by all classes in all situations
than in Japan, and nowhere else is physical violence less
in evidence. At the same time, few people are more
dependent upon orders from above and on long established rules of conduct. The Japanese when thrown on
their own judgment away from their normal environ-
ment seem to be more at a loss than peoples accustomed
to greater freedom of action at home. They are as emotionally excitable as any people, and when they meet
a situation to which their accustomed patterns of cour-
teous conduct no longer apply, they are likely to react
more violently than other people. This may be one explanation for the amazing contrast between the cour-
tesy and docility of the modern Japanese at home and
his cruelty and excesses as a conqueror abroad.

The long peace of the Tokugawa era was, of course,
in many ways a blessing to the land. Yet by holding
back the wheels of normal social and economic progress and fixing on the nation an antiquated political and

social order, the Tokugawa preserved in Japan an outdated feudal structure and mentality far longer than
they could have lasted in a freer society. What had
been essentially a reactionary political and social system when founded in the early seventeenth century
was preserved almost intact until the middle of the
nineteenth century. Then a Japan still intellectually
and socially bound down by an antiquated political
system was suddenly confronted again by the Europeans, who during the intervening two centuries had
made tremendous strides forward in almost all fields of
human endeavor.

❖❖❖❖❖❖❖❖❖❖❖❖❖❖❖❖❖❖❖❖❖❖❖❖❖❖❖❖❖❖❖❖❖❖❖❖

Chapter VIII

SIGNS OF CHANGE BEHIND
THE FEUDAL FAÇADE

Despite the best efforts of the Tokugawa to prevent
any change that might undermine their safely isolated
political system, it was, of course, impossible to stop all
natural processes of evolution and growth within Japanese society. Outward political forms were relatively
simple to maintain, but the internal working of the
society and economy could not be held to a rigidly
unchanging pattern. During the sixteenth century,
Japanese society and economy had developed beyond the bounds of a strictly feudal system. Even
the ruthless Edo regime could not force a return to
simple feudal patterns.

Actually the unity and long peace under Tokugawa
rule made the perpetuation of a feudal economy all the
more impossible. With national unity established, many
of the petty economic restrictions and limitations that
had existed in the days of the Ashikaga were brushed
away. Trade was possible on a greater scale than ever
before, and despite the division of the land into many
Daimyo domains, Japan became essentially a single eco-

nomic unit. Relieved of the feudal fees and restrictions of earlier ages, the merchants no longer needed the protection of closed guild organizations. Guilds gradually disappeared, and independent merchants and firms of merchants or manufacturers took their place in a freer economic order.

The prolonged, complete peace of the Tokugawa period brought to Japan years of unprecedented prosperity, and industrial production and trade grew rapidly. Although the Tokugawa, the Daimyo, and the whole *samurai* class clung tenaciously to the concept that agriculture was the only true source of wealth, and continued to measure their incomes in terms of bushels of rice, in the cities and towns of Japan a vigorously expanding merchant class was creating a commercial economy far beyond anything to be expected in a politically feudal land. Paper credits of all sorts were developed and commonly used in normal transactions, and great rice exchanges with daily fluctuating price quotations grew up at the two economic capitals, Osaka and Edo.

The ruling class had placed the merchants at the bottom of the social scale, but the merchants, with their control of the nationwide rice market, came increasingly to dominate economic life. In an expanding money economy, the Daimyo and *samurai* felt a growing need for money, and as the Tokugawa period progressed many of them fell hopelessly in debt to rich city merchants. In time, Daimyo and *samurai*, despite their social disdain for the merchant class, sometimes married daughters of rich merchants in order to improve their own economic status.

By the early nineteenth century, several merchant families had amassed great fortunes. One family, the Mitsui, which in recent times built the greatest economic empire in Japan, was even then an important factor in the nation's economic life. A genuine capitalist class had appeared, and a large group of experienced business men. The stage was set for the amazing economic modernization of Japan which was to take place once the doors of the country were thrown open again to trade and intercourse with the rest of the world.

The merchants, not the warrior-administrators, obviously dominated Japan economically, but their real supremacy in Tokugawa times is perhaps best seen in the cultural field, for the arts and literature of the period were more an expression of a city bourgeoisie than of a feudal warrior class. The cities clearly dominated Tokugawa culture, and in the cities the gay amusement quarters were the centers of social life. Here the *geisha*, a professional female entertainer, carefully trained in the arts of singing, dancing, and amusing conversation, reigned supreme. To her came the tired business man and the "slumming" warrior-aristocrat for the free social contact with women, denied them by the overly formalized patterns of society, which confined women of breeding strictly to their own homes.

To a surprising degree the art and literature of the time revolved around the *geisha* and the amusement quarters. Artists of the Tokugawa period loved to portray the streets of these quarters and the famous *geisha* beauties of the time; and the great seventeenth century novelist, Saikaku, made the demimonde the normal subject of his risqué, somewhat pornographic novels. The authorities, fearful lest the works of men like Saikaku corrupt public morals, often attempted to suppress them. But with the increased use of printing in the Tokugawa period, this was not an easy task even for the well-organized Edo police, and the novels of Saikaku continued to have a great vogue with city dwellers.

The drama of the age, like the novel, reflected the tastes of the city merchant class. Starting with a puppet drama in the seventeenth century, there developed in the course of the Tokugawa period a new dramatic form known as *Kabuki*, which is still the most popular form in Japan. *Kabuki* stressed realism of action and of setting. It utilized the revolving stage with great success, and the settings it developed were in many respects far superior to those of the Occidental theater. In sharp contrast to the slow moving and sedate *Nō* drama of the Ashikaga period, the *Kabuki* maintained a high degree of emotional tension and dealt freely in scenes of violence and melodrama.

Possibly the influence of the city dwellers may be seen also in the field of poetry, in which there appeared a new and excessively brief poetic form, the *haiku* — a reduction of the classical thirty-one syllable poem to a mere seventeen syllables. In the hands of a master like the seventeenth-century poet, Basho, the *haiku* was a superbly clever creation, conjuring up a whole scene with all its emotional overtones in a simple phrase or two. But its brevity made it even more limited as a literary form than the old classical poem, and the thousands of faddists who took up *haiku* writing during the

Tokugawa period often reduced it to little more than an amusing word game.

Art in the times of Hideyoshi and the early Tokugawa showed in many respects a radical departure from the major trends of Zen art in Ashikaga days. The calm and serenity of the simple landscape paintings were lost in a burst of magnificence and splendor — fitting expression of the military and political might of the age. Primary emphasis was put on erecting and decorating magnificent palaces. Gorgeous decorative screens and panels, with brightly colored scenes and designs laid on backgrounds of gold leaf, were the most typical artistic creations of the time. By the late sixteenth century the deep religious spirit, which earlier had produced supremely beautiful statues of Buddhas and fine portrait-statues of Buddhist monks, was lost; and sculptors for the most part confined their efforts to ornamenting palaces and temples with a superabundance of elaborate, detailed carvings.

The increased industrial output of this period of peace and unification also resulted in a great gain in semi-industrial arts. The making of fine pottery and beautiful porcelain ware, at first under the guidance of Korean potters, became a great industry with high artistic standards. Gorgeous silk brocades were produced by the expanding textile industry, and lacquer ware of great decorative distinction was made in quantity. In pottery making, weaving, and lacquer work the Japanese maintained their aesthetic standards despite increasing production during the Tokugawa period. In these fields and in many other minor industrial arts they have continued up to the present day to

hold a balance between large-scale production, technical excellence, and aesthetic value which is almost un-
matched in the modern world.

The art of the early Tokugawa period was in many
ways already a popular art as contrasted with that of
Ashikaga times, but as the Edo age progressed it grew
even more markedly popular. The work of the sculptor
became largely the production of small, often amusing
trinkets for popular use, and the subject matter of the
graphic arts became increasingly the city people and
their life. Great artists, instead of working to beautify
the palaces of rulers, produced pictures to fit the tastes
and pocketbooks of the bourgeoisie. This was particularly evident in the development of the technique of
wood-block printing, which made it possible to repro-
duce hundreds of copies of a single colored picture and
to sell them at reasonable prices. This art for the masses
reached a glorious culmination in the early nineteenth
century in the work of two great masters, Hokusai and
Hiroshige. The wood block print, as exemplified in
their works, has become the form of Japanese art best
known in the occidental world.

The development of a complicated commercial
economy and a strong merchant class were not the only
ways in which the foundations for a modernized Japan
were being laid during the Tokugawa period. Interest
in Europe and things European was reviving. Christianity and possible foreign aggression had become
such dead issues by 1720 that Edo removed a long-
standing ban on the study of the West and the importation of European books — with the exception, of
course, of anything dealing with Christianity. Soon a

small but intellectually vigorous group of students of the European sciences arose, working through the medium of the Dutch language, which they learned from the Dutch at Nagasaki. Within a few decades, a Dutch-Japanese dictionary was compiled and a text on anatomy translated into Japanese. By the middle of the nineteenth century Japanese scholars were well versed in such Western sciences as gunnery, smelting, shipbuilding, cartography, and medicine. Few in number, they formed a valuable nucleus of scholars to take the lead in scientific work on a much larger scale when opportunity finally offered itself.

The development of a strong national consciousness during the Tokugawa period was another element in setting the stage for Japan's modernization. By the nineteenth century the Japanese were definitely a nationalistic people, and their possession of a fully developed spirit of nationalism perhaps best explains the success and speed with which they transformed their country into a modern nation-state.

As in western Europe, nationalism in Japan was the result of long, slow growth. Why it should have appeared so early and developed so fully in Japan, long before it became significant in other Asiatic lands, is an interesting question. The main reason may have been that the Japanese throughout their history felt themselves to be completely overshadowed by China but still distinct from it. There was no denying that China was the cradle of civilization in the Far East, a far older and greater country than Japan, and that Japan was no more than a small and, for long, a backward offshoot of Chinese civilization. The Koreans and some other East Asiatic peoples stood in much the same relationship to the Chinese as did the Japanese, but the prestige of Chinese civilization, coupled with occasional rule of their lands by the Chinese, persuaded them at certain times in their history to identify themselves with the Chinese, and to look upon themselves as members of the Chinese cultural empire.

The Japanese were saved from surrendering their cultural independence and national initiative by their greater isolation and their freedom from Chinese political control. Living in their own land and speaking their own language, they remained fully aware that they were Japanese, not Chinese. Yet they realized their insignificance when compared with the Chinese. Perhaps in compensation for a sense of inferiority, they early developed a strong consciousness of their national identity and a deep sense of pride in all things Japanese.

Such an attitude was already clearly observable in the Kamakura period, when Nichiren and other religious leaders injected a strong nationalistic note into their teachings. It was clearer in the political writings of the early Ashikaga period. A scholar of this time who supported the cause of Daigo II wrote a history to prove the validity of Daigo II's claim to rule. He gave this history a strong nationalistic tinge by stressing the unique virtues of the Japanese political system, which he attributed to the fact that Japan was a land of divine origin, ruled by an imperial line of divine ancestry.

Shinto priests, who again began to play a part in the intellectual life of Japan during the feudal ages, did much to build up national consciousness. For many centuries Shinto had been completely overshadowed by Buddhism. Its many deities had been given humble recognition as local manifestations of universal Buddhist deities. But during the feudal period Shinto began to free itself gradually from Buddhist domination and to take on new intellectual vigor. Shinto philosophers, by adopting many Buddhist and Chinese concepts, developed their simple cults into a religion suitable to a more advanced people. In the process, Shinto priests came to claim superiority for their religion over Buddhism. They even reversed the old theory of relationship, terming the Buddhist deities foreign, and therefore inferior manifestations of supreme native Japanese gods. Quite naturally these nationalistic Shinto priests felt that native things were superior to foreign importations, and they looked back to the period of Japanese history which antedated Buddhist and Chinese influences as a golden age.

During the Tokugawa period, political unity and complete isolation marked by strong anti-foreign policies made for a rapid growth in nationalism. Strangely enough, even the Tokugawa patronage of the Chinese philosophy of Confucianism did much to strengthen nationalism, for interest in Confucianism led to a revival of historical studies; and the study of Japanese history took scholars back to the myths and legends of ancient Japan, as related in the early histories, the *Kojiki* and *Nihon Shoki*. One important school of historians was founded by the second head of the great Tokugawa branch family at Mito. This group, in the

seventeenth century, started a monumental history of
Japan which was not finally completed until the early
years of the twentieth century.

A group even more responsible for the growth of
nationalism consisted of certain Shinto scholars who
studied the old myths and traditions and reintroduced
them to the educated public. In the latter part of the
eighteenth century one of these Shinto scholars produced a commentary to the *Kojiki*, which did much to
make this early history the primary text of Japanese nationalism. He and other Shinto scholars studied the
primitive pre-Chinese period of Japanese history,
searching for native virtues which would explain to
their own satisfaction the superiority to China which
their unreasoning nationalism now led them to feel.
What they often found was simply naïve myths and
historically absurd traditions, but in their blind zeal
they accepted these as true and foisted them on a nation
which should have been too sophisticated to have taken
them seriously.

One sidelight of the intellectual revival of Shinto was
the sudden appearance in the first half of the nineteenth
century of popular Shinto sects. Some were founded
by women, and several stressed faith healing. All these
sects added many Buddhist concepts and practices to
basic Shinto principles, but generally they were
strongly colored by nationalism. The popular Shinto
sects were not only a sign of growing national consciousness; they also indicated that Buddhism was no
longer able to meet all the spiritual needs of the lower
classes. Converts flocked to the new sects in great num-

bers, and today, after about a century of existence, the thirteen chief Shinto sects number around 10,000,000 adherents.

The interest of historians and Shinto scholars in the early days of Japanese history naturally revealed the high place the imperial family had held in Japan, and nationalists tended to emphasize the divine ancestry of an unbroken imperial line as one of the unique virtues which accounted for Japan's supposed superiority to other lands. The people in general again became aware that there was an emperor in Kyoto, and that in theory he was the supreme ruler of the land. In the late sixteenth century there had been signs of increasing interest in the imperial family, and this interest was fostered by the Tokugawa historians and Shinto scholars. In the eighteenth century, a certain scholar at Kyoto so boldly expounded the right of the emperor to rule that Edo was forced to take disciplinary action against him and his courtier pupils. The emperor and his court of course remained politically impotent, but the imperial line emerged again from obscurity; and the emperor again became a figure of such nationwide importance that many people began to wonder why a Shogun was actually ruling.

During the eighteenth century and the first half of the nineteenth century, Tokugawa rule continued serene and unchallenged, but beneath an unchanging surface, forces were at work remaking the foundations of the nation. Until the middle of the nineteenth century the Tokugawa were able to preserve an antiquated political system and an absurdly outdated political and social philosophy. However, rapid economic growth had produced behind the feudal façade an advanced commercial economy, capable of ready transformation into a modern economic order. Despite the division of the land into a large number of feudal fiefs, the people had developed a strong sense of national consciousness. Japan had become spiritually a modern nation, ready to take over and adopt the more efficient political forms of the modern nation-state.

Chapter IX

THE CREATION OF A MODERN STATE

By the middle of the nineteenth century, political and social changes were long overdue in Japan. Since the political system had been basically reactionary even in the early seventeenth century, it was by now more than two hundred years out of date. The growth of nationalism and the development of a full-fledged commercial economy had made Japan ready for an entirely new political and social order. But so well had the early Tokugawa succeeded in creating a system capable of preserving political stability that the machine was still running relatively smoothly. It took an outside force to disrupt it. This force was provided by the Europeans, who came not only from Europe but also from their newer homes in America.

In the last years of the eighteenth century the Russians, who had crossed the vast land expanse of Siberia and reached the Pacific, began to attempt to establish contacts with the Japanese. At about the same time the English, who had supplanted the Portuguese and Spanish as the chief mariners and traders in Far Eastern waters, began to try to rewin entry into Japan. But the Americans were most interested of all in opening Japanese ports. Their whaling vessels frequented the North Pacific and the waters around Japan, and American clipper ships, bound for China on the great circle route across the Pacific, passed close to the shores of Japan. The Americans wanted permission for their whalers and clipper ships to enter Japanese ports to take on water and replenish their stores, and when steamships came into use, the desirability of a coaling station in Japan became obvious.

Not infrequently, also, American and European sailors were wrecked on the shores of Japan. The laws of the land decreed death for any foreigner entering the country, and although this was not always enforced, those unlucky mariners stranded in Japan who eventually got out by way of Nagasaki usually had tales to tell of extremely cruel treatment.

In the first half of the nineteenth century the Americans, English, and Russians repeatedly sent expeditions to Japan in efforts to persuade the Japanese to open their ports to foreign ships, and the Dutch urged them to accede to these demands. But Edo stood firm on its old policy. A few scholars among the native students of Western science bravely advocated the opening of Japan, but the vast majority of the people, long accustomed to isolation from the rest of the world, were bitterly opposed to permitting foreigners to enter their land. It was obvious that Japan would not voluntarily open its doors.

The American government eventually decided to delay matters no longer, but to force the doors of Japan open. For this purpose, it dispatched a considerable naval force under Commodore Matthew C. Perry. Perry steamed into Tokyo Bay in July 1853. After delivering a letter from the President of the United States to the ruler of Japan, demanding the inauguration of trade relations, he withdrew to the Ryukyu Islands for the winter, with the promise that he would return early the next year to receive a reply.

Edo was thrown into a state of complete confusion over this sudden crisis. The Japanese were appalled by the size and guns of the American "black ships," as they called them, and they were amazed by the steam-powered vessels which moved up the bay against the wind. They realized that their own shore batteries were almost useless against the American warships, before which Edo, too, lay defenseless.

The government split into two factions — conservatives who blindly advocated the expulsion of the foreigners, and realists who saw that Japan could do nothing but bow to American demands. In their own indecision, the Edo authorities did a most unusual thing. For the first time in over 600 years of military rule, the Shogun's government asked the opinion of the emperor on an important problem of state and invited counsel also from the Daimyo. Conservative Kyoto and the Daimyo of the land were of course strongly in favor of expelling the foreigners.

The Edo government was indeed caught on the horns of a dilemma when Perry's fleet returned to Tokyo Bay in February 1854. The emperor and the nation as a whole demanded a policy which Edo was quite incapable of carrying out. Under the threatening guns of the American ships, the Tokugawa had no choice but to sign a treaty with the United States, opening two ports to American ships and permitting a certain amount of closely regulated trade.

Once the door had been pushed open a crack, there was no closing it. Within two years Edo had signed treaties with England, Russia, and Holland, and in 1856 Townsend Harris, the first American consul general, arrived in Japan to negotiate a full commercial treaty. This he concluded two years later, and the European powers soon made similar treaties with Japan. The door was now wide open. Foreigners were permitted permanent residence at five ports and also at the great cities of Osaka and Edo, and free and unrestricted trade relations were sanctioned. Foreign merchants began to set up their business concerns at the fishing village of Yokohama, which grew rapidly and within a few decades developed into one of the great ports of the world.

The Tokugawa realized that because of their own military impotence they could do nothing to check the foreigners. Rather belatedly they initiated reforms designed to modernize their military establishment, starting with the building of a small occidental-type navy. However, the Kyoto court and the vast majority of the feudal domains, which still had seen nothing of the overpowering military might of the Westerners, showed little interest in military modernization and remained completely unreconciled to Edo's action in opening up the land to foreigners. The cry of "expel the barbarians" grew in all quarters of the land.

The Tokugawa branch family at Mito led the oppo-

sition within the Edo government, and men from Mito
in 1860 assassinated the Prime Minister who had concluded the new commercial treaties. Other irreconcilable conservatives from Satsuma murdered an Englishman near Yokohama, and the forts of the great
western Honshu fief of Choshu fired on American,
French and Dutch vessels passing through the narrow
Straits of Shimonoseki at the western end of the Inland
Sea. The Kyoto court, rising to a new sense of authority, began to demand that Edo expel the foreigners.
The emperor even took the unprecedented step of sum-
moning the Shogun to Kyoto, and the Shogun, showing how far Edo had already gone in surrendering authority to the emperor, meekly complied.

All the dissident elements in Japan and particularly
the *samurai* of the great "outer Daimyo" domains of
western Japan, which had been forced to recognize
Tokugawa supremacy for two and a half centuries,
without ever becoming reconciled to it, now saw the
widening cracks in the hitherto impregnable armor of
the Tokugawa. Edo had been compelled by the Western powers to adopt the unpopular policy of opening
the land to foreign intercourse, a policy that ran
counter to the expressed wishes of the emperor. The
Tokugawa were at last vulnerable to attack. Their
opponents, summing up their stand in the double slogan,
"honor the emperor — expel the barbarians," pressed
the attack by intrigues at Kyoto and by military prepa-
rations, which led to pitched battles between Edo and
the western Honshu fief of Choshu. The great Edo regime, still the paramount military power of the land,
was foundering, not because the machinery of govern-

ment had broken down, but because it had lost the confidence of the nation. Even the supporters of Edo had been persuaded by historians and Shinto propagandists to admit the right of the emperor to rule.

The end of the Edo regime came in a surprising way. A son of the Tokugawa Lord of Mito became the new Shogun in 1867, and, as befitted a scion of the family that had championed Japanese historical studies for the past two centuries, he voluntarily surrendered the actual rule of the country to the emperor in the autumn of that year. The year 1868 saw some desultory fighting at Edo and in northern Japan between the supporters of imperial rule and die-hard adherents of the Tokugawa regime, but the end of Tokugawa rule cost surprisingly little bloodshed. Despite its continued efficiency, the Edo system had become so hopelessly unsuited to the mentality of the Japanese nation that, once it started to crack, it collapsed suddenly and completely.

The new imperial government naturally centered around the person of the emperor, for it had been the revived theory of imperial rule which had made the overthrow of the Tokugawa possible. The *coup d'état* came to be referred to as the "Restoration" of imperial rule, but this did not mean that the emperor himself was to be in control. A boy of fifteen had recently ascended the throne, and although this young emperor grew to be a strong figure in the central government of Japan, eventually being recognized as one of the great men of Japanese history, in the early years of his reign he was too young and inexperienced to be a dominant force.

The court aristocracy around the emperor included a few capable men and in time produced some important statesmen, such as Prince Saionji and, later, Prince Konoe, two descendants of branches of the ancient Fujiwara family who were to become Premiers of the new Japan. But for the most part the Kyoto courtiers lacked the experience and the drive to become forceful in the new government. Some of the "outer Daimyo" participated in its work, but few of them were truly important political figures. High posts of government were largely held by imperial princes, court nobles, and Daimyo, but the leadership of the new regime actually was taken by a group of young and often relatively poor *samurai* who had come to dominate the politics of Satsuma, Choshu, and other "outer Daimyo" fiefs in western Japan, and for a decade had been intriguing against the Tokugawa at Kyoto and in the capitals of their own domains.

By tradition these young *samurai* of western Japan were all hostile to the Tokugawa, and they rallied to the imperial cause as the best way to attack Edo. At first they were also bitterly anti-foreign, and until the Tokugawa collapse they echoed the popular cry, "honor the emperor — expel the barbarians." But long before they came to power in the final months of 1867 they had come to realize that it was impossible to "expel the barbarians."

In 1863 a British squadron had bombarded Kagoshima, the capital of Satsuma, in retribution for the murder of an Englishman by unruly Satsuma warriors. The next year American, British, French, and Dutch warships bombarded Shimonoseki in reprisal for the attack

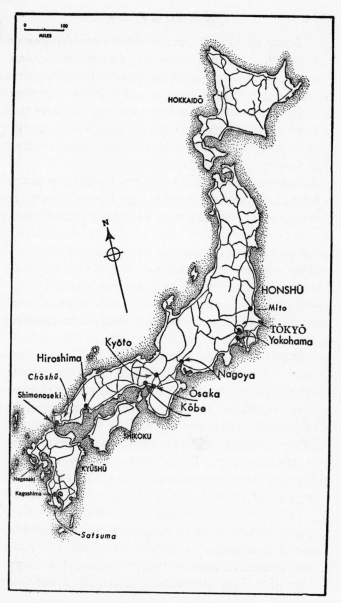

MAJOR RAILWAY LINES OF MODERN JAPAN

by Choshu on Western merchant vessels. The young aristocrats of Satsuma and Choshu saw how helpless their fiefs were against Western naval strength. They learned their lesson at once, and demonstrating an amazing ability to reorient their thinking, they dropped all thought of a narrow policy of isolation and immediately began to study the techniques of warfare that had made the West so strong.

Satsuma soon launched its own small navy along modern lines, and the young officers who began their naval careers in Satsuma were to become the men who created and dominated the Imperial Japanese Navy until well into the twentieth century. Similarly, Choshu, abandoning the concept of a small warrior class, started to create from its peasantry a modern army trained in the techniques of European military science. The success of this attempt was clearly demonstrated in 1866, when Edo dispatched forces to chastise Choshu for its anti-Tokugawa intrigues. The aristocratic warriors of Edo were fought to a standstill by the peasant recruits of Choshu, led by a group of young *samurai* officers who were to become the dominant element in the officer corps of the Imperial Japanese Army. The *samurai* of Satsuma and Choshu, far from remaining champions of anti-foreign conservatism, had ushered in the military and social revolution that would sweep away the last vestiges of the feudal order in Japan.

Finding themselves in virtual control of the new imperial government in the late autumn of 1867, the young *samurai* of western Japan embarked on a daring course of rapid modernization, which amounted to a revolution in Japanese society and government. This revolution did not, like those in nineteenth-century Europe, boil up from below. It was carefully planned at the top and forced upon the people by a relatively small but extremely vigorous group in control of the government. The leaders had the advantage of coming for the most part from the same *samurai* background, and they had arrived at a similar point of view through similar experiences and influences. Since they were young, they were mentally and emotionally more eager for sweeping changes than their elders. And they were extremely talented, having achieved their leadership by demonstrating superior abilities and a capacity for adjustment to new situations in the confused politics of their individual Daimyo realms, and in the intrigues and counter-intrigues of the Kyoto court.

The leaders of the new regime also had another advantage — they inherited the strong and reasonably efficient Tokugawa government almost intact. The central administration had not been eaten away by decay and corruption, as had often been the case in other countries when revolutionary governments came into power. Japan entered its great revolutionary period a unified, centralized nation, unravaged by any prolonged period of political disruption and disunity.

The contrast with China and Korea, Japan's only neighbors, was marked. Both these countries, during the nineteenth century, suffered prolonged periods of political decline. The Manchu dynasty of China, after two hundred years of strong rule, was slowly dying from inner decay, and China was to fall into a sad state of political disruption before Republican revolutionaries seized the disintegrating reins of government in 1911. The contrast between the political unity and efficient administration the Japanese revolutionaries inherited from the Tokugawa, and the political disunity and disrupted central government the Chinese revolutionaries inherited from the Manchu dynasty, does much to explain the more rapid progress the Japanese made in modernizing their country, and the entirely unprecedented economic and military supremacy Japan was soon to win in the Far East.

The leaders of the new imperial regime had all been deeply impressed by the helplessness of Edo, Satsuma, and Choshu in the face of occidental military power, and the humiliation they had been forced to suffer because of their military backwardness. Quite naturally, they were obsessed with the idea of creating a Japan capable of holding its own in the modern world. Since they were military men by tradition and early training, they thought primarily in terms of military power; but they were surprisingly broad-minded in their approach to the problem, realizing that to achieve military strength Japan needed economic, social, and intellectual renovation. They set out to make Japan strong, and they showed a willingness to do anything necessary to achieve this goal.

Early in January of 1868, the new government had the young emperor officially assume direct rule over the nation. The new era was given the name of Meiji, and the transfer of power from the Tokugawa to the group around the emperor came to be known as the Meiji Restoration. Meiji remained the official title for the rest of the emperor's long reign, which lasted until 1912, and the name was then given to the emperor as his personal posthumous title. Two and a half centuries of rule from Edo had made the city so definitely the administrative center of Japan that the young reformers moved the imperial capital from Kyoto to Edo in the autumn of 1868 and renamed the city Tokyo, meaning "eastern capital."

In the early spring of 1869, only a little over a year after they had come to power, the bright young *samurai* started the task of doing away completely with the feudal system under which they had grown up and which had given their class a dominant place in society. They persuaded the Daimyo of Satsuma, Choshu, and other leading fiefs in western Japan to offer their domains to the emperor, and the other Daimyo of Japan felt morally obliged to follow suit. Thus, at one bold stroke the division of Japan into feudal principalities came to a sudden end, in theory at least. Actually, however, during a brief period of transition, the Daimyo were appointed governors of their old fiefs, with one-tenth of their former revenues as personal salaries. Two years later, in 1871, the fiefs were entirely abolished, and the land was divided into a number of new political divisions called *ken*, or "prefectures." This marked the definite end of the Daimyo as feudal lords. The government eventually made an economic settlement with them, giving them fairly generous lump sum payments in the form of government bonds, which helped insure their support of the new regime. The old Daimyo, who had produced few strong political figures in the new government, gradually left the political scene and became merely an element in the growing capitalist class of Japan.

In settling with the Daimyo, the government also gave them titles of nobility in the new peerage it was creating. The old Daimyo were divided into five noble ranks in accordance with the size of their old fiefs, with the last Tokugawa Shogun becoming a Prince and the lesser Daimyo receiving the lowest rank of Baron. Another large element in the nobility was composed of the former courtier families from Kyoto, who had little political influence and were relatively poor. The dominant role in the new aristocracy was in time actually taken by the bright young *samurai* from the western fiefs, who rewarded one another for their services to the nation with titles of nobility.

Freeing Japan from the control of a small and relatively weak group of Daimyo was a far easier task than stripping the many and vigorous *samurai* of the social, economic, and political privileges which had made them the dominant class of feudal Japan. Choshu had already pointed the way toward depriving the *samurai* of their status as an aristocratic caste of warriors, and the new government felt itself strong enough in the winter of 1872–73 to introduce universal military service. Under the able leadership of young officers, such as Yamagata of Choshu, an army of peasants was recruited, first on the French and then on the German model because of the military superiority Germany demonstrated in the Franco-Prussian War.

The loss of his cherished position as a warrior-aristocrat was hard enough on the *samurai*, but a more serious blow was the loss of his privileged economic status. At first the government had assumed the responsibility of paying pensions to the *samurai* in place of the hereditary stipends they had received from their feudal lords. However, the government reduced these pensions to only half the original stipends, which had never been generous. Then suddenly in 1876, the authorities demanded that these pensions be commuted into relatively small lump sum payments. This order, together with one of the same year prohibiting the *samurai* from wearing their traditional two swords, meant the end of the *samurai* as a class with feudal privileges. They had been reduced to the level of ordinary subjects of the emperor and had been cast forth to fend for themselves as individual citizens of the state.

Many of the abler *samurai* were already rising fast in the new government. Some were making careers for themselves in the professions. Others used their lump sum payments to start successful business enterprises. A large proportion of the *samurai* were attracted to the officer corps of the new army and navy, or became policemen, entitled to wear swords, a fact which may account for the traditional prestige and authority of the ordinary Japanese policeman.

Many of the *samurai*, however, found themselves unable to learn new methods of livelihood, or incapable of adjusting themselves mentally to the new world in which they lived. Irreconcilable conservatives among them from time to time defied the authority of the new government. The most serious of these *samurai* revolts occurred in Satsuma itself, where discontented conservatives rallied around Saigo Takamori, one of the young *samurai* of western Japan who had helped establish the new government, but had returned to Satsuma in protest against the policies of his colleagues. Saigo and his followers found themselves in open rebellion against Tokyo in 1877. The peasant army was dispatched against them, and the Satsuma conservatives soon learned that *samurai* armed with swords were no match for peasant soldiers, well-armed and well-drilled. The Satsuma rebellion of 1877 was the last gasp of a fast dying feudal society. In less than ten years the young reformers had rid themselves of this antiquated social and political system and had cleared the ground for more modern and more efficient political institutions.

The leaders of the new Japan realized full well that they could not stop merely at removing the old system. Theoretically, they had engineered a "Restoration" of the imperial rule of the seventh and eighth centuries, and they actually did revive many of the ancient names of offices and of governmental organs, but they knew that this was only theory and nomenclature. What they really desired to do was to establish a strong nation like the leading Western powers, and so naturally they looked to the West for new patterns of society and government.

The Tokugawa in their last years had been sending envoys and students abroad to learn the techniques and sciences of foreign lands, and the new government greatly expanded this program for studying the occidental world. The forty-five years of the Meiji period were essentially a time when the Japanese studied, borrowed, and gradually assimilated those elements of Western civilization which they chose to adopt. This period of learning from abroad was comparable only to the great period when the Japanese imported Chinese civilization over a thousand years earlier, but this time the process of learning from abroad was carried out on a larger scale and much more systematically. Students were chosen with care on the basis of their knowledge and capabilities, and the countries where they were to study were selected with equal care. The Japanese determined to learn from each Western country that in which it particularly excelled. They went to England to study the navy and merchant marine, to Germany for the army and for medicine, to France for law, and to the United States for business methods. The world was one vast school room for them, and they entered it determined to learn only the best in each field.

With its predominant interest in military strength, the new government naturally paid great attention to the creation of a strong army and navy along Western lines, but the young reformers knew that to be truly strong the new army and navy needed behind them an efficient and stable political system, a physically strong and technically competent people, and a sound and industrially advanced economic system. While building up the army and navy, therefore, they by no means neglected the other requisites for national strength.

The new government was in essence an oligarchy in the hands of fewer than one hundred young men. They had no reason to be dissatisfied with their own form of rule, but they saw the advantages of many Western political concepts and institutions as essential adjuncts of government in any strong state. These features of the West they borrowed in rapid succession. They created ministries on Western models in one administrative field after another; and they organized a prefectural system of rule which kept the control of each prefecture in the hands of the Tokyo government. They adopted the Western calendar, but held to the old Chinese system of counting years by "year periods," which beginning with the Meiji "year period" became identical in duration with the reigns of the emperors. They adopted a policy of religious toleration, permitting the propagation of Christianity once more; they modernized the police, the currency, and organized a modern postal system; they revised and standardized the tax system, and created a national banking system, first on American and then on European lines; they established a civil service; and they revised the legal system and courts on French patterns. Finally, they established a Cabinet on the German model, and even drew up a Constitution for Japan, providing for a parliament called the Diet.

The last step showed that the oligarchy was at last broadening the basis of its rule. But unlike the constitutions and parliaments of Western lands, which had usually been the result of popular demand and pressure, the Japanese Constitution and Diet were the gift of the ruling oligarchy to the people. Of course, there was a growing demand on the part of a small segment of the public for a share in the government. This politically conscious group consisted largely of the *samurai* who had not won their way into the oligarchy and had taken lesser posts in the new government or become business men. It also included other members of the business community who, as legal equals of the old *samurai* class, felt that they were entitled to a voice in the government. However, the oligarchy was not forced to make concessions to the public. It did so primarily because influential members of the ruling group had reached the conclusion from their study of Western political institutions that a constitution was essential to a strong westernized state, and that some form of parliamentary government was also a necessary part of the political machinery which helped make Western powers strong.

In 1868, the emperor had made a so-called "charter oath" in which he had given rather vague promises of forming a deliberative council and allowing public opinion a voice in government decisions. In 1879 the government actually experimented with elective bodies when it created Prefectural Assemblies, chosen by the higher tax-payers within each prefecture. Two years later the oligarchy promised to convene a National Assembly by 1890. Ito, a former *samurai* from Choshu, who was eventually to become a Prince in the new nobility, had been at times openly hostile towards demands for a parliamentary form of government, but he was assigned the task of studying Western constitutions and drafting one for Japan. He toured Europe to study the political institutions of the leading powers and was most impressed by the German, which seemed to him best adapted to Japanese needs. The Japanese Constitution was finally promulgated in 1889 in the form of a gracious gift to the people by the emperor. It stated clearly that the emperor was the fountainhead of all authority in the state, and carefully protected his right to rule. This was natural, for the oligarchy had come to power as champions of imperial rule, and the only basis in theory for their continued authority was their status as spokesmen of the emperor, who in a sense had himself become one of the more influential oligarchs.

The great innovation of the Constitution was the bicameral Diet. There was to be a House of Peers, similar to the British House of Lords, made up of elected and appointed members of the new nobility and of a few other privileged groups, such as the highest tax-payers of the land. The House of Representatives was to be elected by males over twenty-five who paid an annual tax of fifteen yen or more. This meant an initial electorate of 460,000, slightly over one per cent of the population at that time.

The first elections were held in 1890, and Japan got off to a belated start in the established occidental path of representative government. In 1892 the new Diet demonstrated that it was beginning to function as an important organ of government when the Cabinet resigned following a defeat in the Diet. However, it should not be assumed that Japan had suddenly become a true democracy. A group larger than the original oligarchy now participated in the work of government, and a little over one per cent of the population had the right to vote, but the young founders of the new government, now grown to solid middle age, still controlled Japan. They had become "elder statesmen," the surviving leaders of early Meiji days, who added the prestige of long years of rule to their native political talents.

They controlled the Privy Council and thus spoke for the emperor. Parties were formed, but they were dominated by the personalities and views of the old oligarchs. Cabinets came and went in rapid succession, but until 1918 the Premiers all came from the same small group of oligarchs or from their political protégés, who kept revolving in office in a veritable political merry-go-round. There was Ito from Choshu; Kuroda, the Satsuma *samurai* who had played a leading military role in the "Restoration" and also in the Satsuma Rebellion; Yamagata, the army builder from Choshu; Matsukata from Satsuma; Okuma, a *samurai* from an important fief in northern Kyushu; Katsura, a Choshu general; Saionji, the old court aristocrat; Yamamoto, a Satsuma admiral; and Terauchi, another general from Choshu. Although the oligarchy had moved from the closed committee room to the open floor of the Diet, it still held the reins of government. Japanese administration had been westernized, but in spirit the government had hardly departed from the traditions of a paternalistic, authoritarian state.

The early Meiji leaders showed great perspicacity in discerning the importance of education in the modern state. They saw at once that a technically competent populace was a prerequisite for a modern power. The army and navy needed soldiers who could read and who knew the rudiments of Western science. Business and industry, in order to build the sinews of war, needed thousands of trained technicians.

In 1871 a Ministry of Education was formed, and Japan embarked on an ambitious program of universal education. It took time to build the thousands of

schoolhouses required and to train the tens of thousands of teachers, but within a few years the Japanese
had set up a broad educational system, embracing virtually all children of school age. Primary schooling of
six years became compulsory for all. This led to Middle
Schools of five years or to special technical schools for
boys, and for girls to Higher Schools of four or five
years. The boys' Middle School led to various higher
technical schools or to the men's Higher School, which
in turn prepared them for a University course of three
or four years, producing doctors, lawyers, scientists,
scholars, and candidates for higher government posts.
The system was well adapted to Japanese needs, teaching the general populace to read, training a large group
of technicians of various degrees of competence, and
producing a small body of highly educated men for the
professions and for government service.

Universal education made Japan the first country of
Asia to have a literate populace. A high degree of liter-
acy explains, as much as industrial strength and military
power, the dominant role Japan was to gain in East
Asia in the first half of the twentieth century. Universal education had been applied with brilliant success
in Japan, but Japan, while borrowing the techniques of
the West, injected into them certain strong native tendencies quite at variance with the ideals of democracy
and equality which lay behind universal education in
occidental countries. To Japanese leaders, education
meant not the development of young minds for participation in a fuller life but rather the training of a
technically competent citizenry to help build a strong
state. Education was essentially a tool of government,

training obedient and reliable subjects who could serve as technically efficient cogs in the complicated machinery of the modern state.

In the early years of Meiji, private Japanese educators and Protestant missionaries from America took an important part in developing schools for boys and girls above the primary level, but the Ministry of Education more and more asserted its authority over all schools and gradually forced them to conform to a strict pattern. The schools became increasingly a medium for teaching the people what to think rather than how to think. Thus Japan pioneered in the modern totalitarian technique of utilizing the educational system for political indoctrination and was, in fact, decades ahead of countries like Germany in perfecting these techniques.

The educational system coupled with military conscription, which fell primarily on the peasants, permitted a thoroughgoing indoctrination of the young Japanese, especially peasants, who were less likely than their city cousins to be subjected to outside influence. The peasants in late Tokugawa times, ground down by crushing poverty, had at times rioted against tax-collectors and usurers, but the heavy Tokugawa rule had made them on the whole a docile and obedient lot, perhaps even less conscious politically than their forbears of the more turbulent sixteenth century. They were easy subjects for the indoctrination they were given in schools and in the army.

In classrooms and army barracks the young Japanese was taught to glory in Japan's military traditions. He came to believe that death on the battlefield for the emperor was the most glorious fate of man, and to believe in the unique virtues of a vaguely defined "national structure" and an even more vague "Japanese spirit." Together the government and army succeeded in a few decades in creating in the average Japanese the fanatical nationalism already characteristic of the upper classes, and an even more fanatical devotion to the emperor, which had been cultivated by historians and Shinto propagandists and fostered by oligarchs around the throne. They even succeeded in convincing these descendants of peasants, who for almost three centuries had been denied the right to possess swords, that they were not a downtrodden class but members of a warrior race. Japanese political and military indoctrination was indeed thorough and spectacularly successful.

In economic life, the merchant class of late Tokugawa days naturally played an important role in developing private industrial and commercial firms. In these they were joined by the old Daimyo, whose lump sum payments had made them capitalists, and also by many *samurai* who had chosen business as their new means of livelihood. Japan as a whole, however, was lacking in sufficient private capital to develop adequately all the new industrial and commercial fields demanding exploitation. For this reason and probably because the government was not content with the slower and more haphazard course of private economic development, the Tokyo administration led the way in building up many of the industries and economic organs of Japan, particularly those considered essential for a strong military power.

The government directly developed and controlled certain services, such as the railways, the telegraph system, and other public utilities, which usually proved extremely profitable from the very outset. It opened the first railway between Tokyo and its port at Yokohama in 1872. Although many other lines were built by private enterprise, the main network of railways has been in the hands of the government. The government aided many new enterprises and industries by loans or by various other means. It constructed paper-mills and cotton-spinning plants, assisted in the development of a modern merchant marine and shipbuilding industry, helped build up the silk industry, and gave aid and direction to many other essentially private enterprises.

Government financial aid and patronage for the few private capitalists of the early Meiji period contributed to a phenomenal growth of certain financial and commercial interests. Relatively small fortunes skyrocketed into great economic empires, which branched out in all directions, forming mazes of interlocking cartels and companies, all controlled by a single parent company or by a small group of financiers. The Mitsui, which in late Tokugawa times had become a wealthy merchant family, created the largest of these economic empires. Next to the Mitsui came the Mitsubishi interests, developed by a *samurai* family, the Iwasaki, from a merchant firm of the Edo period.

Government interest and aid in the expansion of commerce and industry also resulted in greater governmental control of the economic life of Japan than was to be found in most other lands in the nineteenth cen-

tury. When government control of business became
more common during the twentieth century, Japan
proved to be in the vanguard of this world-wide economic trend; and, because of long experience, the Japanese government was better prepared than most others
for periods of war in which modern governments take
over complete control of almost all economic life.

As the first Asiatic land to adopt the industrial and
commercial techniques of the West on a significant
scale, Japan found itself in a unique position in the economic world. Western science and cheap oriental labor
made an excellent combination for low-priced production. The rest of East Asia had cheap labor but as yet
lacked scientific knowledge. Europe and America had
scientific knowledge and far greater natural resources
than Japan, but also much higher standards of living
and therefore correspondingly higher wages. This dis-
crepancy between Eastern and Western standards of
living, and the lag in the industrialization of other
Asiatic lands, gave the new Japanese industries and
commercial enterprises an exceptional chance for rapid
growth. Japanese factories and business concerns soon
became adequate for the essential economic needs of
the country, and Japanese business men began to push
out into the markets of Asia, where the inexpensive
goods made possible by cheap labor were welcomed by
all the natives.

Industrialization and scientific progress slowly raised
the standard of living of the average Japanese well
above that of his Asiatic neighbors, but this improvement was scarcely commensurate with the rate of industrial and commercial development. This was proba-

bly in part because the ruling group was interested in developing a powerful nation rather than a prosperous people, but a much more basic reason was the economic drag of an impoverished peasantry and the counter-current created by a rapidly expanding population. Japan as a nation was growing rapidly in wealth, but as a result of increasing economic opportunities and improved health conditions and medical care, the population of Japan shot up from 30,000,000 in the middle of the nineteenth century to over 70,000,000 by 1940. Because of this phenomenal growth, the per capita gain in wealth remained relatively small.

Japanese peasants at the beginning of the Meiji period eked out a pitifully meagre existence by intensive cultivation of tiny plots of land. Better seed, scientific rotation of crops, and improved fertilizers brought some increase in crop yields in modern times, and careful planning and hard labor squeezed from the soil about as much food as it could yield, but there was no spectacular increase in the per capita production of the individual farmer. In the West, mechanization of farming had made the individual farmer a large producer, but this called for an abundance of land and a minimum of labor, while in Japan there was a minimum of land and an abundance of labor. As long as the ratio of farmers to acres went unchanged, the Japanese peasant of necessity remained poor.

A large and fast growing peasantry created a superabundance of labor for industry, and the expanding labor market was always amply fed from this source. New needs for labor could be met by fresh recruits from villages and farms. Consequently, the laboring class kept close in spirit and often in family ties to the docile peasantry. Unemployed workers returned home to the farm, and farm girls spent years in the spinning mills, living almost like industrial serfs in company-owned dormitories . The worker endured a life of dire poverty, but the cheap labor he performed for highly efficient cartels made Japan one of the leading industrial nations of the world, unchallenged in the mass production of cheap goods.

The young reformers, who started in 1868 to make Japan into a modern nation able to hold its own on terms of equality with the Western powers, saw their ambitions realized within their own lifetimes. With the aid of a strong army and navy, an efficient government, an obedient and technically competent citizenry, and vigorous industry and commerce, they made Japan within a few short decades a world military power and won recognition of equality from the occidentals, who had in the past tended to look upon all Asia as essentially "barbarian" and outside the family of civilized nations.

During the second half of the nineteenth century, the European powers were engaged in a mad scramble to build up colonial empires by carving out new domains in Africa, Asia, and Oceania. Overseas expansion and colonial possessions were the mark of the successful power. Japanese leaders, with their *samurai* backgrounds, enthusiastically embraced the current imperialism of Europe and soon outstripped the Western imperialists in their determination to win colonies. They saw that poor and small Japan needed more natural resources to become a first-class world power, and they believed that control of adjacent territories would yield many of these resources and strengthen the defenses of Japan.

The political decay and military weakness of China and Korea made these lands ripe for foreign aggression, and Japanese leaders eagerly joined Europeans in the game of winning territories and economic privileges from the weaker regimes of Asia. In 1874, the Japanese tried out their armed forces and the European techniques of forceful diplomacy by sending a punitive expedition to China's island dependency of Formosa to chastise the natives for having killed some sailors from the Ryukyu Islands. The expedition was successful, and the Chinese were forced to pay an indemnity, thereby unwittingly recognizing Japanese claims to full sovereignty over the Ryukyus.

Two years later Japan used the same tactics in Korea that the Americans had employed against the Tokugawa. By a show of naval might, the king of Korea was forced to open his land to foreign intercourse and to sign a treaty granting to Japan the special privileges usually demanded by European powers from Asiatic states. For the next two decades the new government contented itself with intrigues in Korea to gain control of the peninsula and to force the Chinese to give up their claim to suzerainty. Men like Saigo, the Satsuma rebel, had advocated a policy of immediate military expansion, but the dominant group in the government insisted that internal reforms must come first.

Not until 1894 did Japan feel strong enough for a real test of arms. In that year she precipitated a war with China over the control of Korea. The Japanese easily seized Korea, destroyed the Chinese naval forces, over-ran Southern Manchuria, and even captured the port of Wei-hai-wei in China proper. The war ended in 1895. In the peace treaty China agreed to pay a large indemnity to Japan, recognized the full independence of Korea, and ceded to Japan the rich island of Formosa, the strategically placed Pescadores Islands between Formosa and the coast of China, and the Liaotung Peninsula at the southern tip of Manchuria. Japan had demonstrated that she had indeed become a modern military power, and had made a successful start in building an empire.

At about the same time Japan finally won recognition from the occidental powers as a true equal and a full-fledged member of the family of nations. Impressed by the rapid and efficient reorganization of Japanese political institutions in conformity with Western patterns, and satisfied that the new legal system was up to occidental standards of justice and humaneness, the British in 1894 agreed to surrender their right to extraterritoriality, the right exercised by most Western governments throughout Asia to have their nationals tried by their own rather than by native laws. Other Western powers followed the British example, and in 1899 Japan became the first Asiatic land to free itself of extraterritoriality. The Western nations also began to relinquish the treaty rights under which they had restricted Japanese tariffs since the late days of the Tokugawa. By 1911, Japan had resumed complete control of her own tariffs.

For the most part, Americans and Europeans were favorably impressed with the rapid strides in modern-

THE FAR EAST IN MODERN TIMES

ization that Japan was making, and greatly admired the
Japanese for the ease with which they defeated China.
But some European powers regarded with grave mis-
givings the appearance of a new competitor in the game
of cutting up the "Chinese melon," as they sometimes
called it. Russia, Germany, and France, banding together, forced Japan to return the Liaotung Peninsula
to China. In 1898, however, these powers cynically
extorted pieces of Chinese territory from the tottering Manchu dynasty. The French took Kwangchow
Bay in South China; the Germans, the city of Tsingtao
and the adjacent Kiaochow Bay area; and the Russians
seized the Liaotung Peninsula which Japan had been
forced to give up two years earlier. Britain, not to be
outdone by European rivals, expanded her foothold at
Hongkong in South China and occupied the port of
Wei-hai-wei in the north.

Although the Japanese were infuriated by the du-
plicity of Germany and France, they clearly realized
that Russia, dominant in Manchuria and interfering
more and more in Korea, was the chief enemy that
must be defeated before Japan could resume its own
program of expansion in Asia. The Japanese knew that
Russia standing alone would be a dangerous foe for
Japan to face and that a coalition of European powers
would be disastrous for Japanese ambitions. Of this
realization was born the Anglo-Japanese Alliance of
1902, a military pact between Japan and the greatest
naval power of the day, in which each country agreed
to come to the aid of the other if its ally, while engaged in war with one power, should be attacked by
another. The British were not averse to seeing their

old rival, Russia, embroiled in a war in the Far East, and the alliance set the stage for war by giving Japan a free hand to fight Russia alone.

The Japanese, choosing their time in February 1904, set a new pattern for modern warfare by first crippling Russian naval strength in the Far East, and then declaring war. Russia was far stronger than Japan, but suffered the disadvantage of having to fight the war at the end of a single-track railway several thousand miles long. Her military operations were further hampered by revolutionary movements at home. The Japanese were consistently victorious, bottling up the Russians in the Liaotung Peninsula ports, which fell after costly assaults, and driving their other armies northward through Manchuria. Russia sent her European fleet from the Baltic Sea to the Far East, but the entire Japanese navy fell upon it in the straits between Japan and Korea and annihilated it. Although Russia was being soundly trounced, Japan was so exhausted that she welcomed the peace arranged in 1905 by President Theodore Roosevelt, who greatly admired Japanese efficiency and pluck.

In the peace treaty, Russia acknowledged Japan's paramount interests in Korea, transferred to Japan her lease of the Liaotung Peninsula and the railways she had built in Southern Manchuria, and ceded the southern half of the island of Sakhalin, north of Hokkaido. Japan, the military ally of Great Britain, the victor over Russia, and the possessor of expanding colonial domains, had become a true world power.

Relieved of Chinese and Russian competition in Korea, Japan quietly annexed the whole of Korea in

1910. There, as in Formosa, she embarked upon an ambitious program of economic development and exploitation, which brought railways, factories, and other outward aspects of the modern world to these lands. The Koreans and Formosans, however, were subjected to the repressive rule of an efficient but often ruthless colonial administration and an omnipresent and usually brutal police force. The natives had even less opportunity for personal economic gain than the lower classes in Japan, and their intellectual and spiritual oppression was severe.

The First World War gave Japan another chance to expand, this time with little risk or effort. As the ally of England, Japan at once declared war on Germany. Little interested in the outcome of the war in Europe, Japan happily proceeded to pick up German colonies in the East, taking Tsingtao and all the German interests in adjoining areas of China, and seizing German islands in the North Pacific, the Marianas, Carolines, and Marshalls — later given to Japan in the form of a mandate by the peace treaty. With the eyes of the rest of the world turned toward Europe, Japan also found this a good time to win more concessions from the Chinese, and in 1915, presented China with the so-called "Twenty-one Demands," which would have made China a virtual colony of Japan. The Chinese Republican government resisted the more sweeping of these demands, but Japan managed to acquire many valuable economic concessions during the war years. The war in Europe also cut off the cotton mills of England and the factories of continental Europe from the markets of Asia. Japanese business men took full advantage of this golden opportunity and made deep inroads into rich markets previously monopolized by the Europeans.

War in Europe permitted Japan to expand both her economic and political empire, and brought unprecedented prosperity to the land. Only fifty years after the "Restoration," Japan went to the peace conference at Versailles in 1919 as one of the great military and industrial powers of the world and received official recognition as one of the "Big Five" of the new international order.

Chapter X

THE APPEARANCE OF LIBERAL DEMOCRATIC TRENDS

The success of the carefully controlled revolution of the Meiji leaders was tremendous. In a few decades the oligarchs had made the strong Japan they wanted. They had no detailed plans when they started, but they did have a clear idea of the general objective, and this objective they had attained by firmly leading their people through a series of amazing reforms and changes.

Accustomed to severe feudal rule, the docile populace expected to be led. The oligarchs had no difficulty in controlling the people, and remained the masters of each new situation. Minor set-backs and endless personal quarrels occurred among the leaders, but all major issues turned out as they wished. Nothing got out of hand. Yet, in a country open to influences from all over the world, with an educated citizenry becoming aware of the ideas and ideals of other lands, strict control by a small oligarchy of the actions and thoughts of all the people became increasingly difficult.

It was in the intellectual field that new and divergent currents first made themselves felt. In the early days of

Meiji, there had been many able young Japanese leaders who, while no less anxious than the Satsuma and Choshu *samurai* to make a new and better Japan, were not thinking primarily in terms of military strength. There were men like the young *samurai*, Fukuzawa Yukichi, who as a student of Dutch in the last years of the Tokugawa, had become aware of Western concepts, and later under the influence of American ideals became a prolific writer, established a great newspaper, and founded an educational institution which was to become Keio University — one of the several great universities of modern Tokyo.

There were also foreigners in Japan, particularly the Christian missionaries, who came largely from America, and they helped found many of the early schools. Here they taught the Christian ideals of the West which, although tolerated by the early Meiji leaders, were quite at variance with their aims and beliefs. Christianity as an organized religion did not spread quickly in modern Japan, but it won a few hundred thousand converts who were drawn largely from the intellectual classes. Through them the ethics and ideals of Christianity had a much more profound influence on Japanese thought and life than one might assume from the fact that less than one per cent of the population became professing Christians.

The culture of the early Meiji period was a strange conglomeration of undigested borrowings from Western civilization mixed with many elements remaining intact from feudal times. In the late years of Meiji, however, the birth of a completely modern and yet indigenous culture was presaged by the appearance of an entirely new literature. This literature was, of course, deeply influenced by Western models. It was so decidedly modern that many of its ideas might have been those of contemporary Russians, Frenchmen, or Englishmen. At the same time, this literature was too good and too sincere to be simply imitative. It was a distinctly Japanese creation, telling the story of the average middle class people with realism, sometimes with deep psychological analysis, and often with considerable humor. In the hands of a master like the novelist Natsume Soseki, a university professor of English, it was a great literature, worthy of standing beside the finest literary works of the Western world. Its appearance toward the end of the Meiji period clearly indicated that, even while the oligarchy ruled, an intellectual class was growing up which was free of the feudal mentality inherited from the Tokugawa and was thinking in terms quite foreign to the oligarchs.

Side by side with the new intellectual class and to some degree merging with it was a second group, also developing opinions divergent from the ruling oligarchy. This group consisted of business men and financiers, who, although in large part made up of former *samurai* and Daimyo, tended to be more interested in taxes and profits than in military strength and colonial expansion.

The business men had joined with the lesser government officials excluded from the oligarchy in clamoring for a larger voice in the government, and the creation of the Diet in 1890 gave them a place in politics which they gradually improved. Political parties at first had centered completely around the old oligarchs, but as time passed the small ruling circle found it increasingly necessary to win the support of this new politically conscious public. Gradually the great financial and industrial interests began to take control of the parties, although the oligarchs still remained their nominal leaders. At the same time the electorate was expanded by lowering the tax requirement for voting. At the end of the First World War, the tax qualifications stood at only three yen, and the electorate had risen to 1,500,000, thus including the bulk of the middle classes, but not the peasantry and urban proletariat.

Despite these political gains of the middle classes and the appearance of new intellectual trends, Japan entered the First World War apparently under the firm control of a small oligarchy, and then, as the war ended and Japan entered the post-war world, it suddenly became evident that there was no longer a small, clear-cut ruling group, but instead, thousands of bureaucrats, military leaders, business men, and intellectuals, all contending for control of the government. There was even a growing demand that all classes be allowed to participate in politics. Within a few years it also became evident that the intellectual life and even the social patterns in the cities of Japan had become strongly westernized. A new Japanese culture, hinted at in the writings of men like Natsume Soseki, seemed to be emerging.

One reason for this rather sudden change was the disappearance of the original oligarchs. The Meiji emperor died in 1912, leaving the throne to his mentally deficient son, who ruled in name until 1926 under the reign title of Taisho. The Taisho emperor was incapable of participating in the direction of government, and in 1921 he had to relinquish even his ceremonial functions to his son, who became the Prince Regent. The death of the Meiji Emperor meant the disappearance of one of the greatest figures in the oligarchy and the elimination of the throne from Japanese politics, except as a symbol, and a tool for those in control of the government.

Ito, framer of the Constitution and four times Premier, had been assassinated by a Korean in 1909. Yamagata, father of the army and himself twice Premier, died in 1922. Two years later only one of the great "elder statesmen" of the Meiji period remained, Prince Saionji, the old court noble and perhaps the least typical member of the whole group.

Meanwhile, a new generation was coming into power. A majority of the generals, admirals, bureaucrats, business men, and intellectuals of the time had been born or at least had grown up since the "Restoration." These men, for the most part, were the sons of former *samurai* who had become army officers, government officials, or business men, but they, themselves, had never been *samurai*. No one group had the prestige or power of the old oligarchy, and on the whole they lacked the common background and singleness of purpose of the Meiji leaders.

Another significant factor was the First World War. It gave a tremendous impetus to commercial and industrial expansion, which helped make the business classes, and particularly the great commercial and industrial interests, increasingly important in Japanese life and politics. They became the heroes of a prosperous new

Japan, and, as they spread their activities throughout the Far East, they began to overshadow the soldier and sailor as the front line fighters in Japan's expanding search for a place in the sun.

In addition, the overwhelming success of the Western democracies in the First World War strongly influenced Japanese thought. The most democratic Western powers, Great Britain, France, and the United States, had emerged victorious, and the least democratic, Germany, Russia, and Austro-Hungary, had collapsed completely. It seemed obvious that democracy made stronger states and was therefore superior to autocracy. This argument was convincing to the average Japanese. There was an upsurge of enthusiasm for democracy, which inevitably brought new powers and prestige to the Diet and the party politician.

With the disappearance of the old oligarchy and the growing influence of extra-governmental groups, the Diet and party system also proved to be handy mechanisms for the balancing of political forces. The great bureaucrats and high military and naval officers came closest, both in position and outlook, to being the heirs of the old oligarchy, but, lacking the unchallenged authority of their predecessors, they found it necessary to seek support through political coalitions in the Diet. The great business empires, which were coming to be known by the pejorative name of *zaibatsu*, found the Diet a convenient bargaining ground with the bureaucracy, while the parties were for them an effective tool for winning political power through the judicious use of financial aid. The smaller businessmen and rural land owners, who from the start had been the backbone of the political parties, naturally were committed to the support of parliamentary government, for that was their only means of exercising direct political power.

For these various reasons, then, the Diet and party system became the meeting ground for the plurality of forces which had grown out of the unity of earlier oligarchic rule. Professional bureaucrats, admirals, and generals, as well as representatives of the great *zaibatsu* firms, such as Mitsui and Mitsubishi, often dominated the leadership of the parties or even occupied the post of Premier, but for more than a decade after the First World War the Cabinets were largely party Cabinets, dependent upon an elected majority in the Diet. Corruption was rife, and the two major parties, the Seiyukai and the Kenseikai (renamed Minseito in 1927), were often the tools of strong individuals or powerful private interests. The Diet, however, had become the key instrument of government, and Japan had become the first non-Occidental land to make full use of democratic mechanisms, even though only a minority of the Japanese people had as yet found political expression through them.

The new system of party government got its start as early as September 1918, when Hara, the Seiyukai leader, was the first commoner and the first professional politician of the new generation to become Premier. Actually the first Seiyukai leader to be Premier had been Prince Ito, but Ito, far from being the political product or agent of the party, had himself helped create it in 1900 in order to organize support in the

Diet for his own policies. Hara, while high-handed in his efforts to dominate the party, was a product of party politics and dependent on Seiyukai support for his influence. Following his assassination by a fanatic in 1921, Cabinets came and went with bewildering rapidity, some backed by one economic empire or another, some more influenced than others by army and navy interests and more inclined to a strong foreign policy. But until the sudden collapse of party government in 1932, the general tendency was for the government to depend on party power in the Diet and to reflect the dominance of business interests over the other groups that constituted the ruling elements in Japan.

The Japanese businessmen of the 1920's, influenced by the philosophies of the victorious Western democracies, tended to look with disfavor on the high taxes required for large naval and military establishments. They were also inclined to believe that economic expansion — building up a great export trade and acquiring economic concessions abroad through diplomacy — was less costly and more profitable than colonial expansion by war and conquest. This seemed particularly true in China, the chief field for Japanese expansion. The Chinese, with a newly awakened sense of nationalism, were beginning to boycott foreign merchants whose governments were considered to be pursuing an aggressive policy against China. Consequently, military intervention in China cost the double price of lost markets and increased military expenditures.

Such attitudes, together with the prevalent internationalist sentiment of the postwar years, soon led to a reversal of the old policy of colonial expansion through military force. In 1922, the Japanese withdrew from Siberia the last of their troops, which together with British and American forces had landed at Vladivostok, Russia's principal Far Eastern port, in 1918, shortly before Hara had come to power. On this expedition the Japanese had sent far more than their share of troops in an obvious effort to fish for possible rewards in the troubled waters of the Russian Revolution, but the new government considered the venture unprofitable and withdrew completely.

In the winter of 1921–22, at the Washington Conference, Japan joined the United States and the principal European powers in recognizing the territorial integrity of China and renouncing the generally accepted policy of cutting up the "Chinese melon." Japan also agreed with other members of the "Big Five" to limit their respective naval establishments. The ratio of capital ships was set at five for Great Britain and the United States, three for Japan, and 1.67 for France and Italy. This ratio, it was thought, would give Japan definite naval supremacy within her own waters but confine her fleet to the western Pacific.

This same winter, by a separate treaty with China, Japan restored to China the area around Kiaochow Bay and the economic concessions in contiguous parts of northern China once held by Germany. Japan also agreed to withdraw all her military forces from these areas. In 1925, the civilian government forced through a reduction of the standing army, and four of the twenty-one divisions were eliminated — a considerable cut in military strength and a saving to the tax-payer.

Thus the Japanese businessmen called a halt to colonial expansion and asserted their right to limit and even to pare down the national military establishment.

From 1927 to 1929, the cabinet of Baron Tanaka, an army general and leader of the Seiyukai, reversed the trend away from militarism. He used Japanese forces in North China to block the northward advance of the new Chinese Nationalist government, but eventually he had to withdraw these troops. His successors returned to the dominant businessman's policy of conciliatory diplomacy with a view to further expansion of a lucrative export trade.

While a greatly enlarged ruling class of military leaders, bureaucrats, *zaibatsu* executives, and politicians representative of small business and rural landowner interests controlled the postwar parliamentarian regime, other classes were beginning to come on the political scene. With the intelligentsia and underpaid office-workers in the van, city dwellers of lower economic status were waking to a new political consciousness. These men, too, belonged to the new generation and were the products of the new education. University professors, teachers, writers, doctors, lawyers, and office-workers, usually with from fourteen to eighteen years of formal education, were thoroughly conversant with the intellectual and political trends of the Western world. Even the city laborers, with their elementary education, could read the newspapers, which exposed them to influences from all quarters. The educated populace demanded a share in government, and with the democratic tide of the day, this demand could not be denied. In 1919, the electorate was doubled, increasing from 1,500,000 to 3,000,000; and in 1925, a universal manhood suffrage bill was passed, making a total electorate of 14,000,000 voters. Now the whole adult male population of Japan, peasants and city workers along with the middle and upper classes, could vote.

Since the lower classes, however, were politically untutored, they took little interest in politics. The peasantry seemed almost untouched by the strong democratic trends in the cities, and only a small element in the city proletariat, largely under the leadership of middle class intellectuals, expressed itself in political action. With the backing of white collar workers and some laborers, intellectuals founded liberal and left wing parties, such as the Social Democratic and the Labor-Farmer, and later the Social Mass Party, born of a union of the two earlier parties. Even a Communist Party was organized, embracing a few radical thinkers and very small groups of laborers and peasants, but it was early liquidated by the thorough and ruthless Japanese police. Of the other parties, only the Social Mass made any impression in the Diet, and that was not until the 1930's, after the Diet had relapsed into relative insignificance.

Although the new parties were not too influential in practical politics, they were significant. During the 1920's, the city intellectuals and white collar workers became a strongly liberal group, not unlike the liberals in the United States who stood slightly left of center. In the 1930's, when the rest of Japan was disowning democracy and liberalism, and the businessmen were weakly surrendering leadership to the militarists, the intellectuals and white collar workers in the middle class districts of the large cities rolled up huge majorities for the few liberal politicians who were allowed to run for election.

The peasantry had not yet awakened to politics, and the urban proletariat was hardly strong; but without doubt the city workers were on their way to becoming a force in Japanese society and politics. Their medium of expression was more the labor union than the political party. Japanese labor unions, which had grown rapidly during the prosperous war years, were strong enough by 1919 to exert considerable pressure through strikes, and strikes became a definite part of the Japanese scene in the 1920's. By 1929, union membership had grown to well over 300,000 and promised to keep on growing. It seemed but a matter of time before the proletariat would join with city intellectuals and white collar workers to form a strong, possibly dominant political force in Japan.

Paralleling these political changes in Japan during the 1920's were even more startling changes in Japanese society and culture. The rural areas and small towns were being modernized only very slowly, but a whole new social structure and life were beginning to appear in the cities. Tokyo naturally took the lead in cultural as well as political changes, for it was both the capital and the greatest city of Japan, with a population which reached about 7,000,000 in 1940. The great earthquake and fire of September 1, 1923, accelerated the speed of social change in the Tokyo area. This tremendous cataclysm, which in three days took close to 100,000 lives and completely destroyed about one-half of Tokyo and almost all of Yokohama, helped to sweep away old, outworn modes of life, and cleared the ground literally for a new city, and figuratively for a new culture.

Downtown Tokyo became a city of wide thoroughfares and of many great steel and reinforced concrete buildings, resembling in sections the cities of Europe and America more than those of Asia. The Marunouchi district around the main Tokyo railway station was the pride of the nation and a symbol of the new modernized Japan. Other cities followed Tokyo's lead, and soon modern office buildings of steel, school buildings in concrete, large movie houses, an occasional great stadium, and sprawling railway stations were the typical architecture of Japanese cities.

Family solidarity, paternal authority, and male dominance remained the salient features of Japanese society, but increasingly the younger generation in the cities joined the world-wide revolt of youth and began to question time-honored social customs. College students, attracted to liberal or radical political philosophies, embraced the freer social concepts of the West, and there was a growing demand on the part of youth to be allowed to make marriages of love rather than marriages arranged by families through go-betweens. Women office workers became a feature of the new social system, and under occidental influence, many middle class Japanese men began to treat their wives almost as social equals. The women of Japan began slowly to free themselves from their traditional position as domestic drudges.

The symbol of the 1920's in Japan, as in the United

States, was the "flapper," called by the Japanese the *moga*, a contraction of the English words "modern girl," and the male counterpart of the *moga* was naturally called the *mobo*. Moving pictures, either from Hollywood or made in Japan on Hollywood patterns, had a tremendous vogue, and American jazz and Western social dancing were popular with the more sophisticated. Taxi-dance halls appeared; all-girl musical comedy troupes rivaled the popularity of the movies; Western style and Chinese style restaurants became numerous; and there was a mushroom growth of so-called "cafés" — small "beer joints," where cheap victrolas ground out American jazz and emancipated young men enjoyed the company of pretty young waitresses of doubtful morals.

The Japanese threw themselves into Western sports with enthusiasm. Baseball and tennis were already extremely popular. Now they concentrated on track and field sports as well, with a view to making better showings at the Olympic games, and they actually came to dominate the Olympic swimming events. Golf links were built for the rich, and the middle classes took up skiing. Baseball, however, remained the great national sport, and university and middle school baseball games drew crowds comparable to those attending major college football and big league baseball games in the United States.

There were many other less striking but even more significant aspects of the new culture of the Japanese cities. The great literary movement started in the time of Natsume Soseki continued with growing vigor. Thousands of books poured off the Japanese presses,

and the literature of the whole world became available
in cheap translated editions. Great Tokyo and Osaka
newspapers grew to have circulations in the millions,
and popular magazines of all varieties were published.
Higher education was sought by more and more young
men from all classes, and higher education for women
finally achieved a slow start. There was much and often
brilliant scholarly activity in many scientific fields and
in the humanities. A growing taste for good Western
music was seen in the organization of symphony orchestras and in huge audiences for visiting Western
musicians. The city people of Japan were beginning to
share in the rich intellectual and cultural life of the
Western world.

The leaders of the early Meiji period had transformed
Japan into a strong military and industrial power, but
the democratic political concepts, the broad intellectual
life, and the liberal social trends which flowered spon-
taneously from the state they created were something
they themselves could never have imagined or understood. The carefully controlled revolution of the Meiji
period was developing into a runaway liberal movement of the urban middle classes.

Chapter XI

THE NATIONALISTIC AND MILITARISTIC REACTION

The political and intellectual liberalism of the 1920's was for the most part limited to the cities. Peasants and residents of the thousands of villages and small towns, who still constituted the bulk of the population, looked on at what was happening in the cities with wonderment and often with disapproval; and certain elements among the more educated classes regarded the liberal and sometimes radical political theories of the city intelligentsia and the antics of the *moga* and *mobo* with growing hostility and resentment. Army and navy officers, rural landowners, lower middle class citizens of the smaller towns, and many petty government officials found it quite impossible to accept or even to tolerate the growing challenge to established political and social authority.

These men, too, were members of the new generation and products of the new education, but with them the heavy nationalistic and militaristic indoctrination of the school system had weighed more heavily than the opening of new horizons and the influences from abroad. They were in complete sympathy with the authoritarian rule at home and the strong expansionist program abroad of the Meiji leaders, and the post-war liberalism and internationalism seemed to them signs of weakness and perversion. From the Meiji leaders they had inherited a compelling nationalistic urge to make Japan even stronger, but too much nationalistic and militaristic indoctrination had robbed them of the breadth of view of the Meiji leaders they sought to emulate.

Ultra-nationalist and militarist sentiments from time to time found expression in political parties, but these essentially reactionary elements, with their inherent distrust of representative government, leaned more to direct action through private pressure groups and extra-legal cliques than to political action by means of the ballot-box. Ultra-nationalistic secret societies quite naturally developed as one of their major forms of political expression. Some of these exerted considerable influence on Japanese politics by terroristic activities and virulent propaganda directed against their opponents. The best known of these ultra-nationalistic secret societies was formed by anti-Russian propagandists who, believing that the Amur River in Siberia should be Japan's frontier, named their group the Amur Society. A literal translation into English has given us the very sinister sounding name of Black Dragon Society.

The reactionaries all tended to look to the armed forces as their idols and champions, for the army and navy were less tainted with the prevailing democratic views and business man's ideals of the 1920's. The army and navy, furthermore, were the natural organs for the continued military expansion advocated by these reactionaries. The officer corps reciprocated by leaning heavily toward the expansionist and nationalistic views of the reactionaries. Older generals and admirals were often men of broad outlook, who from long and intimate association with business leaders had come to accept much of the business man's point of view, but the younger officers were mostly of a different breed.

The new officer caste was largely composed of sons of officers or of rural landowners, or sometimes even of peasants. Coming from such conservative backgrounds, they were given an even more conservative education. The army recruited most of its future officers at about the age of fourteen, and from that age on the young cadet was subjected to a narrow militaristic training which often made him incapable of understanding democratic concepts of government, or even the civilian mentality. Since these young officers were victims of over-indoctrination, it is not surprising that they increasingly found themselves in violent opposition to the trends of the time and completely out of sympathy with the more moderate and broadminded generals and admirals.

From the start the army had relied on the peasantry as its chief source for enlisted men, and a very special relationship had grown up between the army and the peasants. On the one hand, the army in general and army officers individually had a paternalistic interest in their men and saw to it that they were well cared for while in service, and thoroughly indoctrinated with fierce national pride and a fanatical sense of devotion to the emperor — and to the army as the visible symbol of imperial might and authority. The peasants, on the other hand, denied their share of economic prosperity and still too untutored to take their part in politics, found army life far less onerous than did the city youths, and looked upon the army and the reservist organization for discharged soldiers as their only means of achieving personal glory and prestige in an otherwise humdrum, miserable existence. As peasants they were insignificant members of a poor and downtrodden class. As soldiers they were honored members of a mystic elite corps, participating directly in all the glories of Japan as a world power.

The army officers, with predominantly rural or small town family backgrounds and an intimate and paternalistic relation with peasant soldiers, came to have a deeper understanding of the peasant and a more genuine interest in his welfare than did the representatives of big business interests or the city intellectuals, who more often looked upon the peasant as hopelessly backward and outside the pale of the new Japanese culture. Younger army officers, resenting the political and economic domination of businessmen, doubtful of the ethical or even the economic value of the whole capitalistic system, and distrusting deeply the liberal philosophy of the intelligentsia, gradually came to champion the economic interests of the peasantry against the big city groups, particularly the capitalists. In return, the peasantry gave the army and its officer corps blind but inarticulate support.

The recrudescence of military sentiment and the

abandonment of parliamentarian government in Japan are often portrayed as a simple return to earlier Japanese patterns and a revival of feudal tendencies, but such an interpretation misses the real significance of what happened in Japan. The military officer was no *samurai;* in fact, in the new society he represented the lower classes more than the privileged classes of wealth and aristocratic birth. In the army there was far less place for hereditary prestige and power than in either business or politics, and in this sense the army was further from the feudal past than the rest of Japanese society. The younger officers of the army and navy, with their rural distrust of the cities and big business, were scarcely defenders of the *status quo;* nor were they advocates of a return to an earlier economic balance. They were in actuality moving toward a revolutionary hatred of capitalism and were beginning to champion vague but definitely radical programs to better the economic status of the underprivileged peasantry.

Naturally the nationalistic and authoritarian reaction could not have occurred in Japan had it not been for certain fundamental qualities of the Japanese as fashioned over the centuries. Their smouldering nationalism needed little fanning to break forth again into full flame. Hundreds of years of rule by men of the sword had made the people ready to accept the claims of the militarists to leadership. Centuries of docile obedience to authoritarian rule had left most Japanese almost indifferent to the reimposition of authoritarian patterns. In fact, many were ill at ease with the intellectual and political freedoms they were winning and were anxious to rediscover the emotional security of life under outside authority. Without these strong influences surviving from the feudal past, it seems improbable that the reaction of the 1930's would have occurred at all, but this does not mean that the reaction itself took the form of a return to feudalism. Japan, as a largely modernized industrial nation, could not return to the past in that way. Instead it started on a course taken by certain lands of the Western world, where, as in Japan, the spiritual heritage of an authoritarian past had lived on into an industrialized present and had merged with it to create the egalitarian slavery of totalitarianism — fascist or communist.

Modern Japanese totalitarianism, thus, was not merely an outgrowth of Japan's authoritarian past but was equally a product of the centralizing power of the modern economic and political machine. Modern communications as well as modern techniques of political and economic organization had given even the parliamentary government of the 1920's far greater control over the lives of the Japanese people than any emperor, Shogun, or Daimyo had ever exercised. Universal education, the newspapers, the radio, and, of course, universal military service had given those in power far greater control over men's minds than could have been dreamed of in earlier ages. Totalitarian patterns were certainly as natural an outgrowth of the Meiji modernization as liberal ideals and democratic institutions. It took time for these contrasting products of modernization to mature, and they emerged from the chrysalis of the controlled Meiji revolution at about the same time.

Viewed in this light, the strange mixture in Japan of what have been traditionally considered antithetical forces of left and right takes on a new and sinister meaning. We have in recent decades become all too familiar with the totalitarian perversion of egalitarian ideals and scientific knowledge in the more backward parts of Europe. Japan, as the most advanced country of Asia, was the first to show us that this terrible pattern could also appear in Asia.

These disturbing tendencies grew slowly and almost unnoticed during the 1920's; then in the early 1930's the blatant militarism, fanatical nationalism, and anti-liberal and anti-democratic prejudices of the younger army and navy officers and of other reactionary groups swept over Japan in a sudden reversal of the dominant trends of the preceding decade. The parliamentary coalition of the bureaucrats, big business, and the politicians, with more or less active support from the urban middle classes, had been the first successor of the Meiji oligarchy. Now it was pushed aside by the militarists, with the noisy backing of ultra-nationalistic societies and the tacit support of the rural population.

The exact time and speed of the reaction against liberalism and democracy were certainly influenced, if not determined, by outside forces, just as the rapid growth of liberal tendencies had been fostered by the external factor of the First World War. For one thing, the world-wide disillusionment with democracy, which followed soon after and helped to create fascist totalitarian regimes elsewhere, did not go unnoticed by the Japanese. Many of them were impressed by the vaunted "superiority" of totalitarian governments and their points of agreement with traditional Japanese concepts of authoritarian rule.

Another outside influence was the world-wide depression of 1929 and the resultant collapse of international trade. Japan started its own depression with a bank crisis in 1927, but it was of little consequence compared with the raising of protective tariffs throughout the world as an aftermath of the 1929 depression. This seemed to spell ultimate disaster for Japan's foreign trade. The businessman's program of continued economic expansion and prosperity through a growing export trade was suddenly revealed to be dangerously dependent on the good will and tolerance of foreign powers. Huge political units like Russia, the United States, and the British Empire could ride the storm of world depression, for they had their own sources of supply for most raw materials and their own consuming markets. But a smaller unit like Japan, which depended on other lands for much of its raw materials, and on China, India, and the Occident for a vital part of its consuming market, seemed entirely at the mercy of the tariff policies of other nations.

The problem was all the more acute for Japan because of the tremendous increase in population. There were now more than 60,000,000 Japanese, far more than could be supported by a simple agricultural economy, and with government encouragement the rate of increase was about 1,000,000 persons a year. For the maintenance of this expanded population in the narrow islands of Japan, foreign markets for exports were essential. Consequently, the Japanese viewed any threat to their overseas economic enterprises with grave concern.

In the early 1930's many Japanese believed that the only answer to rising protective tariffs in other lands was for Japan to resume its old program of colonial expansion and win for itself the sources of raw materials and the markets needed to make it self-sufficient and invulnerable as a world power. Such reasoning seemed obvious to the reactionary and militaristic groups. Those businessmen and intellectuals who remained moderate and international in their views were not able to refute these arguments to the satisfaction of the Japanese public.

There was a gradual swing of popular support to the military expansionists. As these same groups also stood for authoritarian rule within Japan, much of the support for imperialist aggrandizement abroad readily became popular backing for the attack on democratic institutions at home. The incipient Japanese totalitarians, however, did not wait until growing popular support should bring them victory at the polls. That might never have come, and, in any case, it was a means to power which they, as a matter of principle, repudiated. Instead they began a direct, frontal attack on liberal beliefs and democratic institutions. They had no well-defined philosophy or central, conspiratorial organization, such as had helped the German Nazis and Russian Communists to win power. The attack was made piecemeal by individuals or small organizations, but it was almost as effective as the better coordinated efforts of the totalitarians in Europe.

Scores of small groups of fanatical nationalists

stirred up popular support for the militarists and hacked away at the foundations of parliamentary government. Occasionally young hotheads were inspired by their rabid elders to commit political assassinations, which not only eliminated their unfortunate victims but, through intimidation, silenced large numbers of other potential opponents. Most important of all, the army on its own authority embroiled Japan in foreign wars of conquest, which, while forcing the nation back to the strategy of military conquest, also aroused the nationalistic emotions of the people and, thus, won their support for the authoritarian as well as the imperialist aims of the militarists.

The ease with which the Japanese totalitarians stifled the growth of democracy in Japan illustrated the obvious fact that the roots of liberalism were still shallow. It also revealed certain specific weaknesses in the democratic mechanism, attributable to its authoritarian background and haphazard growth.

One basic flaw in the whole Japanese political system had been deliberately fashioned by the Meiji oligarchs and carefully preserved by the parliamentary groups of the 1920's until it contributed to their own undoing. This was the mystic position of the emperor as a demi-god whose personal will, in theory, took precedence over all law. The Meiji leaders, who had come to power by championing the right of the emperor to rule, had created and fostered this tradition, since it gave them, as the men who surrounded the throne and spoke for the emperor, far greater authority over the people than they could have achieved otherwise. By building up an elaborate state cult of

Shinto, centered on the person of the emperor and the imperial line, and by indoctrinating school children with fanatical devotion to the emperor and blind faith in all statements said to represent his will, they secured for themselves the unquestioning loyalty and obedience of the people. The parliamentary leaders who succeeded to power chose to perpetuate this system, for it seemed to give them, too, an unassailable position of authority as spokesmen for the emperor. Consequently, they permitted the wildest sort of utterances by members of the lunatic fringe of ultra-nationalists and militarists, because they were couched in terms of devotion to the emperor; but they vigorously and ruthlessly suppressed all radical thinkers who challenged the validity of the emperor concept.

In 1925, the same year in which universal manhood suffrage was adopted, the Diet passed a new Peace Preservation Law, further limiting the rights of free speech and free political action. Under the new law the government became increasingly involved in efforts to stamp out "dangerous thoughts." Any thought was considered dangerous which questioned the position of the emperor or challenged other basic political or economic beliefs of the ruling groups. Although anti-capitalist prejudices were perhaps most prevalent in extreme militaristic circles, the businessmen and bureaucrats were far more afraid of Marxist intellectuals, and the early victims of this thought purge were largely students of liberal or radical tendencies. The embryo communist movement was completely crushed, and many students who had nothing more than vague radical leanings were thrown into prison and forced to recant their "dangerous thoughts."

The parliamentary leaders made their fatal error in failing to see that the reactionary ultra-nationalists and militarists presented the most immediate threat to their continued supremacy. These groups neatly turned the tables on the civil government by claiming that they, not the government, represented the true imperial will. The claim in the case of the army had a certain validity, for in theory the armed forces were the personal army and navy of the emperor, enjoying under him a status of equality with the civil government and therefore equally qualified to speak for him. Profiting from this break in the solid front of government authority and taking advantage of tacit army approval, individual extremists were able to go even further in claiming imperial sanction for their personal views and deeds. Acts of aggression abroad and, at home, acts of civil disobedience, political murders, and open mutiny were all justified as being in accord with the true will of the emperor, whose views, it was claimed, were misrepresented by the corrupt politicians around the throne.

Confronted with this monstrous perversion of their own policy, the weak-kneed parliamentarians failed to take drastic measures or even to stand firm and united. Instead, they all but openly admitted the justice of the charge by remaining silent and by compromising with their attackers. The more liberal elements in the urban population, while dismayed, were too weak politically and, for the most part, too timorous to fight back. The general rural and small-town population accepted these acts of supposed devotion to imperial will at their face value and created an atmosphere so sympathetic to political assassins and other extremists that such offenders were usually given only absurdly light punishment.

The theory of the imperial will, thus, was a fatal flaw in Japan's political structure, but the militarists could not have exploited it so successfully if the armed forces had not in practice enjoyed considerable independence of public control and autonomy within the government. This was another serious constitutional flaw. Diet control over the Cabinet was never fully established even in the 1920's, because the Diet never won full control over the purse strings. If the budget were rejected by the Diet, the Cabinet had the right to continue in force the budget of the preceding year.

The army and navy, moreover, maintained considerable independence of the Cabinet by insisting that the army and navy ministers be active officers of high rank and therefore subject to military discipline and available for service in the Cabinet only with army and navy approval. This ruling, first made in 1895 and given imperial sanction five years later, permitted the armed forces to destroy Cabinets or prevent undesirable leaders from taking the premiership simply by refusing to let any qualified officers accept portfolios in the government. The use of this stratagem as early as 1912 and 1914 indicates the growing divergence in opinion between military and civil officials even at that early date. This ruling was subsequently dropped, only to be revived in 1936, when it proved a valuable asset to the militarists in their bid for power. The armed forces, thus, had not only established their independence of the civil government but had rewon a virtual veto power over the Cabinet. The way was open for any action the army wished to take.

Throughout the 1920's certain high government officials had advocated colonial expansion and a strong military policy. There was, for example, Baron General Tanaka, who intervened in the Chinese civil war in 1928. Although the so-called Tanaka Memorial, a purported secret government document recommending a policy of conquest and empire in East Asia, is no longer generally accepted as an authentic document, views such as it expressed were advanced by many officials at the time. These men, however, had tried to win acceptance of their program by normal political procedures; moreover they had been willing to accept defeat when overruled by other groups in the parliamentary coalition.

The turning point between the more liberal 1920's and the reactionary 1930's came in 1931, when certain military forces, without the approval or knowledge of the civil government, started their own war of territorial aggrandizement. In September, Japanese army units stationed in Manchuria to protect the great South Manchurian Railway and other Japanese interests, embarked upon the conquest of all Manchuria on the flimsy pretext that Chinese troops had tried to blow up the railway. Within a few months, Manchuria had been overrun. Meanwhile, Japanese naval forces had been landed at Shanghai in central China. After a sanguinary fight, they seized the Chinese portions of this key city and some surrounding territory.

Early in 1932, Manchuria was made into the puppet state of "Manchukuo." The League of Nations and the United States looked with strong disapproval on this outburst of military aggression in the Far East. But since neither did more than censure Japan verbally and withhold recognition of Manchukuo, Japan found their policies all bark and no bite. Her answer to their criticism was simply to withdraw from the League of Nations.

There could be no doubt that the Japanese army in Manchuria had been eminently successful. At relatively small military cost, and with only a temporary loss in exports to China because of boycott activities, the army had brought under Japanese control a vast new area, rich in natural resources and inhabited by some 30,000,000 industrious Chinese. It was a promising first step toward the creation of the self-sufficient economic empire which would make Japan invulnerable to economic or military attack.

The people as a whole accepted this act of unauthorized and certainly unjustified warfare with wholehearted admiration. Many businessmen and bureaucrats, instead of denouncing the militarists for acting against the will of the government and therefore against the will of the emperor as interpreted by the government, happily accepted this expansion of the national domain and attempted to justify the acts of the military before a critical world public. The Japanese government, in fact, steadfastly maintained the fiction that there had been no war and called the whole conquest of Manchuria simply the "Manchurian incident."

Meanwhile, other military extremists at home had brought a sudden end to party rule by another form of direct action — political assassination. On May 15, 1932, a group of young naval officers and army cadets, claiming that they were attempting to free the emperor from evil advisers, assassinated Premier Inukai, a professional politician and the head of the majority Seiyukai Party. The army, profiting from this incident, demanded the end of party Cabinets, and the bureaucrats, while condemning the act of violence, tacitly accepted it as judgment against party government. Viscount Admiral Saito, a professional naval man of moderate leanings, was chosen to be the Premier of a compromise "National Government," in which the Cabinet was made up of a central bloc of professional bureaucrats, with other contingents from the political parties and the armed forces balancing each other.

Such compromise governments became typical of the rest of the 1930's. The military element in succeeding Cabinets tended to grow and party representatives slowly dwindled in number, but the professional bureaucrats retained the central and, theoretically, the dominant position throughout the decade. However, the militarists definitely took the lead in creating new policies of government. With the success of their Manchurian venture assured and with the support of sporadic acts of terrorism by individual extremists, they forced as much of their program as they could on the compromise governments.

By simply refusing to recognize the authority of the Diet over the Cabinet, the militarists robbed the Diet of one power after another, and by the end of the decade they had reduced it to little more than an impotent and very timorous debating society. They did not dare to do away with the Diet entirely, because in theory it had been a gift from the Meiji Emperor, but they made it meaningless as a parliament.

The militarists also increased the already strong imperialistic and militaristic indoctrination of the people and did their best to whip the masses up to a frenzy of nationalistic fervor. General Araki and his colleagues invented an undefined state of "national crisis," with the strong implication that war was imminent. There was open encouragement of anti-foreign prejudices, and the people were taught to look upon all foreigners as possible spies.

The Japanese had long hated Russia. Now bitter anti-American and anti-British propaganda was encouraged to spread and to increase in virulence. Frequent reference was made to the abrogation in 1924 by the United States of a "gentlemen's agreement" with Japan, by which a small trickle of Japanese immigrants had been allowed entry into the United States. In its place, the American Congress had passed a bill classing the Japanese with the other Asiatics entirely excluded on the grounds of race. The Japanese took this as a direct insult. This old sad story was revived in the 1930's, coupled with much talk and speculation about a great naval war with the United States.

At the same time, the attention of the Japanese public was focused on the Asiatic colonial possessions of Britain and other European powers. Japanese leaders, coveting these rich territories, began to speak of freeing colonial Asiatics from oppression by the white races. Since it was obvious that the Japanese merely wished to substitute their own rule for that of the European powers, not many of the peoples of the Far East were deceived by this new line of propaganda. The Japanese themselves, however, accepted it completely and came to believe that Japan was the champion of the downtrodden peoples of Asia and would some day free them from their white oppressors.

On the home front, all things not to the liking of the reactionary militarists were termed un-Japanese and, if possible, were suppressed. Western ballroom dancing was severely condemned and taxi-dance halls were sometimes closed. Golf and other luxury sports were frowned on. An effort was made to stop the use of English scientific and technical words in conversation and writing, while street and railway signs, which had once been bilingual, were remade with the English omitted. Students in the men's higher schools and universities, which had been noted for their independence of thought, were forced into the same patterns of rote memorizing as pupils in lower schools; participation by women in the intellectual life of the nation was discouraged; labor unions were deprived of all influence; freedom of expression in newspapers and journals was curbed even more rigorously than before; and a rather successful attempt was made to have the people replace rational thought on political and social problems with the use of semi-mystic phrases, such as "national crisis," "Japanese spirit," and "national structure."

The militarists also sanctioned and encouraged a

veritable witchhunt for all persons whose slightest word or deed could be construed to be *lèse majesté*. Liberal educators were forced to resign their academic positions on the grounds that they had handled the Imperial Rescript on Education improperly, and leading statesmen were driven out of political life because of some unfortunate historical allusion involving an emperor. Even the two great Imperial Universities at Tokyo and Kyoto, which had always enjoyed great prestige and considerable academic freedom, were condemned for harboring "red" professors and were subjected to purges. In 1933 a group of liberal professors was forced out of the Law Department of Kyoto Imperial University, and two years later Professor Minobe of Tokyo, a leading authority on constitutional law and a member of the House of Peers, was forced into dishonorable retirement because he had described the emperor as an "organ" of the state. Social scientists, liberal educators, and moderate politicians soon learned to remain silent if they could not express themselves in the mystical terms of ultra-nationalism and abject devotion to the emperor.

The ultra-nationalists and militarists made skillful though possibly unconscious use of the smear technique. They exploited to the full each example of parliamentary corruption, making even minor incidents into major scandals which were thought to discredit all democratic government. Since the *zaibatsu* interests did exert an undue influence over the political parties, it was not hard to turn the vague economic unrest of the peasantry and the more conscious distaste for capitalism shared by various other groups in

Japan into a distrust of democracy. Since the policy of imperialist expansion had been halted by the party governments, it was also easy to turn concern over the economic future of Japan during a world depression into opposition to democracy. Since both capitalism and democracy had developed under strong Occidental influence, it was not hard to convert the hitherto latent resentment of Western power and prestige into an animosity for the political and economic institutions derived in such large part from the West.

Here was a sort of guilt by association, applied perhaps more to institutions than to individuals. Greedy capitalists, corrupt politicians, and an economically menacing but reputedly effete Western world were lumped together in an amorphous but horrible totality, in which each helped to discredit the others and which contrasted sharply with the supposed native purity and selfless loyalty of the military man and the nationalistic fanatic. One or the other of these discredited forces — capitalism, democracy, internationalism, or Westernism — especially when portrayed in these biased terms, was sure to arouse an adverse emotional response in the heart of the average Japanese, and an antipathy for one was easily transformed into suspicion, if not open hatred, for all. The appeal was emotional, not rational, but the would-be defenders of liberal internationalism and parliamentary government, instead of exposing the irrational basis of the attack, remained timidly and ineffectually on the defensive, until they were eventually robbed of all power to fight back.

A major reason for the weakness of the defense of parliamentary government in Japan was that many members of the parliamentary coalition had little faith in democracy as such and looked upon the Diet and party government merely as convenient mechanisms through which they could exert their own influence. Such groups were won over with relative ease to a new coalition of forces, which had little trouble in silencing the weak and inexperienced elements still committed to democracy. The transition from the parliamentary 1920's to the increasingly totalitarian 1930's, thus, came about through no political upheaval but rather through a small shift in the make-up of the forces which stood behind the government.

Even when party governments were in power, the professional politicians and the popular vote they represented constituted only one of the forces in the coalition. There were also the *zaibatsu* interests, with their great financial power. Most important of all, there were the civil bureaucrats, who enjoyed the prestige of government position and manipulated the mechanisms of government control. And finally, but by no means least, there were the military bureaucrats, the army and navy officers, forming a strong deterrent drag, if not a positive pull, on the politically conservative side. The center of political gravity rested perhaps somewhere between the civil bureaucrats and the party politicians. Only a small shift of the center of gravity to a point somewhere between the civil and military bureaucrats spelled the end of parliamentary government.

Some party politicians, of course, fought bitterly to

preserve their hold on the government, but the only method they knew was that of the ballot-box, and with the decline of the Diet, elections meant less and less. Whether they won elections or not, the party politicians were gradually losing all control of the government. Some cabinets even excluded party men altogether, and those politicians who did not swing around to timid support of the extreme militarists found it best to abandon political life, or at least to keep silent.

The story might have been different if the politicians had received strong vocal support from the public they represented. The political parties had always been dominated by the small businessmen and rural landowners. By the 1920's the white-collar urban vote was beginning to exert a noticeable pull toward the left, but the peasantry and urban labor still had no clear political influence. The parties, thus, represented primarily a conservative, propertied group, which fell easy prey to nationalistic slogans and the patriotic fever of war times. As a result, they allowed themselves to be stripped of their parliamentary means of political expression with hardly a murmur of protest. In 1940 the parties meekly voted themselves out of existence and merged in the Imperial Rule Assistance Association. This organization, which had been designed to be a totalitarian political party, proved to be stillborn. However, with the old parties now gone, the Cabinet had nothing more to fear from the Diet or the voting public it represented, except for an occasional pointed question from some exceptionally hardy politician left over from an earlier age.

Since the less conservative urban public had only been on the fringes of the parliamentary coalition, it was disposed of with even greater ease. Labor's start toward self-expression through union organization was quickly squelched, and the Social Mass Party of the city white-collar workers, swayed by the dominant currents of the day, itself developed certain fascist leanings before leading the procession of parties into the political morgue of the Imperial Rule Assistance Association. Many liberal intellectuals remained in determined opposition to developments at home and abroad, but they were forced to limit their activities to veiled criticisms which had no immediate political influence.

While the voting public was being squeezed out of the governmental coalition, the *zaibatsu* interests were making a practical compromise with the anti-capitalistic militarists. The *zaibatsu* had stood behind the parties, but they had also stood behind a strong centralized government and rigid police control of the people. They were no more committed to parliamentary government than to autocracy. Business meant far more to them than political principles. The vast new field for economic exploitation provided by the militarists in Manchuria became to a large extent the special domain of a newly risen group of *zaibatsu*, but the wars and rearmament programs of the militarists led to a rapid development of heavy industry and of certain other specialized war industries to the benefit of all the big industrialists. The average *zaibatsu* executive remained afraid of the risks and expense of a major war, but he was not averse to cooperating with the militarists in minor colonial ventures and in the profits of building an empire. The militarists for their part, while initially suspicious or openly hostile toward big business and capitalism in general, discovered early in their Manchurian venture that they could not fully exploit the empire they were conquering or develop the war industries they needed without the full and willing cooperation of big business.

The coalition of the military with the *zaibatsu* interests was perhaps nothing more than a marriage of convenience, but it was nevertheless a successful working arrangement. And as time went on, it began to be something more. *Zaibatsu* firms, such as Mitsui and Mitsubishi, in many respects represented monopoly capitalism, but at the same time, because of their very size, they made the transition to a state-controlled economy easier than it would otherwise have been. In preparation for the unspecified "national crisis" of the militarists, the government increasingly assumed direction over broad segments of industry and commerce, and the great *zaibatsu* combines, which were coming to be run by professional managers rather than by their owners, were convenient units of governmental control. The pressures of war hastened the growth of such controls, and the *zaibatsu* combines tended more and more to become economic branches of the state. Japan appeared to be taking the first steps toward a curious sort of state socialism, born of *zaibatsu* capitalism and sired by militaristic authoritarianism.

The civil bureaucrats, unlike the business interests, had not found parliamentary government a new means of political self-expression but had looked upon it rather as a dangerous challenge to their own power. They had compromised with the democratic upsurge of the 1920's, but in doing so they had fancied themselves as guiding rather than yielding to it. One of the weapons they had developed to insure that democracy could be kept under control had been the army, which, with the police, could be counted on, if necessary to support the government against the people. Now the bureaucrats, with little regret over the collapse of democratic forms of government, attempted to ride the new forces of militarism and ultra-nationalism, and again they imagined themselves as compromising with these pressures the better to guide them.

Throughout the 1930's the bureaucrats kept up the appearance of being in the political saddle, balancing the party politicians and big business interests against the militarists; but as the politicians and big business interests declined in power, it was more and more evident that the militarists, if not in the saddle, were at least leading the horse. All the bureaucrats could do was to exert a restraining influence on them. The bureaucrats were in no sense liberals, but they were at least moderates. Some even believed in parliamentary forms of government; most of them believed in the capitalist system, which the more extreme militarists were ready to discard; and many of them were undoubtedly apprehensive about the ultimate outcome of the aggressive foreign policy the militarists were pursuing.

This group of moderates included some of the older army and navy leaders, who in contrast to the younger officers believed that the civil government rather than the army and navy should determine foreign policy. But the chief strength of the moderates was to be found in the Privy Council and other groups around the throne. One moderate stood out in particular. He was the old court aristocrat, Prince Saionji, the last of the *Genro*, or "elder statesmen" from the Meiji period, who served as a definite moderating influence until his death in 1940. Prince Saionji's chief political protégé, drawn from the same old court aristocracy, was Prince Konoe, who was twice Premier between 1937 and 1941. Konoe's feeble attempts to keep the militarists in check were nullified by his own readiness to compromise with them, and his efforts merely paved the way for the complete domination of the government by the militarists when General Tojo became Premier in 1941.

Another figure who might be classed with the moderates was the emperor himself. In 1921, he had become Prince Regent for his mentally incompetent father, the Taisho Emperor, and in December 1926, he had himself ascended the throne, with the reign title of Showa. The political views of a person so sheltered from all normal contact with the outside world as the Showa Emperor cannot be determined with certainty. But it seems not improbable that he was and is at least a moderate and possibly even a liberal at heart. He grew up at the time of the First World War, when democratic trends were strongest; he traveled in Europe in 1921; and he has usually been surrounded by moderate if not always liberal men. He is a man of scholarly tastes with a deep interest in marine biology, which alone would make literal belief in his own divinity improbable. Moreover, he made definite efforts to discourage his so-called advisers from leading Japan into war with the United States. The views of the emperor, however, meant relatively little in practical politics. What counted was not what was in his mind, but what the people were led to believe was in his mind, and this the militarists determined for themselves.

The restraining influence of the civil bureaucrats on the militarists, thus, was never strong and in the end failed completely. In part this was the result of the virtual independence of the army and navy. An even more decisive factor was that direct action on the part of the army or of individual extremists always resulted in an increase in the influence of the militarists. The general public, reverting to the feudal tradition of rule by military men, accepted the claims of military extremists at their face value and judged these men to be "sincere," while accusing their opponents of "insincerity" as scheming politicians or selfish capitalists. Increased military influence in the government lead to an increase in the militaristic indoctrination of the people, which in turn produced greater public tolerance of direct action on the part of the militarists. Here was a vicious circle which, when once started in motion, drew Japan inexorably onward in a fatal spiral toward war.

At times the motion was hardly noticeable on the surface, for it consisted of many small though significant compromises or surrenders on the part of the moderates in inner government decisions. The fight, however, was not only between the civil bureaucrats and the armed forces. Much of the struggle for control between the extremists and moderates took place within the army itself, sometimes in the full glare of public notice. In 1935, for example, a lieutenant colonel, representing the younger officer faction, murdered one of the leading generals of the Army Ministry, because he was thought to be carrying out a sweeping program of reassignment of high officers in order to rob the extremists of influence.

In the general election of February 1936, the voting public definitely endorsed the more liberal candidates, indicating very strong support still for parliamentary government. Military extremists, startled by the recalcitrant attitude of the public, struck swiftly. Before dawn on February 26, a group of young officers from a Tokyo regiment, leading fully-armed enlisted men, went to the homes of several leading statesmen and slaughtered them. Premier Okada and Prince Saionji narrowly escaped the assassins; but General Watanabe, the inspector general of military education, Takahashi, the venerable and able finance minister, and Admiral Saito, keeper of the privy seal and one of the closest advisers of the emperor, were all murdered. In 1932 Saito had been the compromise candidate for Premier to succeed the murdered Inukai. In 1935 he in turn fell prey to the extremists.

The conspirators had hoped to seize the government by this bold move and for a while held out in downtown Tokyo in defiance of all government pleas and threats. Within a few days, however, the rebels were persuaded to capitulate in the face of overwhelming military might brought against them by the group around the throne, which for once took a determined stand. The ringleaders of the revolt were severely punished, but the militarists as usual emerged from the incident nearer their goal of complete domination. Thus, step by step, incident by incident, the militarists and extreme nationalists strengthened their hold on the nation.

Chapter XII

WAR

The early course of reaction had proved smooth sailing for the nationalists and militarists. Direct action at home and abroad had brought the nation around to their policies and had put control increasingly in their hands. It was a risky game, but so far had proved eminently successful and had not involved themselves or Japan as a whole in any serious consequences. The next fateful step, however, though seemingly no more hazardous than the others, landed them in the midst of a quagmire from which they were to find no escape. A second supposedly limited war in China, though designed to be just another "Manchurian incident," was not to end until Japan herself had been destroyed.

The Japanese militarists, on one pretext or another, had been pushing from Manchuria into North China and Inner Mongolia, slowly winning control over the war lords and the business interests of these regions; but during these years the Chinese Nationalist government had been steadily growing stronger in Central and South China and even gaining influence in the north. The Chinese Nationalists were bitterly opposed to the special privileges of all foreign powers, and it was becoming evident that the old days of happy hunting for concessions and territories in China were fast coming to an end. If Japan were to consolidate her gains and seize additional territory from China in another cheap local war, she would have to move fast before China became too determined or strong.

In July 1937, following the precedent of the "Manchurian incident," military extremists provoked a new "incident" near Peking in North China. Again the grounds for conflict were extremely flimsy, and again the local Japanese units were acting without the knowledge or the expressed approval of the government. But again the Japanese civil government meekly supported the war brought on by the militarists. Japanese troops quickly seized the two principal cities of North China, Peking and Tientsin, and overran large parts of North China and Inner Mongolia. Fighting again broke out around Shanghai as it had during the conquest of Manchuria.

The aim of the militarists was obviously to bite off as much of North China and Inner Mongolia as possible before Chinese Nationalist authority over that region became too strong. But the militarists had miscalculated; it was already too late to seize North China by a localized war. The Chinese were determined to protect themselves from further foreign encroachments.

Chinese resistance irritated the Japanese militarists, but it did not worry them. They would accept the challenge and crush all opposition by capturing the capital at Nanking. The campaign around Shanghai, although costly, was pushed to a successful conclusion, and Japanese armies marched on to Nanking, which fell in December. When the Chinese government withdrew up the Yangtse River to Hankow, in the geographic center of China, the Japanese realized that they were in for a hard fight, but they pushed on and captured Hankow in October 1938. The indomitable Chinese then withdrew their government farther inland, past the rugged gorges of the Yangtse to Chungking, which lies in a great mountain-rimmed plain, almost impregnable to attack even by vastly superior military forces.

The Japanese now saw that their "incident" was becoming a protracted war. They held the cities and rail lines of most of northeastern China and Inner Mongolia, the major ports of the southern coast of China, and the great central cities along the Yangtse River, which constitutes the main artery of China's trade and commerce. Yet the war had reached a stalemate because the Chinese, although pushed into the more remote and backward parts of the country and cut off from foreign aid and the industrial production of their own cities, simply refused to surrender.

Even so, the Chinese military and economic position appeared hopeless in the long run. The Japanese, holding the richest parts of China and strangling the rest of the land economically, decided to wait the Chinese out. Alternating between acts of terrorism and conciliatory gestures to the puppet government they had created at Nanking, the Japanese forces settled down to wait for the collapse of the Nationalist government.

But Japan had miscalculated again. The Chinese government did not collapse, and the fighting spirit of the supposedly pacifistic Chinese people fed upon the blunders the Japanese militarists themselves committed. Their narrow-minded and domineering attitude toward the Chinese made cooperation with them almost impossible, and the excesses they permitted their troops, as in the mad orgy of rape and murder which followed the capture of Nanking, made even the politically apathetic Chinese peasants determined and irreconcilable foes of Japan.

The outbreak of war in Europe in 1939 must at first have looked like a fortunate event to the Japanese. In 1936, Japan had joined with Germany in an anti-communist pact, to which Italy also subscribed the following year. Now Japan's European allies seemed on the point of crushing her potential European enemies. The eyes of the world were diverted from close scrutiny of the Far East, and the collapse of France in 1940 permitted Japan to start upon a gradual military and economic penetration of French Indo-China in the heart of the European colonial domains of Southeast Asia.

The war in Europe, however, aroused the American public to a consciousness of the true significance of Japanese aggression in China. It came to be realized that the militaristic regimes of Germany and Japan, if victorious, would constitute a perpetual menace to the peace and freedom of America, and of the world. While gradually swinging to the aid of Britain against

JAPANESE EXPANSION ON THE CONTINENT
BEFORE DECEMBER 1941

Germany, the United States also began to take a more positive stand against Japanese aggression. The old policy of verbal protests and non-recognition of Japanese conquests was slowly supplemented by economic sanctions, which hurt Japan far more than a thousand verbal protests. Valuable shipments of scrap iron were eventually stopped; Japanese assets abroad were frozen; and with the cooperation of the British and the Dutch, shipments of oil were cut off. Imports of scrap iron and oil were vital to the Japanese economy and war machine.

By the summer of 1941, Japan was confronted with a most difficult and momentous decision. Four years of war in China had strained her economy, and the tightening blockade imposed by the Western democracies would, if permitted to continue long enough, seriously impair Japanese economic strength and greatly reduce her military effectiveness. The Chinese war would become increasingly difficult to wage, and Japan would eventually lose her military supremacy in the Far East. Obviously the policy of waiting for China to collapse was no longer feasible, and action was called for.

Two choices were open to Japan. One was to bring an end to the war in China by generous concessions, withdraw her troops as the United States demanded, and settle back to profit economically from the new war in Europe as she had done with such splendid results during the First World War. Here was clearly the course of economic self-interest. With the factory power of Europe temporarily cut off from Asia and threatened with more permanent destruction, Japan could take another great step forward toward the establishment of an economic empire in Asia without the attendant costs of conquests, if she could but disentangle herself from the war in China.

But economic self-interest was not to carry the day. Withdrawal from China seemed to the militarists a national loss of face which they could not tolerate. It also would have been interpreted in Japan as an open admission that the militarists' program of prosperity through conquest had failed. Inevitably there would have been a shift in sympathies which would have endangered their hold on the government. For the militarists the only satisfactory solution of the impasse was to break the economic blockade by war on the Western democracies. The moderates, appalled by the danger of war against a coalition of foreign powers but aware that the army would never be willing to withdraw empty-handed from China, desperately sought some compromise which would satisfy both the United States and the militarists at home. The United States, however, refused to compromise with aggression.

As the year 1941 wore on, it became obvious that war was inevitable. Although the activities of certain extremists in the past had threatened to embroil Japan in war with the West, the moderates had always managed to stop short of it. The crisis caused by the wholly unwarranted sinking of the *Panay*, a United States Navy gunboat bombed by Japanese planes flying over the Yangtse River in December 1937, had been settled. Numerous clashes with Russian troops on the Manchurian-Siberian border, culminating in a

month-long battle in 1938, had never been permitted
to develop into war. But now the government saw
war with the West staring it in the face. Prince Konoe, unable to face the ultimate consequences of his
own policy of weak compromise, resigned the Premiership in October 1941, making way for General
Tojo and his war Cabinet.

The Japanese did not enter the war in a spirit of
wild bravado. The decision on the part of the militarists, who were now definitely in the saddle, was
cool and calculated. They knew how weak the American, British, and Dutch forces in the western Pacific
were, and how easily the Japanese could overrun
the rich lands of Southeast Asia. There they would
find the minerals and oil so desperately needed. These,
it was hoped, would soon make the Japanese economy
stronger than ever. Russia, apparently on the verge of
collapse, seemed to be out of the picture. Britain was
in far too critical a situation at home to do much in
the Far East, and the United States could never dare
concentrate all its power in the Pacific as long as Germany was undefeated.

Germany was thus the first line of Japan's defense.
If she won, Japan was safe. If she lost, she would at
least have fought a rear-guard action in behalf of Japan, tiring their mutual enemies and giving Japan time
to bring China to her knees and to build an invulnerable economic and military empire, containing enormous natural resources and many hundreds of millions
of industrious people, protected from attack by the
vast expanse of the Pacific and Indian Oceans.

It was a fateful decision. As the result of small initial

wagers in 1931 and in 1937, Japan was now forced
into a position in which she either had to withdraw
ignominiously from the game and lose what was already won, or else make a win-all, lose-all play. In
Tokyo in the autumn of 1941, the chances for success
seemed good, and the rewards of victory promised to
be the creation of the most populous and perhaps the
richest empire the world had ever seen.

But again the Japanese miscalculated, not so much
on geographic, economic, or military as on human
factors. They counted heavily on their own moral superiority, the famed "Japanese spirit," and the supposed degeneracy and pacifism of the Western democracies, particularly America, which they believed
to be corrupted by too many luxuries. They were
convinced that Americans did not have the will to
fight a long and costly war. In this delusion the Japanese showed themselves to be so blinded by their own
nationalistic and militaristic propaganda that they
were unable to evaluate the spirit of other peoples or
to judge their reactions correctly. They entirely mis-
read the character not only of the Americans, but of
the British and Russian peoples too. The Russians did
not collapse; the British continued a valiant struggle
with growing determination and strength; and the
Americans entered the war with a resolution and
vigor the Japanese had not dreamed possible.

The Japanese even failed to judge correctly other
Far Eastern peoples. Japan had developed a telling
propaganda technique, and phrases such as "East Asia
for the East Asiatics," "A New Order in East Asia,"

and "The East Asiatic Co-Prosperity Sphere" had a ready appeal for other Asiatics. However, warned by Japanese actions in China and disillusioned by the brutality and arrogance of their conquering troops, the native populations gave the Japanese little support. The Chinese, encouraged by the appearance of powerful allies in their war against Japan, took new heart in the stubborn fight against the invaders. The Filipinos, far from welcoming the Japanese, fought stoutly alongside the Americans; and other peoples of Southeast Asia either stood by indifferent to the outcome or gave only lukewarm aid to their new masters.

Repeating the tactics used against Russia in 1904, the Japanese started the war with a brilliantly successful surprise attack on Pearl Harbor at dawn on Sunday, December 7, 1941. They crippled the American navy with this single, sharp blow, virtually eliminating it for the time being, and thus cleared the way for an easy conquest of Southeast Asia and the islands north of Australia. The attack on Pearl Harbor was indeed an unqualified military success for Japan. But it was also a psychological blunder, because it united the American people, who had been bitterly divided over the question of participating in the wars in Europe and Asia, and they took up arms determined to crush Japan and Germany.

With a speed that must have appalled the Japanese, the Americans rebuilt their navy, created an air force against which the Japanese were no match, and dispatched strong army and marine units to the Pacific to hold the line against Japan. In the summer of 1942, the

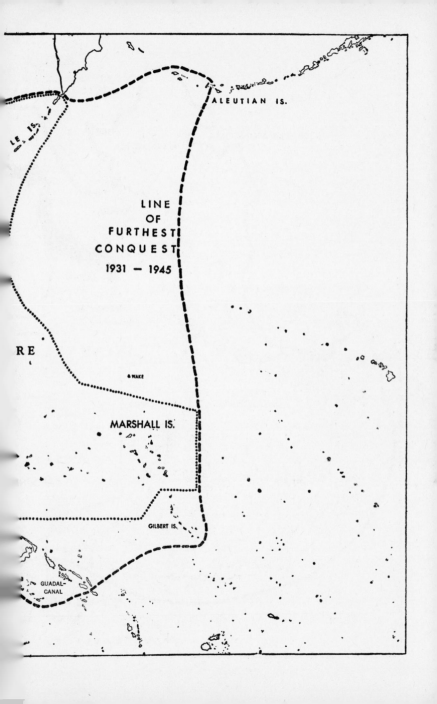

Americans stopped the Japanese advance at Midway and at Guadalcanal, and in 1943 they took the offensive.

The vast natural resources and tremendous productive power of America were pitted against the meagre resources and relatively feeble productive power of Japan, already weary from four years of war and needing far more time to benefit from the rich territories conquered in Southeast Asia. The United States, while making a major contribution to the war in Europe, could still spare enough to win control of the skies and seas in the Pacific. Her ships, submarines, and planes drove the Japanese navy back to its home waters and virtually destroyed it; they cut the lifeline of Japan to Southeast Asia, and eventually to China; and they isolated the islands of the Pacific, both from one another and from the home base in Japan, so that these enemy outposts could be attacked singly and their garrisons destroyed piecemeal.

The Japanese fought with a fanaticism born of long indoctrination. Taught to believe that surrender would mean disgrace for their families, and torture and death for themselves at the hands of the enemy, the soldiers in the field usually fought on doggedly to the last man. Even civilians sometimes chose death rather than surrender. But the Japanese were to learn that blind fanaticism was not enough in the face of superior weapons in the hands of a determined foe. The Americans broke through the island barriers of the central Pacific; they knifed their way along the New Guinea coast and recaptured the Philippines; and they established themselves in the heart of the Japanese

Empire by seizing Okinawa, the main island of the Ryukyu chain.

By the early summer of 1945 it was clear that Japan had lost the war. Her cities were being wiped out one by one; her factories were fast being destroyed; her navy and merchant marine were largely gone; her overseas armies, though on the whole intact, were almost isolated from the homeland; and the final collapse of Germany meant that the entire strength of the United States and Great Britain could be turned against Japan. The Americans were obviously poised for an assault upon the home islands of Japan. With the crushing superiority of American arms, and the blind determination of Japanese soldiers and civilians to fight to the death, as they had been trained to do, a terrible massacre of the people and complete destruction of the nation seemed inevitable.

The Japanese people themselves, fatalists by long tradition, and victims of militaristic and nationalistic propaganda which taught them to obey orders without question, stoically watched their homes burned by incendiary raids and their friends and relatives killed. They appeared to be either unaware of their impending doom or else resigned to it. But fortunately for Japan there were men in the government who could comprehend the situation and who preferred the disgrace of defeat to national suicide.

The growing disasters brought on by the war had tended to discredit the leadership of the militarists, and the government had been slowly gravitating again into the hands of the more moderate bureaucrats. These men were spurred into immediate action by the dropping of the two atomic bombs on August 6 and 9, all but wiping out the cities of Hiroshima and Nagasaki, and by the Soviet declaration of war against Japan on August 8. Despite the frantic efforts of die-hard militarists, they accepted on August 14, 1945, the "unconditional surrender" formula of the Allied Powers as embodied in the stern but just terms for surrender issued by the United States, China, and Great Britain at Potsdam on July 26 and subsequently adhered to by the Soviet Union. The emperor gave determined and possibly decisive support to the peace party and shattered all precedent by personally announcing the surrender by radio to his people. The war came to an abrupt end, and for the first time in its long history Japan came under the control of foreign conquerors.

Chapter XIII

OCCUPATION

On September 2, 1945, the representatives of the Japanese government signed the terms of surrender on board the battleship "Missouri" in Tokyo Bay, and Japan entered upon one of the most significant phases, and certainly the most unusual, of its long history. Indeed, the period of six and a half years of American occupation and tutelage was to prove unique in the record of human experience. Never before had one advanced nation attempted to reform, from within, the supposed faults of another advanced nation. Never before had a military occupation of one world power by another proved so satisfactory to the victors and at the same time so tolerable to the vanquished. When the peace treaty finally went into effect on April 28, 1952, most Americans and Japanese shared a feeling of general satisfaction with the period of occupation which was coming to an end. There were, inevitably, ample grounds for criticism and complaint on both sides. And yet, to Americans, Japan in 1952 appeared to be one of the few bright spots in the outside world, and, while many Japanese greeted the return of sovereignty with apprehension and viewed their new treaty relationships with open misgiving, Japan itself seemed to them to be a far better place to live in than they had imagined possible in the days of their defeat.

The Japanese and Americans share the credit for the remarkable and, in large part, unexpected accomplishments of the occupation. The Americans showed basic good will as well as self-interest in their effort to reform rather than chastise their enemy, and they demonstrated imagination, enthusiasm, and, on the whole, good sense in carrying it out. The Japanese, too, showed remarkable good will as well as self-interest in their patient acceptance of tutelage. Instead of resisting this unasked for outside help, most of them profited from it by responding with wholehearted co-operation and energetic efforts to do their part. Thus, to the great unplanned changes brought about by the pressures of war and defeat were added the reforms of the occupation authorities, furthered by the active cooperation of the Japanese people. The net result was a period of rapid change and evolution in Japanese society, as a strong new start was made toward the development of a working democracy in Japan.

The Japanese attitude in defeat and occupation was, under the circumstances, fortunate both for Japan and the United States. It was, at the same time, extraordinary in terms of normal human responses – an unusual product of inner traits and external circumstances. It was based in part on old Japanese habits of acceptance of authority, re-enforced by the preceding fifteen years of growing authoritarian control. When the emperor and his government surrendered, the army of occupation became the new and unquestioned locus of authority. The people were astounded by this turn of events but obedient to their new masters. The latter, as Americans, were perhaps easier to accept than any other foreign people. The long influence of American teachers, missionaries, and businessmen in Japan and the great admiration of many Japanese for America, despite all the propaganda of the militarists and because of, rather than despite, the overwhelming military victory of the American forces, made American tutelage less objectionable than it otherwise would have been.

Equally important in shaping the Japanese attitude was the complete and disastrous failure of Japan's former leaders. The militarists' program for prosperity through conquest had not only lost the whole of the empire but had also brought devastation to the homeland. Japan's vital foreign markets were all gone; so also was the merchant marine on which foreign trade depended. The factories were either destroyed or closed for lack of materials. The cities of Japan were for the most part destroyed. All but the hard central core of concrete buildings and the wooded suburban fringes of Tokyo had been wiped out in two great fire bomb raids in the spring of 1945, in which over 100,000 lives had been lost. The city people were homeless and destitute. The militarists' efforts to interpret the imperial will had led to a slaughter of his loyal subjects and had forced him personally to take the lead in accepting surrender.

Never in modern times were an advanced people so thoroughly disillusioned with their leadership, and the very strength of their indoctrination made the repudiation of the past all the easier. The falseness of the claims of the militarists, the hatred for Japan in China and other Asian lands, the excesses of the Japanese troops abroad, all came as shocking surprises to most Japanese. To people who had been steeling themselves first for death in an unequal struggle and then for rape and pillage by their conquerors, the orderliness and open friendliness of the occupying forces produced a grateful and enthusiastic response. The average Japanese felt that he had been very wrong, but only because he had been misled. Some may have been resentful of their leaders, but few felt any personal guilt. They were ready to turn over a new leaf and were willing to let their erstwhile enemies show them how.

The Japanese attitude was no more surprising than the resolution and skill with which the Americans started about the task of turning the page for the Japanese. All too often in recent years the United States has not been prepared for the responsibilities which world leadership has forced upon her, but she was ready for the task in Japan. The very nature of the war against Germany and Japan had directed American attention primarily toward these countries. For years the State Department had been preparing for the problems of postwar Japan, and in the months preceding the surrender an over-all American policy had been agreed upon through the agency of SWNCC, the State-War-Navy Coordinating Committee.

Drawn up by experts unhampered by external political pressures, this policy showed the mark of true statesmanship. It was based on the realization that a policy of revenge would only breed hatred and unrest; that a policy of mere retribution would reduce the Japanese to desperation without wringing from them any substantial amends; and that only through a policy of enlightened reform could Japan change her role from destroyer to promoter of the peace and welfare of her part of the world.

The policy was stern but generous. Japan was to be deprived of its empire; her military might was to be completely destroyed; she was to pay what reparations she could to the lands she had despoiled; but the Japanese were to be given a chance to survive economically and were to be given aid and guidance in developing along peaceful and democratic lines. This policy was first outlined briefly in the Potsdam Proclamation, which by its just and realistic terms made possible, or at least facilitated, the Japanese surrender. It was further elaborated in the *United States Initial Post-Surrender Policy for Japan* of August 29, 1945, which set the course and tone for the whole of the occupation.

Execution of a policy is often more difficult than its formulation, but in this case it was no less successful. The choice for Supreme Commander for the Allied Powers, or SCAP as he came to be known, fell on General Douglas MacArthur. This was a happy choice. The job and the person fitted each other well. MacArthur was an administrator of great experience and skill. More important, he had a forcefulness of character, a deep sense of mission, and an almost messianic vision, which appealed at once to the demoralized

Japanese. The chief of their conquerors became their symbol of hope — the unfaltering leader who saw with confidence beyond the destruction of war and the despair of defeat to a brighter Japan of the future. The Japanese desperately needed leadership and hope, and these MacArthur supplied them in full measure.

MacArthur was also a good choice from the point of view of domestic American politics as it was to develop during the next few years. As the spokesman in Japan of the Democratic administration and the hero of its most bitter political enemies, he enjoyed the confidence of both sides. This factor together with the obvious success of occupation policies kept Japan out of American politics in the postwar years. It remained the problem of the experts, not a political football to be kicked by each new aspirant to political notoriety. When MacArthur was abruptly dismissed from all his posts by President Truman in the spring of 1951, it was solely because of disagreement over the prosecution of the war in Korea, and Japan still did not become a political issue. Fortunately, a prominent Republican, John Foster Dulles, had already taken over responsibility for negotiating the Japanese peace treaty, and through his efforts American policy toward Japan remained not bi-partisan so much as non-partisan.

The occupation personnel supporting MacArthur fell into three major categories: first, an army of occupation, which, while predominantly American, included some Australian and other British Empire elements; second, a headquarters staff in Tokyo, subdivided into a series of Sections, each responsible for the direction of one phase of the undertaking; and third, a series of Military Government teams responsible for the implementation of policy in the individual prefectures. All three branches were originally staffed by combat troops, who, though often little informed on Japan, came to their tasks with a saving sincerity and enthusiasm bred of battle experience. Gradually these men were replaced by others not always so well qualified to do the work. The youthful and undisciplined draftees who took the place of the war veterans in the army of occupation could not retain the respect of the Japanese public. The civilian employees and professional military officers on routine assignments who succeeded to the posts of many of the original staff officers, while for the most part conscientious and devoted workers, could not recapture the full enthusiasm of the men they replaced.

Another difficulty of the occupation was its organization. Stemming from a wartime army and led by a professional army man, it inevitably remained a strictly military organization, operating through the usual military chain of command. But the military aspect of the task all but dwindled away, while the political and economic complexities of the undertaking grew. The strict military organization proved less and less adequate to the needs of the situation. No basic reorganization, however, was ever attempted. The difficulty of such a move and hope for the early conclusion of a peace treaty were always felt to outweigh the need for drastic change.

The occupation was in name international, for MacArthur was the Supreme Commander for the

Allied Powers, but in fact it was almost entirely American both in composition and in policy. While the Potsdam Proclamation had been issued jointly with Great Britain and China and had subsequently been endorsed by the Soviet Union, it was of American inspiration, and the *Initial Post-Surrender Policy*, under which MacArthur launched his program, was purely American.

The Moscow Agreement of December 27, 1945, provided that the supreme policy-making organ for the occupation should be a Far Eastern Commission in Washington and that an Allied Council for Japan should be created in Tokyo to assist MacArthur. Neither body proved effective. The Allied Council, made up of representatives of the United States, the Soviet Union, the British Commonwealth, and China, never was more than a forum for angry but futile debate between the American and Russian representatives and soon lapsed into a moribund condition. The Far Eastern Commission, made up at first of eleven and subsequently of thirteen nations which had participated in the war in the Far East, went through the motions of establishing policy, but only rarely did it do so in actuality. MacArthur, once provided with his original policy directives, was little inclined to welcome any further policy guidance from his own government, much less from an international body. Moreover, the United States was in a position to all but dictate to the Far Eastern Commission, for it not only shared the veto power with the Soviet Union, China, and Great Britain, but also had the right to issue interim directives to MacArthur pending a decision by the Commission. The net result was that the Commission usually did little more than adopt without significant change the American policies which MacArthur was already putting into effect.

The American occupation of Japan fell into three successive phases, which might be called the periods of reform, retrenchment, and revision. While not separated from each other by sharp divisions of time, each was characterized not only by differing types of activity but also by distinctive attitudes on the part of both the Americans and the Japanese.

The first and by far the most important phase lasted from the surrender until 1948. This was the period of rapid and often drastic reform. The American concept was that through reform Japan was to be made a more democratic and therefore more stable and peaceful country. But this was not envisioned merely as a political problem. If Japan were to be more democratic, it needed a new deal — a fairer division of power and wealth between the peasants, city laborers, and the more privileged classes. The United States sponsored a social as well as a political revolution in Japan.

American policy called for sweeping changes, and MacArthur and his staff proceeded to carry these out with speed and thoroughness. The mood of the Americans was one of enthusiasm, hope, and boundless confidence. Everything seemed possible. A violent attack was started on what appeared to the Americans to be the non-democratic aspects of Japanese institutions. This included a wholesale offensive against the *status quo* — against prestige, political power, and also wealth. Traditional legal guarantees were sometimes slighted in the process. Men were purged from office by category, not on their individual records, and others were deprived of their property with little recompense. In the confusion of the early days of the occupation, a few leftist sympathizers among the occupying forces even acted as if they were preparing Japan for a socialist or communist revolution. The leftists were in time weeded out by MacArthur, but his reform measures remained perhaps as much revolutionary as evolutionary in nature.

Here was a radicalness which has not often characterized American thinking or action. The United States, which has usually appeared to be the champion of the *status quo* elsewhere in the world, was clearly a revolutionary force in Japan. It was a surprising situation, but it can perhaps be explained by two common American concepts of the time which had grown out of the war experience. One was that the defeat of Germany and Japan had solved all the major problems of the world and all that was now needed was the reform of the two international culprits. The other was that Japan, as the disturber of the peace, was all bad and that drastic measures were needed to reform her. A popular argument was that an extreme policy of a type neither desirable nor justified in the healthier society of the United States was necessary to correct the extreme evils of Japanese society.

Neither concept was entirely accurate. Japan and Germany were by no means the only or even the most difficult problems of the postwar world. Nor was Japan as wholly bad as Americans had judged in the excitement of war. Without broad foundations within Japan for the democratic reforms that were attempted, few of these reforms, however radical, would have meant much. They depended entirely on certain basic features of Japanese society which the Japanese themselves had been creating during the past century—such fundamental things as universal education, efficient communication facilities, and experience with democratic processes. The supposed lack of democratic foundations made the American reform program radical; their actual presence made it successful.

The radical approach of the Americans in the early postwar years in Japan, thus, was postulated in part on errors, but it was nonetheless successful, at least in the short run. It fitted the situation in Japan. The Japanese were dazed and bewildered; they welcomed strong, positive leadership. Revolutionary zeal made the Americans more imaginative and more forceful than they otherwise would have been. They were ready to strike hard while the iron was still hot. Some of what they did was overhasty and ill-advised. Yet, this radical approach accomplished much that was worth doing and which otherwise might never have been done. Japan on the whole profited from it, and American postwar policy toward Japan, revolutionary though it was or perhaps just for that reason, still appears to have been the most successful phase of postwar American policy toward Asia.

The Japanese for their part accepted the reforms without much open protest and frequently welcomed them with enthusiasm. Their leaders, while often doubtful or dismayed at some of the things that were being done, limited themselves to half-hearted obstructionist tactics. The mass of the people accepted the American reforms with the same unquestioning faith they had shown in their former leaders. In the desperate struggle for mere existence in the economic chaos of postwar Japan, they found comfort in the realization that determined and apparently inspired men were preparing for a better day. They were more than ready to grant MacArthur the omniscience he seemed to claim.

It was comparatively easy in the first two years of the occupation for the Americans to reshuffle the top leadership in Japan and make mechanical adjustments in political and legal processes. The entire army and navy were rapidly liquidated; political prisoners, including Communists, were released; the power of the police to control the speech and thought of the citizens was eliminated, and as an accidental byproduct, the morale and effectiveness of the police in maintaining law and order was reduced to an alarmingly low level; laws were revised to insure legal respect for the civil liberties regarded as fundamental by Americans; and those organs of the government which were felt to restrict the normal freedoms of the citizen were either abolished or greatly limited in power. The most notable change of the latter type was the elimination of the old Home Ministry, which had had a strong hold over the lives of the people through its control of the police and the prefectural administrations.

All former leaders who were felt to share in any

way in the responsibility for Japanese aggression or for individual atrocities during the war were either punished through war crimes trials or were purged by being barred from public office. The trials affected substantial numbers of men who were guilty of atrocities but who were of little political consequence in Japan, as well as twenty-five high military and political leaders, including Tojo, who were considered primarily responsible for the war. Seven of the latter were hanged in December 1948 and most of the rest sentenced to life imprisonment, though their sentences were subsequently shortened.

A far more important move was the purging of all professional military officers, Diet members, high-ranking bureaucrats, and important business and intellectual leaders who were believed to have been associated through their acts or posts with Japanese aggression. For example, all high *zaibatsu* executives and all Diet members who had been sponsored by the Imperial Rule Assistance Association were dismissed from their posts and barred from further public life. Many new and usually younger men, along with a few old leaders who by luck or conviction had remained aloof from Japan's aggressive policies, took the places of the purged leaders in an almost complete turnover of all top positions. Nearly 200,000 men were involved in the purges, but the change in the quality of leadership was not so great as these numbers imply. Many men of distinctly more liberal stripe than the prewar leaders did come to the fore, but in most cases the younger men who took the places of their dismissed predecessors had differed from the later during the war and prewar years, not in ideas, but only in rank and seniority. And, in any case, most of the purged leaders were subsequently restored to public life. It was the changing attitudes of the Japanese as a whole rather than the shift of individuals that was chiefly responsible for the changes that did occur in Japanese leadership.

The most important single reform of the occupation was the revision of the Constitution and of its supporting legislation. This was done in order to eliminate the constitutional flaws which had helped block democracy before the war and to create a set of political rules under which democratic forces could express themselves more easily and successfully. The draft of the new Constitution, which was drawn up by the Japanese government—though with considerable advice and pressure from the occupation authorities—was made public in March 1946 and was subsequently adopted with little change by the Diet, going into effect on May 3, 1947. Although constitutional revision was carried out in the manner provided for by the prewar Constitution, it produced an important change in Japanese political procedures and an even more abrupt shift in political theory.

A major change in the realm of theory concerned the position of the emperor. The attitude toward the emperor had at first been the most controversial aspect of occupation policy in the United States and in other foreign countries. Many Americans had advocated the trial of the reigning emperor as a major war criminal and the abolition of the monarchy by force. To do so, however, would have been neither wise nor just. The

Potsdam Proclamation had promised that the future government of Japan would be "established in accordance with the freely expressed will of the Japanese people"; the vast majority of the latter continued to venerate the emperor; moreover, they were aware that he personally should not be held responsible for the war and that it was in part his intervention which had made the surrender possible and had assured the ready acceptance of MacArthur's authority in Japan. The imperial institution had helped the militarists to gain power, but that did not mean that the emperor personally deserved punishment or that the whole institution should be abolished in the face of strong opposition by the Japanese people. Its danger had lain, not in the emperor himself, but in the attitude of the people toward him, and this could scarcely be changed by punishing him or abolishing the institution against their wishes.

What was needed was the development of a different attitude toward the emperor and his role, and this the new Constitution attempted to facilitate by making a fundamenal redefinition of his status which would eliminate, at least on paper, the whole dangerous theory of the imperial will. The first chapter of the Constitution starts with the statement: "The Emperor shall be the symbol of the State and of the unity of the people, deriving his position from the will of the people with whom resides sovereign power." It then goes on to specify that the emperor can act in matters of state only as provided for in the Constitution and with "the advice and approval of the Cabinet" and that "he shall not have powers related to government."

This was a startling break with older Japanese political theory but one which the Japanese people readily accepted, just as they had accepted without surprise or disapproval the emperor's denial of his own divinity on New Year's Day, 1946. Acceptance came easily because the new Constitution was merely bringing theory in line with practice, for the last two emperors had, in fact, acted only on the advice of their advisers and, with the exception of the surrender decision itself, had never really exercised any power related to government. The monarch had been slowly becoming a symbol in the British manner, and the new Constitution merely recognized this fact officially.

Another important constitutional change concerned the relationship between the legislative and executive branches of the government. In prewar days the Diet had never been able to establish unquestioned control over the Cabinet and the vast bureaucratic structure it administered, nor had the Cabinet been able always to control the armed forces. The second problem had been drastically solved by the elimination of the army and navy, but it was left to the new Constitution to make clear and absolute the control of the Diet over the Cabinet and the whole bureaucracy. It specifies that "the Diet shall be the highest organ of state power, and shall be the sole law-making organ of State." At the same time, it provides that the Prime Minister shall be chosen by the Diet from among its own members and that a majority of his Cabinet officers also be from the Diet. The Cabinet, thus, has become merely an executive committee of the Diet, and, in the British manner, it can be forced to resign by a vote of no confidence on the part of the House of Representatives, unless the Cabinet instead puts its mandate to popular vote by dissolving the House and holding a general election.

The new Constitution thus restored the system of party government based on a parliamentary majority that had been starting to develop in Japan in the 1920's. At that time it had had neither constitutional guarantees nor long practice to support it. Now it is so deeply imbedded in the new Constitution that only sweeping alterations or flagrant disregard of that document could destroy party government or Diet control of the Cabinet.

A third important change was in the composition of the Diet. While the House of Representatives had been elected since 1928 by universal manhood suffrage, membership in the House of Peers had been largely hereditary or appointive, and those members who were elected were chosen only by certain small, privileged groups. Under the new Constitution, with the peerage entirely abolished, the House of Peers was replaced by a purely elective body, the House of Councillors, and the electorate broadened to include all adult women. The 250 Councillors are now elected for six-year terms, 100 from the nation at large and the remainder from the forty-six prefectures. The 467 members of the House of Representatives are elected in much the same way as before the war, with three to five Representatives chosen from each of 118 electoral districts. Since each voter has only a single vote, this system results in a form of proportional representation.

The House of Representatives takes precedence

over the House of Councillors. Budgetary matters do not need the latter's concurrence, and other acts of the lower house become law if the House of Councillors fails to vote against them within 30 days or if its negative vote is overridden by a two-thirds vote of the House of Representatives.

A fourth consitutional change concerned the status and rights of citizens. Not only were the Japanese people recognized as the locus of sovereignty, but a long chapter in the new Constitution also enumerated their rights. These included all those familiar to Americans from their own Constitution, plus other more recently defined "rights," such as "the right to maintain the minimum standards of wholesome and cultured living," "the right to receive an equal education," "the right and the obligation to work," "the right of workers to organize and bargain collectively," "academic freedom," and equality of the sexes in marriage.

A fifth constitutional change concerned the judiciary, which in prewar Japan had been merely a branch of the executive, controlled through the Justice Ministry. The new Constitution set up an independent judiciary under a Supreme Court, which, as in the United States, became the final arbiter of constitutional matters. Approval of the membership of the Supreme Court is submitted to popular vote every ten years.

A final major political change written into the new Constitution and its supporting legislation was the strengthening of local self-government. The Constitution specified that the chief officers of all local public entities, such as prefectural governors and mayors, and the members of all local assemblies, should be elected by their respective constituents. At the same time, local authorities were given far greater powers for taxation and legislation than they had ever enjoyed before, and the control of the police was transferred from the now defunct Home Ministry to the municipal or prefectural authorities. In an effort to further stress the importance of local self-government, an Autonomy Ministry was created to take over the remaining functions of the Home Ministry. Some of these efforts, however, did not have much effect in relatively small and uniform Japan. After witnessing the confusion of multiple police jurisdictions, the Japanese preferred to restore some measure of centralized police control. Moreover, local governments failed to make full use of their constitutional powers of taxation and legislation. In short, the Japanese continued to parallel the French or British pattern of political centralism, despite the efforts of the occupation authorities to introduce the American type of broad local self-rule.

The occupation authorities did not stop at mechanical changes in the Constitution but went beyond these to sweeping reforms in Japanese society and education in the hope of insuring that there would be a citizenry capable of operating the new political system.

In the field of education, the main emphasis of the reforms was on extending, equalizing, and liberalizing education and on teaching children *how* to think rather than *what* to think. Textbooks were entirely revised to eliminate militaristic and nationalistic propaganda, and the old courses on "ethics," which were thought to have inculcated these doctrines, were banned in favor of new courses in the social sciences. Control over education was largely shifted from the Education Ministry to the local municipalities, though the effort to adopt the American type of elected Boards of Education proved a failure and was abandoned in 1956. Compulsory education was extended with no great difficulty from six to nine years, since even before the war most children had sought some further education beyond the required six years. The standing of schools at each level was, at least in theory, equalized, so that the next level of education would be open to all those who had completed the preceding one. In addition, the levels beyond the initial six years of primary school were made over, amid great confusion, to conform to those used in America: the three-year junior high school, three-year senior high school, and four-year college, or university as it is always called in Japan. In the process, most of the old five-year middle schools added another year to encompass both junior and senior high schools, while the various types of three-year higher schools, by dropping their lowest year and adding two higher years and then combining with other higher schools, became multi-faculty universities, paralleling in name if not in reality or prestige the old prewar universities.

The new educational system has greatly spread educational opportunities and has produced more spontaneous and uninhibited students than did the old system, but many Japanese feel that the quality of education has suffered in the process. The chief blame is laid to what seems to many the entirely unnecessary revision of the levels of education, which however has been such a massive change as to appear irreversible.

The occupation authorities showed equal vigor in carrying out social reforms. At the most basic level, women were not only given the franchise but also full legal equality with men and equal educational opportunities. Similarly, laws which echoed the feudal past in giving authority to family heads over adult members of their families and to main family lines over branch families were all abolished.

The occupation authorities devoted special efforts to breaking up the great concentrations of wealth in the hands of the *zaibatsu*, both on the dubious argument that the *zaibatsu* system had been responsible for Japan's imperialistic aggressions and on the more valid grounds that such great concentrations of wealth in a relatively poor country were not conducive to the development of a healthy democratic system. Members of *zaibatsu* families and their chief executives were purged, their assets frozen, and the bulk of their holdings taken over by the government in a general capital levy, which was graduated to run from 25 per cent on modest holdings of 100,000 yen to 90 per cent on fortunes of more than 15,000,000 yen. Steeply graduated income and inheritance taxes were also imposed, making the future accumulation of great wealth much more difficult than it had been in the past. In this way the financial power of the *zaibatsu* themselves was drastically reduced; yet, the many large companies of which their empires had consisted continued to exist. At one time it had been planned to break up more than 300 of these, but this large-scale trust-busting operation proved both difficult and inadvisable in the face of continuing economic stagnation in Japan and was scaled down by 1949 to less than a score of companies.

The reverse side of the coin was an effort to develop the political consciousness and power of industrial labor and the peasantry. Labor legislation was revised to conform to the most advanced concepts of Europe and the United States, and veteran Japanese labor leaders from the 1920's, with the active encouragement of the occupation, built up a rapidly burgeoning and often violently assertive labor movement. By 1949 more than six and a half million workers had been enrolled in labor unions. From the start, Communists controlled a large share of the unions, and the movement further differed from that of the United States in that a high percentage of the organized workers were government employees—either as teachers, white-collar workers in government offices, or laborers on the national railroad or in other nationalized industries. As a result, the occupation authorities soon discovered to their distress that organized labor showed less interest in bargaining with management than in political agitation, which seemed a more direct way to effect government wage scales or achieve Communist ends.

The most daring and sweeping of all the occupation reforms was aimed at improving the lot of the peasant and awakening his political consciousness. This was the land reform program, which while slow to get under way was carried out with thoroughness. Almost two decades earlier, the Japanese government, worried by the rapid increase of tenancy, had managed to stop its further growth, and the figure for tenant cultivated lands had remained since then at a trifle under 50 per cent of all farm land. Now the figure was rolled back to a mere 10 per cent. This was done by abolishing absentee land ownership and by limiting members of farm communities to the ownership of the land they themselves cultivated, plus an area roughly equivalent to one average-sized farm, which in Japan tends to be about two and a half acres. Generous credit terms were made available to the former tenants, and, since the sale price of the land did not take into consideration the runaway inflation that followed the war, payment was relatively simple. This procedure, however, naturally entailed a sharp reduction in the wealth of the former landowners.

The shift from the reform phase of the occupation to that of retrenchment was a gradual process, but it had become quite evident by the latter part of 1948. For one thing the reform work was by then largely completed. There was a definite limit to what could be accomplished in the democratization of Japan by foreign dictation. The Constitution and laws had been revised; the military power destroyed; wealth and power were being redistributed. The mechanical changes had largely been made. What was now needed was for the Japanese themselves to adjust the new rules by assimilation and adaptation to Japanese realities, and to gain experience in living and governing themselves according to democratic processes. The rate of reform slowed down noticeably, and in some cases reforms already started were modified or even abandoned.

Another factor in the shift to retrenchment was the American re-evaluation of the world situation and

Japan's relationship to that situation. Hopes for a united and peaceful world were rapidly being chilled by the cold war forced upon the West by intransigent Communist hostility. China was in the throes of civil war. Much of the rest of Asia was convulsed by political disorders and economic disruption. The world was dividing into two hostile armed camps, and Japan was close to the borderline between them, both geographically and ideologically.

It was becoming obvious, in fact, that Japan itself was a primary battlefield in the cold war. The American occupation of Japan was clearly an experiment in democratic reform and rehabilitation, and the success or failure of that experiment would inevitably have a great ideological impact on the billion odd people of Asia. The future role of Japan, the only area in Asia of great immediate industrial capacity, had also become a vital question. At the end of the war Japan had seemed a hopelessly defeated and isolated nation, facing a united and triumphant world. In a divided world she was a crucial factor in the balance of power —militarily, economically, and politically.

The American effort in Japan, thus, was clearly far more important to the United States and the whole free world than had at first been supposed, but its success in the meantime had become more doubtful. Japan had suffered economically from the war perhaps more than any of the other major combatants, and she had recovered less. She was entirely dependent on foreign trade, and this had shown little sign of revival. Cold war, civil war, and economic decline in Asia had, at least for the time being, eliminated Japan's chief markets. She was living at a bare subsistence level, and at that on American largess—a dole of close to half a billion dollars a year. Democracy or political stability of any sort would be impossible in the long run without economic stability. Political and social reform, desirable in themselves, had little chance for eventual success unless there was a sound economic structure.

Consequently, there were some grave reappraisals of the economic side of the occupation and a resultant shift of emphasis. Economic recovery now became a major objective, and certain reforms which conflicted with this, notably the trust-busting effort, were either modified or dropped. The original plan for transferring a large part of Japan's remaining industrial plants as reparations to the countries she had devastated had proved impractical and was first scaled down and eventually abandoned. In December 1948, it was decided to force upon the Japanese government a thoroughgoing economic retrenchment. The labor unions, which the occupation authorities had so actively built up, were restrained from actions which would cut seriously into production. More and more efforts were devoted toward actively promoting the revival of Japan's export trade.

This change in emphasis was accompanied by a growing divergence of opinion and some loss of assurance among the Americans, and by an even more marked resurgence of self-confidence and critical judgment on the part of the Japanese. The despair and confusion of the early postwar years was wearing off, and many Japanese began to realize that not all that was distinctively Japanese was bad and not all that the Americans were attempting was wise. Most Japanese remained impressed by the good will and enthusiasm of their American mentors and sympathetic toward their major objectives, but they came to see that in many details the occupation had been following American patterns too closely and, thus, had been sometimes attempting to do either the unnecessary or the impossible.

Criticism of American policies grew and was accompanied by increasing resentment of the privileges and luxuries which the American conquerors had arrogated to themselves, often at the expense and inconvenience of the Japanese people. Resentment of this sort was inevitable in such a situation, and, though it was surprisingly slow to develop, it became an important factor during this second phase.

The time had obviously come to end the occupation. On the negative side it was beginning to build up forces which militated against the success of its reforms. What was needed was more initiative and experience in democratic practices on the part of the Japanese, not more outside direction. MacArthur's original estimate of about three years as the desirable duration of the occupation was not far off the mark. In 1947 the government in Washington began efforts to bring the occupation to an end through a peace treaty, but in a divided world this was not easy to do. The Soviet Union blocked all efforts to hold a peace conference by insisting that peace terms should be decided solely by the great powers and that the Soviet Union must have a veto right in such a decision. Since the Russians had no desire to see the democratic experiment in Japan succeed, they would no doubt have used the veto to sabotage the peace treaty as envisaged by the Americans and their allies. Here was an impasse which prolonged the occupation for several years longer.

With the passing of the years, however, the need to bring an end to the occupation grew, rather than diminished, and eventually the United States decided to proceed with the Japanese peace treaty without Russian participation, if the Soviet Union did not change its attitude. With the appointment of Dulles as a State Department advisor in April 1950 and the announced decision to enter into preliminary discussions of the peace treaty the following September, the stage was set for the negotiations which were to lead to the signing of the peace treaty at San Francisco on September 8, 1951. In the process of these bilateral negotiations between the United States and each of the other interested countries, the text of the peace treaty was agreed upon in advance of the conference. This was a new departure in diplomatic procedures, made possible by the increased facilities for rapid communication between the various capitals of the world.

The occupation was obviously entering a new and final phase. The terms for its liquidation were already being drafted; and Japanese and Americans alike began to look forward to the imminent restoration of Japanese sovereignty. Earlier plans for the peace treaty had envisaged certain formal Allied controls over Japan lasting into the post-treaty period. The long delay in the treaty, however, had made such controls seem undesirable. Japan was to be restored to full sovereignty and would soon be in a position to revise the postwar reforms as she saw fit. The remaining days of the occupation gradually turned into a period of transition in which the Japanese could reassume responsibility for their own affairs and begin the inevitable process of adaptation and revision of the work of the occupation.

The process of transfer of authority and revision of policy was accelerated by two external factors. One was the invasion of South Korea by the Communist regime of North Korea on June 25, 1950, and the heavy involvement of the United States in the war which resulted. The attention of the American authorities in Japan and of the government in Washington became focused primarily on military developments in Korea rather than on civil reform in Japan, and at the same time the American army sharply increased its purchases of goods and services in Japan, producing a marked improvement in the economic situation there. Japanese self-confidence and economic independence were growing fast, just when American interest in domestic Japanese affairs was declining.

And then, as a by-product of the Korean War, MacArthur was dismissed on April 11, 1951. The Japanese at first were shocked and apprehensive lest this meant a sudden change in American policies toward Japan. When they saw that this was not the case, they were not only greatly relieved but also began to look upon the dismissal as a valuable object lesson in democracy. For all the American preaching about democracy during the earlier occupation years, the Japanese were amazed and deeply impressed to see that a single message from the American civil government could in actuality end the authority of a great military proconsul, who to them had seemed all-powerful. MacArthur's last lesson in democracy for the Japanese was by no means his least.

General Matthew B. Ridgway was appointed to succeed MacArthur as SCAP as well as in his other posts, but he could not really take his predecessor's place in Japan. MacArthur's role had been unique, and no one could replace him as the great reformer of postwar Japan. Ridgway wisely made no attempt to do so. Instead he encouraged the Japanese to assume leadership with only a minimum of assistance and direction from the occupation authorities.

The transition from occupation to independence was now fully under way. Already the Japanese were being allowed to resume normal relations with the outside world. At home, the process of revision had started and was to be seen most clearly in the growing numbers of persons and groups removed from the purge classification given them in the early days of the occupation. When the treaty was signed in San Francisco on September 8, 1951, it was only an incident in the process of transition—a clarification of the rules for the formal transfer of authority, which finally took place when the treaty went into effect on April 28, 1952.

Forty-eight nations signed the peace treaty with Japan, but not her two giant neighbors, Communist China and the Soviet Union. The latter, to everyone's surprise, had come to San Francisco, but only to refuse to join in the treaty. Since the United States recognized the government of the Republic of China, while several of the signatory nations recognized the Chinese Communists, it had proved impossible to decide which Chinese government should be invited to San Francisco. The next most populous Asian country, India, had also abstained from the conference, largely as a protest against the exclusion of China. Subsequently, however, both India and the Republic of China signed treaties of peace with Japan.

The peace treaty specified Japan's acquiescence to the dismemberment of her empire, which had already taken place in conformity with the Potsdam Proclamation and the terms of surrender. Korea once again had become an independent though tragically divided nation. Formosa and the Pescadores Islands had reverted to China and had become the sole remaining refuge of the Chinese Nationalists. The North Pacific Islands, which the Japanese had held under a mandate from the League of Nations, had been formally transferred to the United States in 1947 as a trusteeship territory under the United Nations. The Soviet Union, in accordance with the Yalta Agreement of February 1945, had occupied Southern Sakhalin and the Kurile Islands. The United States similarly had occupied the Ryukyu and Bonin Islands, administering them as areas separate from Japan. In the peace treaty Japan agreed to support proposals for placing the Ryukyus and Bonins under United States trusteeship and renounced its claims to all these other territories. Thus the treaty confirmed the limitation of Japan to the four main islands of Honshu, Kyushu, Shikoku, and Hokkaido and the smaller islands which adjoined them.

The treaty, however, did not specify the ultimate disposal of some of these areas. Nor did it resolve certain other basic problems. Reparations, while referred to, were left in an uncertain state. Since imports still exceeded exports, the Japanese economy remained dependent on American aid, and thus in the economic field no sharp line could be drawn between the occupation and post-occupation periods. Japan also remained heavily dependent on the United States in the field of defense. At the time of the peace treaty, Japan possessed only an embryonic force, and its public was sharply divided on the need for any armaments. Thus the only solution to Japan's defense problems in a dangerously divided world was a bilateral security pact with the United States, signed on the same day as the treaty and providing for the continuation of American bases in Japan.

Chapter XIV

POSTWAR JAPAN

The American occupation wrote a remarkable page in the long history of Japan, and the reforms it brought were nothing short of spectacular. But it was the energy, skills, and wisdom of the Japanese themselves that made this episode the significant turning point in history it has proved to be, not only for Japan, but for the world around it.

The Japanese needed no preachments from the Americans to grasp the fundamental meaning of their defeat and of the emergence of nuclear power as an entirely new magnitude of military might. Obviously Japan, with its limited resources, could never again hope to be a first-class military power, and therefore the militarists' dream of prosperity through conquest had vanished into thin air. Indeed, it was clear that Japan, dependent as it is on large-scale trade for its very existence, would henceforth have to be a champion of world peace and international trade. Showing their characteristic energy and economic skills, the Japanese also seized every opportunity the postwar

years offered to rebuild their devastated land, until it
was far more prosperous than it had ever been before. Philosophically accepting the changes that war
and occupation had brought, they built on their past
experience with democracy and the institutions of an
industrialized society to fashion a political and social
system that, in its stability and capacity to cope with
the problems of the modern world, does not compare
unfavorably with the advanced countries of Europe
and North America. In short, the nation whose economic fears helped plunge the whole world into war
became the economic miracle of the free world; the
wartime pariah was turned into a shining model for
rapid political and social development. The American
occupation certainly aided in this great transformation, but it probably deserves no more than an assist
on the play. Obviously the Japanese themselves de-
serve most of the credit for what they have achieved
in the years since 1945.

The war left Japan a thoroughly devastated and demoralized land. Probably none of the other major par-
ticipants suffered proportionately such heavy damage,
and no other industrialized country was so slow in
starting to show signs of recovery. Approximately half
of the urban housing of Japan had been burned to the
ground by American air raids. Tokyo's population had
shrunk by more than a half, Osaka's by almost two-
thirds. With the destruction of the cities and the virtual disappearance of the merchant marine, which had
maintained the flow of Japan's economic lifeblood, industrial production had plummeted, standing in 1946
at a mere seventh of the 1941 figure. The people were

clothed in rags, ill-fed, and both physically and emotionally exhausted.

The Japanese farms, though deprived of manpower,
fertilizers, and new investment throughout the war,
had maintained themselves better than industry, but it
had been a long time since domestic agriculture, even
under the best of circumstances, had been able to feed
Japan's rapidly expanding population. Naturally it was
the city dweller who suffered most. His caloric intake
fell to the semi-starvation level of 1500 calories. Those
whose homes had not been burned out made exhaust-
ing trips to the countryside to seek food from the
farmers in exchange for their remaining family possessions. This peeling off of successive layers of their
goods they wryly called an "onion existence." Others
attempted to supplement their diet with pathetic crops
grown on whatever scrap of land they could find—a
disused roadway or the burned-out site of their former
home. Runaway inflation further plagued the wage-
or salary-earner. The yen fell to less than a hundredth
of its prewar value, finally being stabilized by the occupation authorities in 1949 at 360 to the dollar. Only
the black market prospered, but it was dominated in
large part by Koreans, who had been accorded the
status of victors standing above the laws of Japan.
During the war large number of Koreans had been
forced into Japan's mines and factories, and some 600,-
000 of these elected to stay after Japan's defeat.

No matter how far one looked into the future, the
prospects appeared bleak. Even before the war, more
than 70,000,000 Japanese were crowded into a land area
smaller than the state of California, only 16 per cent

of it arable and blessed with few natural resources. Immediately after the war some six million soldiers and civilians from Japan's overseas empire and conquests were poured back into the country, and the resultant reunification of long-separated families produced a frightening boom in the birth rate. It was a valid question if the Japanese, despite all their energy, could ever develop on their narrow islands even a minimally viable economy. For years much of the population was kept above starvation levels only by an American dole.

The Japanese, however, long accustomed to restoring the natural devastations of earthquakes and typhoons, threw themselves with characteristic determination and vigor into the work of restoring their country from the greater man-made holocaust of war. A scum of shacks began to cover the burned-out wastes of the cities, and these were replaced in time by progressively sturdier buildings, until eventually the downtown sections were crowded with ten-storied steel and concrete structures far more imposing than the prewar buildings that had stood there. Similarly, Japan's war-devastated industries started to stir again, slowly restoring their lost production with what remained of their old industrial plant, and then with growing speed replaced their worn-out prewar equipment with the most efficient modern machinery, often becoming in the process more efficient producers than their less modernized industrial competitors overseas.

While traditional Japanese industries, such as textiles and steel, surged back to new highs of production, there was even more spectacular growth in such newer industrial fields as shipbuilding, electronics, and photographic equipment. Indeed, in certain of these areas Japan had achieved world leadership by the 1960's. These newer industries characteristically called for advanced technological skills, which Japan shared with only the most advanced Western nations, together with relatively high labor requirements, which gave her advantages over these same countries because of their higher wage structure.

In agriculture, too, there was a surprising surge forward as the accumulated scientific advances of the decades since Japan had embarked on its venture in conquest were applied to its farms. Year after year in the late 1950's Japan's all-important rice crop set new records. Eventually it became clear that Japan was not merely being favored by an extraordinary stretch of climatic good luck but had achieved a new technological level, resulting from the optimum application of chemical fertilizers, improved insecticides, and better seed strains. Aided by a fall-off in per capita rice consumption, as dietary habits shifted to a larger intake of bread and meat, Japan became self-sufficient in rice for the first time in the century and at the same time greatly expanded her production of fruit, vegetables, meat, and dairy products. And all this happened despite a drastic decline in farm population, made possible on the one hand by burgeoning job opportunities in the cities and on the other by the advent of "bean-size" tractors and other mechanized equipment designed to fit Japan's miniscule fields. Between 1955 and 1962 the percentage of the total labor force engaged in agriculture dropped from 41 to 29 per cent, or in absolute terms a decline took place from around 17 to 13 million farm workers.

While agricultural production inched ahead and industrial production rushed forward with seven-league boots, Japan's population growth, on the other hand, started to taper off, with the result that, unlike most of the other countries of Asia, little of Japan's postwar economic growth has been nullified by the need to feed more mouths. Facing few if any religious or sociological scruples, the government, aided by the big companies, has disseminated birth-control information very widely. At least of equal importance is the common practice of abortion. The laws permit abortion for medical reasons, and there is little effort to check illegal abortions, which are extremely numerous. The growing urbanization of the population promises to put an even more permanent damper on population growth, because in Japan, as elsewhere in the world, city populations tend toward a lowered birth rate. After the early postwar baby boom, the rate of growth soon declined to less than one per cent, or around 900,000, per year. In 1963 the population stood at only 96,000,000, and the experts predict a complete stabilization at only a little over 100,000,000. This number Japan has already proved that it can not only maintain, but can provide with rapidly rising living standards.

The statistics of Japan's postwar economic growth are staggering. In 1946 her gross national product had sunk to an abysmal 1.3 billion dollars, or $17 per capita. By 1950 these figures had risen to 10.9 billion and $132, respectively. As we have seen, the outbreak

of the Korean War resulted in heavy procurement
by the United States in Japan, helping to shove the
gross national product up to 15.1 billion in 1951. By
1962 it reached 53.6 billion (or 44.8 billion in terms
of the 1955 value of the dollar). Meanwhile per
capita income soared far beyond prewar standards and
in 1962 reached $564 (or $471 in terms of 1955
values). In 1963 further gains of around 13 per cent
were registered in the economy as a whole.

One should not, however, exaggerate Japan's economic prosperity and strength. While standing out as
the only major industrialized and rapidly growing area
in the world, outside of North America and Europe,
Japan's geographic base remains pathetically small as
compared with the major industrial countries of Western Europe, to say nothing of the United States and
the Soviet Union; and Japanese living standards, while
becoming comparable to those of Southern Europe, are
still far behind those of West Germany or England, let
alone those of the United States and Canada.

Japan also continues to face many difficult economic problems. One is the serious imbalance between
the private and public sectors of the economy. One
of the main reasons for the rapid growth of the past
decade and a half has been the concentration on investment in the private sector of the economy, particularly industry, at the expense of the public sector.
By the 1960's such fields as housing, schools, roads
and harbor facilities had fallen far behind the rest of
the economy and threatened to put a brake on future
economic growth unless they received a far larger
share of available capital than in the past.

Other problems are rising prices, which are beginning to eat heavily into economic growth as estimated in money terms, and the so-called "dual structure" of the Japanese economy. While much of Japanese industry, because of its modernized postwar plant, is highly efficient, other large areas of the economy remain relatively backward. Feeding into the large industrial plants are thousands of small-scale sub-contractors of varying degrees of efficiency. Except for the giant and ultra-modern department stores, retailing and the other service industries remain for the most part divided into a myriad tiny units that use labor in a lavish and wasteful manner. And Japan's pitifully small-scale agriculture, for all its scientific skill, new machinery, and high yields per acre, remains a low producer in per capita terms, requiring heavy government subsidies. Since the wages of industrial laborers have gone up commensurately with the increase in their productive capacity (annual wage increases of around 10 per cent have been common in Japan) and since general economic prosperity has begun to raise the demand for labor beyond the supply, workers in the less productive sectors have also shared in wage increases beyond the increase in their productive capacity. The result in the early 1960's has been sharply rising prices, which have raised serious political and social problems.

There are only two long-range solutions possible for the "dual structure" problem of Japan's economy and the resultant up-creep of prices. One is the transfer of workers from the less productive activities into big industry, as can be seen already in the rapid drop of the agricultural population. The other is the rationalization of the less efficient economic fields, as in the substitution of supermarket for corner grocery, which is starting to take place, and the expansion of the farm unit, which still appears to lie in the future. But changes of this sort entail vast sociological as well as economic upheavals. The rebuilding of Japan's "dual structure" into a single efficient level of economy will obviously take time and travail.

Perhaps Japan's greatest economic problem is its permanent dependence on the outside world for much of its food and foodstuffs (such as soybeans, wheat, and other cereals), virtually all of its oil (which is fast replacing coal as the major source of power), and most of the raw materials for industry (such as cotton, wool, rubber, and virtually all of the minerals). To pay for this, Japan must, of course, export on a vast scale, and the question always remains whether foreign markets can keep up with Japan's extraordinary rate of growth. Running on a very narrow margin, Japan has constantly been on the edge of balance of payments problems. Too rapid a rate of domestic growth so stimulates or "overheats" the economy that imports and domestic consumption rise more rapidly than exports, necessitating a belt-tightening operation to cut down on domestic investment and imports and to maximize exports. Such crises were faced, periodically, in 1953, 1957, and again in 1961. In each case the Japanese showed an unparalleled ability to control their economy, throwing the brakes on the domestic economy softly but just firmly enough to restore the

balance they needed within about a year without losing much of their forward economic motion.

The end of Japan's period of rapid economic growth
is obviously not in sight. In view of the various problems cited above, it seems probable that the average
annual growth rate of the late 1950's, of around 8 or
9 per cent in real terms, will drop off slightly in the
remaining years of the 1960's, but there is no reason
not to expect Japan to remain for some years to come
one of the fastest growing economies in the world.

Japan's postwar economic resurgence has frequently
been called a miracle, and, as the term implies, it is
easier to describe than to explain. The primary ingredients, of course, have been the energy, organiza-
tional skills, and high technological and educational
levels of the Japanese people—in other words, the
same characteristics that accounted for Japan's phenomenal economic growth between the 1870's and the
1930's. Another factor has been Japan's particular
free-enterprise system. The Japanese economy has left
plenty of room for the full exercise of the boundless
initiative and energy of the Japanese entrepreneur and
businessman. It is of no small significance that the
free economy of postwar Japan has in sustained
growth easily outstripped any of the planned economies of the world, regardless of the far richer geographic bases some of them enjoy. At the same time,
the Japanese, as their record with balance of payments
crises has shown, have demonstrated an amazing skill
at directing free enterprise into the most constructive
channels. They appear to have in practice, even if not

in theory, an informal but effective integration of the banking community, big business, and government leadership that permits a higher degree of planned utilization of economic resources than is to be found in the other major free-enterprise countries.

One final reason for Japan's rapid growth has been its special and close relationship with the United States. As we have seen, American aid helped see the Japanese through their desperate early postwar years. We have also seen how United States' purchases occasioned by the Korean War of 1950 gave a special fillip to the Japanese economy. Another factor is that the American military presence has allowed the Japanese to avoid heavy investment in military defense. Even in the early 1960's, only a little over one per cent of the Japanese gross national product went into military expenses—a mere fraction of the amount devoted to defense by any other major industrialized nation. As we shall see, the immediate reason for this situation has been the determined opposition of large sectors of the Japanese public to the maintenance of any military establishment. On the other hand, to those who believe that twentieth-century conditions still necessitate military defense, it has appeared that such Japanese attitudes have been tenable only because the United States was bearing gratis a large part of Japan's natural defense burden.

The chief contribution of the United States to Japan's economic recovery, however, has been through mutually beneficial trade and economic cooperation. As Japanese industry began to get on its feet again, technical know-how from the United States, embodied in hundreds of agreements on patents and affiliations between American and Japanese firms, made a huge contribution to the reviving economy. So also did an immense flow of American credit to capital-hungry Japan, in the form of corporate investments, large amounts of short-term credit, and growing long-term investments in Japanese securities. The United States also became Japan's greatest market, steadily absorbing about a quarter or more of its exports. In return, the United States accounted for even more of Japan's imports—roughly a third. In fact, Japan has come to stand second only to Canada as an export market for the United States, and is its best market for agricultural products. Usually, United States exports to Japan exceed imports by a few hundred million dollars annually, though American military expenditures in Japan and the providing of capital tend to turn the balance of payments in Japan's favor. In this tremendous economic relationship there has constantly been a fringe of hotly contested trade problems, such as the levels at which Japan would limit its cotton textile exports to the United States. But these problems have been small as compared with the over-all size of the Japanese-American economic relationship. By the early 1960's trade between the two countries topped the $3 billion mark, making it by all odds the greatest trans-oceanic trade the world has ever seen.

The destruction of war and upheavals of the occupation were enough to set off vast sociological changes in postwar Japan, but these were accelerated and heightened by the breakneck economic pace and the unaccustomed affluence it began to produce. Wartime and early postwar exigencies, particularly the need to patronize the black market, led to a general breakdown of morale and widespread disrespect for law and government. The disaster of defeat tended to discredit all traditional authority and values, and agreement on new values was difficult. The vast dispersals of population caused by imperialist expansion and wartime air raids and the grinding poverty of the early postwar years disrupted the traditional patterns of life. And then, when recovery did come, it brought broad new adjustments: a vast further urbanization of the population; dislocations resulting from increasing automation; the blighting of mining areas, as imported oil replaced domestic coal; and changing patterns of relationships and an accelerating pace of life, as prosperity introduced an intense, almost frenetic, new tempo of activity.

The Japanese family has been deeply affected by all this. Prewar tendencies for the typical family to shrink to the conjugal pair and their pre-adult children and for women and youths to challenge the authority of the *pater familias* have been greatly strengthened. Long before the war, industrialization had made most young men in the cities economically independent of the older generation, and this had been accompanied by a growing spirit of independence. The wartime labor shortage, by greatly increasing the employment possibilities for women, gave them, too, far more economic independence than ever before. It was not surprising, therefore, that the postwar legal reforms, which freed younger adult males from subordination to so-called family heads and gave women equal status with men, were readily accepted by the public. The women, when given the franchise, made enthusiastic use of it and did not hesitate to elect a considerable number of their sex to high office. All in all, the postwar years have shown a rapid trend in the same general directions that American society has been taking ever since the latter part of the nineteenth century.

The educational changes of the occupation too have brought significant modifications to Japanese society. The nine years of compulsory education for all were easily accepted, and some 60 per cent of the students now continue on to high school. More surprising is the great number who attend college—the highest percentage, next to the United States and Israel, in the whole world. As we have seen, the broadening of educational opportunities has resulted inevitably in some lowering of standards, to the great distress of the older generation, but the Japanese remain a nation of avid readers. Their book-publishing statistics rank near the top in the world. Weekly and monthly magazines of every description pour forth in vast numbers. Their newspapers are in circulation among the greatest in the world and in quality among the finest: the three largest national dailies together publish some 10 million papers each morning and only a little less each evening. The new emphasis in primary education on thinking for oneself rather than on rote memory work has produced what seems almost like a new breed of young Japanese—direct, casual, sometimes undisciplined and rude as compared with their prewar predecessors, but at the same time eager, spontaneous, and encouragingly fresh and openminded.

Nothing is more strikingly evident in postwar Japan than the rapid rate of urbanization. While all prefectures with a predominantly rural make-up are losing population, every city is growing in size, and the larger they are the more rapid the pace. Tokyo has become a sprawling monster of more than 10 million, hemmed in by several million more in surrounding prefectures. Only metropolitan New York can contend with it for the dubious honor of being the world's largest conglomeration of human beings. All the larger cities are hopelessly crowded both for living and for moving around. Mushrooming *danchi* (developments), which in most cases are serried rows of four- to six-story concrete apartment houses located in the far suburbs, have still made only a small dent in the housing problem. The superb rail network and the tremendous urban commuting systems (supplemented in Tokyo by subways) are absurdly overcrowded. Inadequate roadways are the scene for the world's worst traffic snarls. Water supplies fall to dangerously low levels, and sewage disposal is entirely inadequate. Juvenile delinquency, though small by American standards, has become a serious worry. In short, most of the problems of twentieth-century urbanization faced by the United States and the other Western nations have shown up in Japan, often in exaggerated form.

But for all these problems, the chief impression given by the cities of Japan is one of vitality, gaiety, and unbounding vigor. All the arts, both native and Western, flourish exuberantly. Tokyo alone has six professional symphony orchestras. Intellectual life is vigorous and prolific. The literary scene bubbles with creativity. The scurrying crowds look young, purposeful, and happy.

Japan has produced its own version of the affluent society, decidedly less fat than that of the West but probably for that very reason more lively. The pleasure districts of Tokyo, with their night clubs, cabarets, bars and fantastically variegated neon lights, are probably the biggest, gaudiest, and gayest in the world. The family car is beginning to come to the middle classes with disastrous consequences for overcrowded roads and resorts. The great majority of Japanese homes boast television sets, and two government networks and a number of private ones are available to most viewers. Washing machines and electric refrigerators have become commonplace, and no people in the world are better supplied with fine cameras. The most popular word of 1962 was the English word "leisure," replaced the next year by the French word "*vacances*."

Even rural Japan shares in the new life. A television set bringing its citified fare into the peasant household, a motorcycle, or a party phone operated by the local agricultural cooperative can affect bigger changes in the ways of life and thought for a farmer than for his urbanized cousin.

Social change, urbanization, and affluence have all brought their share of new problems together with their blessings, but the Japanese appear capable of handling these with much the same degree of competence as the industrialized societies of the West. Their legal system and courts seem adequate to the new burdens placed on them, and government services in general show a relatively high degree of honesty and efficiency. It is true that Japan lags far behind the West in such major areas as housing, roads, and social security, but the rate of progress, at least, is probably greater than in many Western countries. Certainly the road building, subway laying, and building construction going on in Tokyo and some of the other major cities defies comparison anywhere else in the world.

Japan's record-breaking economic pace and the apparent ease with which it has taken great sociological changes in stride are in themselves remarkable but become all the more surprising when one considers that, ever since the war, it has been an intellectually confused and emotionally divided nation. The war, defeat, and subsequent occupation were all great shocks, leaving deep wounds on the Japanese psyche which have healed only slowly. All old values were cast into doubt, and new ones remained bitterly disputed in a rapidly changing situation. All that was clear was change itself—swift, upsetting change—but toward what end and for what purpose remained the question. Imagine the innovations that have swept the United States or Western Europe since the 1930's and multiply these by a factor of three or four and you will have some idea of what the Japanese have been through.

Differences of attitudes by generation are marked enough in the West, but they are vastly greater in Japan. A youth coming to his majority in the 1960's, his father who reached maturity in the war years, and his grandfather who graduated from the university in the early 1920's are the products, not just of different generations, but of different worlds. Their experiences and the outlooks these have produced are so dissimilar that the different generations hardly speak the same language.

The gulf between occupational groups is sometimes almost as wide. In any case it is incomparably greater than in our own more fluid society. The government official or big businessman lives in a different world from the so-called intellectual, or *interi*. The latter is a term of pride in Japan, used for a wide group of people, particularly university professors, writers, and the like, yet including almost anyone who has received a higher education but who has not become a businessman or government official. The latter two groups probably attended the same universities as the "intellectuals," receiving the same Germanic sort of theoretical, idealistic education, but they have abandoned that point of view, often with reluctance, to become pragmatic men of affairs, while the "intellectuals" cling tenaciously to their bookish theories, unsullied by any compromise with supposedly sordid reality. Such differences are not unknown in the West, but the gap is much greater in Japan.

A similar cleavage exists between the farmer and the intellectual and the latter's young cohorts among university students. The farmer has his own well-established pattern of pragmatic democratic politics, based on personal associations, patronage, and other local considerations. All in all it is a political pattern not unlike those of the rural areas of Western democracies. The student contemptuously rejects all this as "feudalistic," insisting with fanatical intolerance on his own particular brand of Utopian democracy or Communism, two terms which in his special dream world are easily merged.

Industrial labor and management also view each other with a degree of suspicion and hostility that is almost unknown in the industrialized West today, although it was not uncommon a few decades ago. In a sense these labor-management attitudes in Japan are surprising, because employment practices there still retain some of the desirable humane qualities of the pre-industrial past. Employers tend to feel a lifetime obligation to employees and normally do not consider lack of work or profits as sufficient reason for dismissal. As a result, Japan has virtually no unemployment, though there is a great deal of underemployment. Wages, which are much more heavily in the form of fringe benefits than in the West, tend to be paternalistic, based more on length of service and family needs than on the value of services performed. Yet, despite these characteristics of the employer-employee relationship, organized industrial labor and big business often regard each other quite openly as "the enemy."

Postwar Japan has been characterized by four other major psychological tendencies which must be clearly grasped if one is to understand what has been going on there. The first is the loss of self-confidence brought on by defeat and occupation. Nationalism and patriotism were so misused by the earlier militaristic leadership that contemporary Japanese are reluctant to employ these terms. Even the national flag is used sparingly. Anything international is automatically viewed with favor; anything strictly national is viewed, at least by younger Japanese, with a certain degree of suspicion. Despite their remarkable postwar accomplishments, the Japanese tend to underrate themselves. In part this is so because, with unconscious snobbery, they compare themselves only with the most advanced countries of Western Europe and North America, which, with their head start in modernization and richer geographic bases, are quite understandably ahead of Japan in many ways. In international circles they prefer to speak softly and carry no stick at all. Remembering the deep animosities their wartime conquests stirred in neighboring lands, they hold back from taking leadership even among those countries which obviously need their help and have much to learn from them. Postwar Japan has been compared to the big boy who prefers to sit quietly in the back of the classroom in the hope that no one will notice him.

Another even more important psychological factor in postwar Japan is the deep longing for peace and the resultant idealistic pacifism that emerged from the disaster of the war. However bewildering the postwar world might be, certain things seem crystal clear to most Japanese: that the militarists were tragically wrong, that war does not pay, and that Japan must at all costs avoid any involvement in future wars. As the only people who have ever suffered nuclear attack, the Japanese have shown particular sensitivity to nuclear weapons. Ever since the war they have overwhelmingly resisted any thought of the introduction of such weapons into Japan, even for defense purposes, and have passionately protested their development and testing by other nations, particularly by the United States.

It was because of their abhorrence of war and deep longing for peace at any price that the public enthusiastically accepted in the new Constitution the now famous Article IX, renouncing war "as a sovereign right of the nation" and promising never to maintain "land, sea, and air forces." Subsequently it became clear to many Japanese that the surrounding areas of East Asia remained in an unsettled and often warring condition and that the Communist powers were still dedicated to their basic philosophy of destroying through one means or another all other forms of society. The result was successive treaties of mutual security with the United States, which were based on a clear American commitment to the defense of Japan and permitted the continuance of American bases there.

The Japanese government also started to build up a small defense capability under a liberalized interpretation of Article IX. In 1950 a paramilitary National Police Reserve of 75,000 men was started to back up the weak and locally divided police forces. Renamed the National Security Force in 1952, it added a naval arm that same year. In 1954 an air arm was started, and all three elements were reorganized as the Self-Defense Force under a Defense Agency of sub-cabinet status. By the early 1960's it totaled around 200,000 men, with more than a thousand planes and an efficient naval arm boasting vessels up to the destroyer level.

Thus Japan does have a modest military force and a

strong defense alliance with the United States, but the questions of defense and pacifism remain deeply divisive factors in Japanese society. The Self-Defense Force was viewed with contempt during its early years, and even today many Japanese tolerate it only with reluctance. Large elements remain adamantly committed to the belief that greater safety for Japan lies in complete, unarmed neutralism than in alliance with the free world, while a few would seek the protection of close association with the neighboring Communist colossi on the continent. Moreover, the great majority of Japanese, whether they be supporters of the government policy of maintaining a small defense capability and an alliance with the United States or members of the opposition, remain opposed to any association with nuclear weapons and deeply committed to the concept that whatever forces Japan possesses must be used only for the defense of the homeland.

A third intellectual factor of the greatest importance is the deep penetration throughout Japanese society of the Marxist interpretation of history. Marxism had a heavy impact on Japanese intellectual circles in the 1920's and 1930's, just when conservative thought was retreating behind the mystical concept of the "imperial will" and liberal, democratic thinkers found themselves ground between this obscurantist doctrine and the emerging reality of totalitarian controls. While liberal thought withered, Marxism helped father, on the one side, the totalitarian extremism of the young officers and, on the other, the determined opposition of various Communist and Socialist groups.

When the militarists and emperor-centered conservatives went down in ignominious defeat, the Japanese public assumed that their Communist and Socialist critics had been proved right. Perhaps the single greatest failure of the American occupation authorities was their inability to see this situation and remedy it by adequate intellectual antidotes. The field was left open instead to the Communist and Socialist brands of Marxism. They came to dominate the magazines and newspapers. University faculties, and naturally their student bodies, became thoroughly imbued with Marxist doctrines. The powerful Teachers Union of primary and secondary school teachers has been dominated by extreme leftists, many of them open Communists, ever since it was formed. The reforms of the occupation and the Japanese institutions these helped produce were fully grounded in the liberal, democratic tradition, but Japanese thought took on a heavily Marxist flavor.

Japanese Marxism remains much truer in doctrine to the classical Marxism of the nineteenth century than do most of the Marxist derivatives in the rest of the industrialized world, whether they be in Communist, Socialist, or so-called capitalistic countries. According to this doctrine, it is a truism that a stage in history known as "capitalism," which is Marx's analysis of the early industrial societies of Western Europe and what he assumed would happen to them, will inevitably be followed by an historical stage called "socialism," which is his Utopian dream of the future, in which all persons work according to their capacities and receive according to their needs. Since "capitalism" is said to be the breeder of imperialism and the latter the cause for war, all international tension is to be laid at "capitalism's" door.

Japanese Marxism has proved an extremely hardy plant. Its failure to correspond to the facts of twentieth-century history, even as these unfold within Japan itself, has not blighted it. The true believers and even many conservative Japanese, who are unaware of how much they remain influenced by their Marxist education, seem hardly to have noticed that so-called capitalism has turned into something far different from what Marx assumed it would become and that the supposedly socialist societies have approximated Marx's dream only in words and superficial details. Marxism has flourished even despite a most infertile emotional soil. Grass-roots Japan remains basically conservative in disposition, and the Japanese as a whole are an extremely pragmatic people. Moreover, deeply ingrained prejudices run against the major so-called socialist countries and in favor of the principal so-called capitalist countries. No people are more suspected and feared in Japan than the Russians, and the attitude toward Chinese is probably more that of affectionate condescension than real respect. By contrast the United States remains not only the best known but overwhelmingly the best liked and most respected foreign country, with such other major free-world nations as the United Kingdom, France, and West Germany not far behind. Yet, despite all this and despite Japan's enormous economic success, large sectors of the Japanese public still debate with all seriousness whether it is "Japanese monopoly capitalism" or

"American imperialism" that is the chief enemy of the Japanese people.

A fourth major characteristic of postwar Japanese thought is what may be called the "American fixation." This is scarcely a surprising phenomenon. It was after all the United States that crushed the Japanese Empire and occupied and ruled the nation for seven years, and it is still the United States that defends Japan militarily and looms overwhelmingly in its economic life. Japan's ties with the United States—economic, military, and cultural—are many times greater than those with any other nation, near or far. Adult Japanese assume all Occidentals in Japan to be Americans unless there is clear proof to the contrary, and children quite simply call them all Americans instead of *gaijin*, or "foreigners," the usual term for Westerners.

Every issue of political, economic, or social importance has its American aspect. Those who champion absolute neutralism, to say nothing of those who advocate a Communist alignment for Japan, find in the American military alliance and American bases the natural target of attack. Those with a dogmatic belief in primitive Marxism find the United States, as the "leader of the capitalist camp," the obvious enemy. Those who disapprove of the purges or the economic, social, or educational reforms of the occupation period —and these are largely to be found among Japanese conservatives—not unnaturally concentrate their blame on the United States. Those who look with disfavor on one or another of the great sociological changes sweeping Japan—and these include both leftists and conservatives—are all too prone to attribute whatever they consider to be the ills of the modern age to an excessive "Americanization" that is destroying the "real Japan." Those who have fears about Japan's external markets, the inflow of foreign goods, or future economic conditions think in all cases primarily about the economic relationship with the United States. Japan's relationships with other countries, be they Communist, democratic or less developed, almost invariably involve Japan's relations with the United States, or at least so it seems to the average Japanese.

The Japanese-American relationship is indeed a unique one in history. Never before have two countries established such extensive, cordial, close, and mutually profitable relations across such broad barriers of space, language, and differences in cultural background. But the Japanese attitude, while understandable, is something of a psychological complex nonetheless, going well beyond the realities of the situation. The United States becomes too easily involved in the Japanese mind in every nuance of domestic or foreign politics and in every aspect of Japanese society or the economy.

While the four basic attitudes described above have characterized Japan ever since the end of the war, they, like everything else in Japan, are not static. Increasing contact with and knowledge of the outside world, and perhaps a growing understanding of Japan's own recent history as well, have tended to blur all four of them. Japan's huge economic success has naturally begun to restore some sense of self-confidence and has

shaken Marxist dogmatism, but not as yet to the extent
one might have asumed. The "American fixation" has
faded a bit, and there has been increased acceptance of
the need for self-defense. Thus all four of these psychological tendencies, though still strong in the early
and mid-1950's, have shown signs of weakening in
the early 1960's. What will happen to them in the
years ahead will go a long way toward determining
the future of Japan.

Despite the breakneck economic pace of postwar
Japan, its vast sociological upheavals, its psychic
wounds, and its deep intellectual cleavages, the course
of postwar Japanese politics has been amazingly steady,
even if often turbulent. This is so perhaps because
postwar politics was not the complete break with the
past that most people have assumed, but instead has
reflected in large part the continued flow of prewar
tendencies, some in the ascendant, others in decline.
It is true that one of the major prewar forces, the
predominance of the armed forces and their philosophy of imperialist aggrandizement, has been eliminated from the scene. Discredited by defeat, rooted
out by the occupation, and scorned by the temper of
postwar Japan, the old type of militarism appears to
have been banished beyond recall. For the rest, however, the power groups of contemporary Japan have
all grown from prewar roots. Japanese and Americans alike are all too prone to assume that the postwar
political system was the creation of the occupation,
when actually the occupation reforms succeeded only
to the extent that they coincided with natural tendencies. They were not new seed but fertilizers and

poisons, accelerating the growth of some tendencies and impeding others.

The civil bureaucracy had been a major power group, or rather a series of power groups, in prewar Japan. Now freed from the shadow of the military, it flourished with new vigor. The prestige and authority of government had in the meantime become seriously tarnished in the public mind, and the new Constitution made clear the supremacy of the elected Diet over the bureaucrats, but such powerful ministries as the Foreign Office, the Finance Ministry, and the Ministry of International Trade and Industry remained influential elements in the making of policy as well as in carrying it out.

A prewar tendency for bureaucrats to switch to elective politics also became strengthened. Unable to advance beyond the post of Vice-Minister, ambitious bureaucrats would run for election with the hope of subsequently becoming Ministers or possibly the Prime Minister. It is a significant fact that, for all but three and a quarter years since the end of the war, Japan has been under Prime Ministers of bureaucratic origin; and it is no mere accident that for eight of the first nine postwar years, when the most important function of the Japanese government was to deal with the occupation authorities and subsequently with the United States government, Japan was led by three Prime Ministers who were all products of the Foreign Office.

The Diet is, of course, now supreme in Japanese politics, but the parties that are active in it and the groups they tend to represent are all derived straight from pre-

war days. The two major prewar parties, both conservative by contemporary standards, usually went
under the names of the Seiyukai and Minseito. Beaten
down by the militarists during the 1930's and entirely
eclipsed during the war, they re-emerged vigorously
after the surrender, under much the same old leadership and drawing votes from the same old sources.
The Seiyukai group usually operated under the name
of Liberals, with the Minseito group alternating between the labels of Progressives and Democrats, until
the two groups merged late in 1955 as the Liberal-
Democratic Party.

Drawing well over half the total votes in all but the
first postwar general election, and always occupying
over half of the Diet seats, these successors to the two
major prewar parties have dominated postwar Japanese
politics. Their local base of power is the personal
drawing power and supporting organizations of the
individual Diet members in their respective constituen-
cies. On the whole these local vote-getting organizations, as before the war, are stronger in rural
communities than in urban centers. At a higher level
the conservative politicians maintain close contacts
with big business, which supplies the bulk of their
political funds, though many businessmen hedge their
political bets by contributing also to the opposition
parties of the left. All in all, a remarkably close and
effective relationship exists between the conservative
political leadership and the highly integrated leadership of the banking community and big business. The
two groups cooperate with each other smoothly and
closely, often seeming to be coordinate branches of

an undefined but very real "establishment." Thus, the conservative politicians, today as when their parties first took shape well over a half century ago, are most closely associated with rural Japan and the business community.

Even the factionalism that has characterized postwar conservative politics is a direct derivative from prewar days. Perhaps old traditions of personalized relationships have contributed to this tendency for Diet members to break up into leader and follower groups. Certainly the multi-seat election-district system has strengthened factionalism by pitting candidates of the same party more against one another for their respective shares of the local party vote than against opposition candidates, whose supporters would be more difficult to woo away. The lack of a really effective centralized fund-raising organization in the conservative party has also contributed to factionalism, by making individual politicians look primarily to influential political patrons for financial support. Of course, factionalism within political parties is scarcely unkown in other democratic countries, and it has perhaps been overemphasized in Japan by the typically East Asian love of classifying and categorizing. In any case, factions, despite much talk about their abolition, were still a prominent feature of the Liberal-Democratic Party in the early 1960's.

Most analysts usually divided the party's membership in the House of Representatives into about eight factions, varying in size from less than a score to 60 or more members, each under its own "man of power" or "division commander," as the leaders are facetiously called. Much attention is always paid to factional membership in deciding the composition of a Cabinet. While the faction leaders sometimes differ sharply on policies, their respective factions can be classified as liberal or conservative only in a most general way. Perhaps a more significant cleavage exists between leaders of bureaucratic background and the straight party men who have worked their way up entirely through elective politics.

The parties of the left have almost as old antecedents as those of the right. The Communist Party, deriving directly in leadership from the tiny, outlawed prewar party, has not developed a truly mass appeal. Except for the 1949 general elections, it has never drawn more than 4 per cent of the popular vote. The Socialist Party, on the other hand, as the direct successor of the much larger Social Mass Party of the 1930's, has proved vastly stronger. The Socialist vote, though sometimes divided between battling factions of the left and right, has varied between 15 and 36 per cent.

The leftist vote, whether Socialist or Communist, has tended to come largely from those elements in society that began giving their support to the parties of the left before the war. These are first of all the so-called intellectuals and the urban white-collar workers, or "salary-men," as the Japanese more accurately designate this functional group. An even more important group both in numerical and power terms is composed of the labor unions, which as efficiently organized forces have tended to exercise disproportionate influence on the leftist parties.

The left-wing groups show the same factional ten-

dencies as the conservatives, and, since these are reinforced by much greater doctrinal differences, party
splits have not been uncommon. The Communists,
themselves faction ridden, have never been able to
join forces effectively with the Socialists, despite repeated "united front" attempts on their part. The
Socialists have from time to time spawned and re-
absorbed splinter groups, but a basic left-right division
has persisted throughout. Between late 1951 and late
1955 this resulted in an openly divided party, and
again in January 1960 the more conservative elements
broke off to form the Democratic Socialist Party.

Back of the party and factional divisions of the left
are parallel divisions in Japan's labor movement. Although its postwar revival was sponsored by the
American occupation, the labor unions, as we have
seen, early fell under Communist domination. Repeated anti-Communist reform efforts divided the
movement from time to time, until it finally settled
down into a general three-way split. On the left, is the
largest grouping, known as Sohyo, which in 1962
embraced 45.9 per cent of the total union membership of 8,971,156 workers. Of the remainder, 13.4
per cent in 1962 were in Zenro and affiliated groups on
the right (known collectively as Domei Kaigi), while
the rest were in independent unions or various in-
between organizations. The unions of the extreme left,
commonly made up of government workers, tend to
advocate, together with the usual Communist causes,
direct political action rather than wage bargaining,
since government rather than business sets their wage
scales. The true blue-collar workers, particularly those

in the more modernized industries, tend to be more conservative, and are increasingly approximating the wage-bargaining stands and attitudes of unions in the United States. While some of the Communist-leaning Sohyo unions give political support to either Communist or Socialist candidates, the majority support only the Socialists, while the Zenro unions support the Democratic Socialists.

When one looks only at the conservative-leftist division in Japanese politics, ignoring the divisions within these groups, one fact stands out with startling clarity. The leftist vote, from national down to local elections, has been growing at a slow but remarkably steady pace for a long time, approximating a one per cent shift of voters per year from the conservative to the leftist side. Actually this trend might be traced back to prewar days, because it is discernible up through the last reasonably free prewar election in 1936 and picked up after the war at about the level where it could have been charted if one had extended the curve established a decade or more earlier. Another fact, consistently revealed by polls, is that the voting trend to the left is most marked among the lower age groups, the groups with higher education, and those living in more urbanized areas. Since young people are always replacing their elders on the voting rolls and since Japan is racing toward ever greater urbanization and higher educational standards, one cannot assume that the leftward voting trend will not continue.

In recent national elections the once overwhelming conservative majority has shrunk to around the 60-40 level, and one could easily jump to the conclusion that Japanese politics will move decidedly to the left in the not too distant future. There are a number of reasons, however, for viewing such a conclusion with scepticism. For one thing, the conservative majority, which is still impressive enough in national elections, tends to be even greater the more local the election, although conservative candidates in local elections very commonly prefer to use the label of "independent." In other words, at the grass-roots level Japanese politics remains very conservative indeed, and only on the more remote and abstract level of national policy do the parties of the left have strong appeal.

Another factor which one should keep in mind when reading the palm of Japanese politics is the gradual change of attitudes within Japan. The penchant for Marxism and the other psychological factors described above, which have all been most characteristic of the leftist groups, are, as we have seen, tending to weaken. As they do, the leftist parties will either lose some of their appeal to voters, or, as appears already to be happening, will tend to shift their stand bit by bit toward the center. In time, a large part of the Marxists may, like the Socialists of Western Europe, lose their Marxism without dropping their Socialist label.

The persistence of the leftward voting trend despite the declining appeal of leftist concepts suggests that many people are attracted by the image of the left rather than by its ideology and thus may be voting more for images than for policies, as is sometimes the case in Western democracies too. A member of a labor

union, a salaried white-collar worker, or an "intellectual," whatever his political views, finds it hard to vote
for what he regards to be the party of big businessmen
and unenlightened farmers. In turn, farmers and small
as well as big businessmen are repelled by the image
of the leftist parties as the tool of organized labor.
And young people tend to look with disfavor on the
Liberal-Democrats as the party of old men of prewar vintage, though they find little comfort either in
the elderly, prewar leadership of the parties of the left.
Thus, the leftward voting trend may be more a sociological than a political phenomenon, reflecting population shifts rather than changes in attitudes.

But even if the leftward voting trend does continue
to the point where the Liberal-Democrats drop below
the median mark, one should not conclude that the
government would pass automatically into the hands
of the parties of the left, because these are likely to
remain deeply divided. At one end of the leftist spec-
trum, the small Communist Party is wholly committed
to the usual Communist goals. At the other end, the
Democratic Socialists have made quite clear their ir-
revocable commitment to parliamentary democracy
and their abhorrence of totalitarianism, be it Communist or Fascist. The Socialists, who include the great
majority of the leftist forces, spread all the way from
one extreme to the other. On the left they include a
large number of fellow travelers who have rejected the
Communist label either out of distaste for Russians
or in the vain hope of unifying the leftist movement.
On the right is another large group who sympathizes
with the Democratic Socialists but refused to join the

schism in 1960 in the hope of maintaining party unity. In between are myriad shades of viewpoint. Conceivably, the leftists, now divided into three parties, might reshuffle into two, the pro-Communists and those who stand for parliamentary democracy along with Socialist economic views, but it is almost inconceivable that they can merge into a single effective unit.

Japan's postwar political history falls into three phases. First there was the occupation, then a transitional period after the peace treaty in which many of the attitudes and much of the flavor of occupation days lingered on, though in diminishing degree, and then, after the great riots in the late spring of 1960, the Japanese clearly entered a new phase, in which they began to feel and act like an entirely sovereign nation.

During the occupation period, particularly in its early years, there was great confusion and political fluidity. Many politicians were elected to the Diet as independents, and minor parties came and went. People did not know what to expect, and, except for the Communists and more dogmatic Socialists, they were not even sure what they hoped for. Leftist unions battled with management for control of the ruins of Japanese industry. The leftists let loose a flood of propaganda. But most Japanese remained confused by all the rapid changes going on and benumbed by the difficulties of mere existence.

Yet, surprisingly, the result of all this was not political chaos. The ultimate political authority, after all, was not the Japanese government but the American occupation, backed up by adequate military force.

However confused the people and unsteady the government, the occupation provided firm stability and guidance.

Prince Higashikuni, a member of the imperial family, had assumed the Prime Ministership on August 17, 1945, in order to help insure the peaceful transition to occupation rule. But immediately after the formal surrender, the old parliamentary leaders started reorganizing their disbanded parties, and on October 9 Shidehara Kijuro, an ex-diplomat and former Foreign Minister, who had been the prime figure in Japan's liberal, internationalist foreign policies of the 1920's, became Prime Minister as the head of the Progressive Party.

A few days earlier, General MacArthur had freed from prison the veteran Communist leaders. Joined in January by Nozaka, their most popular colleague, who had spent the war years on the continent with the Chinese Communists, these old activists got the now legal Communist Party off to a much publicized start.

The occupation authorities felt that their purge and reform programs had advanced sufficiently to permit the first postwar general elections on April 10, 1946. About a third of the vote went to independents and minor parties, 17.8 per cent to the Socialists, only 3.9 per cent to the Communists, and the remaining 42 per cent to the two conservative parties, with the Liberals winning a plurality. Their leader was the veteran politician Hatoyama Ichiro, but as he had been purged at the last moment by the occupation, the Prime Ministership went instead to his successor, the veteran ex-diplomat Yoshida Shigeru, who was to hold on to it for seven of the next eight and a half years.

The next test of the public's political preferences came in April 1947, when a series of elections were held under the new laws in preparation for the formal inauguration of the new Constitution on May 3. On April 5 the 46 prefectural governors were elected for the first time in history and with them over two hundred mayors and more than ten thousand town and village heads. The immaturity of local politics was reflected in the fact that virtually two-thirds of the governors, more than two-thirds of the mayors, and over nine-tenths of the town and village heads were elected as independents. The electorate also showed itself to be preponderantly conservative and to some degree traditionally minded by electing an overwhelming majority of conservative candidates, including several former appointive incumbents among the governors.

The same tendencies were apparent in the April 20 election for the House of Councillors, in which 110 of the 250 candidates elected ran as independents and several were well-known former peers. There was, however, another aspect to this election. This was the apparent tendency of the electorate to turn away from the party in power. This appears to have been a natural tendency throughout the occupation period, perhaps because the party in power was, inevitably, more the agent of the occupation than the master of Japanese destinies and thus was likely to receive the blame for what was unpopular but little credit for what met with public approval. In any case, the

Socialists topped the popular vote of the Liberals and won 46 seats in the House of Councillors, to 40 for the latter.

This last tendency became even clearer in the election for the House of Representatives on April 25, in which the Socialists and also the Democrats (as the Progressives had been renamed) both virtually equalled the Liberals in the balloting and, because of a better distribution of votes, won 143 and 131 seats respectively, to 124 for the latter. The Communists suffered a slight loss, while independents received less than a third of their 1946 vote, indicating that during the intervening year there had been a considerable clarification of political alignments among candidates and voters as well. As a result of these elections the Socialists became the plurality party, and Katayama Tetsu, the Christian head of the party, became Prime Minister on June 1, 1947, with a coalition Cabinet which included the Democrats and the small People's Cooperative Party.

The new Cabinet was the first postwar government to come in with the support of a clear majority in the House of Representatives, but it was weakened by inner cleavages, for the Socialists tended to divide into right- and left-wing factions, and neither of these had much in common with the Democrats. Moreover, the Katayama Cabinet stood in an even more anomalous position as the agent of the occupation authorities than had its conservative predecessors. As a result of growing internal strains and finally an open revolt of the left wing of his own party, Katayama resigned in February 1948 and was succeeded on

March 10 by Ashida Hitoshi, another former diplomat and at the time head of the Democrats. Ashida organized a second coalition Cabinet made up of the same three parties, but it fared even worse than that of Katayama, and finally was forced to resign in October by the defection of the Socialists, amid widespread charges of corruption.

Meanwhile, Shidehara and other former Democrats had changed allegiance to the Liberal Party, considerably enlarging its Diet support and causing it to adopt temporarily the name of Democratic Liberal Party. With this increased but still minority support, Yoshida, on October 14, 1948, again became Prime Minister and set the stage for the third major test of political sentiments in a general election held on January 23, 1949.

Since the Katayama and Ashida Cabinets had been backed by a centrist coalition, the reaction against them produced a distinct swing toward the two extremes: the Socialists lost votes to the Communists; and all the coalition parties lost votes to the Liberals. The Liberals won an outright majority of 264 seats in the House of Representatives, and the Communists obtained almost three times as many votes as they had received in the election less than two years earlier, winning 9.8 per cent of the popular vote and a total of 35 seats. The Democrats and Socialists fell to a mere 68 and 49 seats respectively, and the minor parties and independents to less than 10 per cent of the total. With this clear mandate from the people, the Yoshida Cabinet continued vigorously on into the final stages of the occupation, thus becoming the Japa-

nese government in power at the time the peace treaty
went into effect.

The tendency toward political polarization, revealed in the 1949 elections, was a dangerous trend,
but perhaps a not unnatural one under occupation
conditions. The Japanese, as they emerged from the
first shock of their defeat, were becoming increasingly
restive under foreign rule. The gradual relaxation of
American controls in the years that followed and the
end of the occupation in 1952 were major factors in
halting this trend. The Communists themselves contributed to its end by overplaying their hand. Some
cases of violence and sabotage in the summer of 1949,
generally attributed to the Communists, helped
tarnish their appeal, for the Japanese public since the
war has reacted with strong distaste to all open violence. Furthermore, on January 6, 1950, Moscow
openly censured the Communist leader, Nozaka, for
his compromising and gradualist attitude—he had even
stressed the concept of a "lovable Communist party"
—and, when in response, the Japanese Communists
took a more intransigent stand, the occupation authorities retaliated by making the government purge
the Communist leaders, thus forcing them under-
ground. The sudden invasion of South Korea by the
Communist North Korean regime on June 25, 1950,
may also have damaged the Communist cause, though
Japanese for the most part, absorbed in their own
problems, paid relatively little heed to the desperate
war being fought at their doorstep.

The violence of the anti-American riots, which swept
downtown Tokyo on May 1, 1952, as an outgrowth

of the first post-occupation May Day celebration, showed that it was indeed high time for the United States to have ended its control over Japan. With the coming of independence, it was also time for new elections, which were held on October 1, 1952. In these the Liberals lost slightly, but maintained an absolute majority of 240 seats. The Progressives, as the Democrats had again been renamed, rose to 85 seats, and the Socialists, though split in late 1951 into independent right- and left-wing parties, won a total of 111 seats, fairly evenly divided between the two groups. The Communists, however, fell to a mere 2.6 per cent of the popular vote, and for the first time won no seats in the House of Representatives.

The lifting of the purge bans, largely in 1951, had in the meantime restored Hatoyama and many other former leaders to politics. Not unnaturally, Hatoyama made a determined effort to recapture leadership of the Liberals from Yoshida, bolting the party to form his own Liberal Party in March 1953. As a result, the Diet was dissolved and new general elections were held on April 19, but Hatoyama's adherents made only small inroads into the Liberals' Diet representation. Although the Progressives lost slightly and the two Socialist parties made small gains, the general Diet balance was little changed, and Yoshida thus remained in the saddle.

Hatoyama's next bid for power proved more successful. In November 1954, he reorganized the smaller of the two conservative parties, once again under the name of Democrats. The Liberals then made an effort to unite all the conservatives under the leader-

ship of the veteran politician Ogata. When this failed
and Ogata threatened to desert Yoshida, the latter,
already discredited by government scandals, resigned
in December 1954, passing on the Prime Ministership
at last to Hatoyama, who at once called for new
elections. Held on February 27, 1955, these made the
Democrats for the first time the plurality party. The
Liberals lost about half of their Diet seats, while
the two Socialist parties again registered small
gains.

As independents and minor parties gradually faded
out of the picture, Japanese politics settled down to
a four-way split between the two Socialist and two
conservative parties. There were obvious advantages
in unification for both the Socialist and the conservative camps, and it was a foregone conclusion that, if
one succeeded, the other would be forced to follow
suit. The Socialists, on October 13, 1955, were the
first to achieve this goal, and a month later, on November 15, the conservatives coalesced into the Liberal-Democratic Party. Prime Minister Hatoyama
continued as Prime Minister and was elected the first
President of the party the next spring.

One of Hatoyama's major aims while in office was
that of clarifying Japan's amorphous position with the
Soviet Union. When the latter in December 1955
again vetoed Japan's candidacy for membership in the
United Nations, as it had on previous occasions, this
re-emphasized the fact that no peace settlement had
as yet been made between the two countries. Hatoyama set out to correct this situation, managing to
obtain a fisheries agreement with the Russians in May

1956, and, eventually, on October 19, relations were normalized between the two countries through the issuance of a joint statement. This, however, was by no means a full settlement. The chief stumbling block was the Kurile Islands. While the Japanese had renounced all claims to them in the earlier peace treaty, they demanded the return of certain small islands off the coast of Hokkaido, which they insisted were not part of the Kuriles. They also maintained, with much validity, that some of the southern Kurile islands, by all rights of discovery and development, really belonged to Japan. Japanese resentment of the Soviet Union also ran high on other counts. The latter had been slow in returning Japanese prisoners of war, and many thousands never came back, presumably the victims of conditions in Siberian prison camps. Following the settlement, however, the Soviet Union did not again veto Japan's membership in the United Nations when it once more came up in December 1956, and a small but growing trade also developed, following the signing of a treaty of commerce in December 1957.

Hatoyama's health meanwhile had failed, and this together with general dissatisfaction, because his handling of the negotiations with the Soviets had left the issue of the northern islands unsettled, forced him to resign in December 1956. Since his most obvious successor, Ogata, had died earlier in the year, a sharp struggle ensued over party leadership, from which Ishibashi Tanzan emerged victorious, but he almost immediately fell ill, and his chief rival, Kishi Nobusuke, soon succeeded him, becoming Prime Minister on February 25, 1957.

Kishi, an ex-bureaucrat, handled the factional divisions within his party with skill, and, when he held general elections on May 22, 1958, the results proved satisfactory to the conservatives. It is true that the Socialists again scored slight gains in popular votes and Diet seats, but the Liberal-Democrats emerged with a strong majority of 61.5 per cent of the seats in the House of Representatives.

Problems, however, were building up for Kishi beneath the surface. The unification of the hitherto divided conservative and Socialist groups had, of course, accentuated the confrontation between left and right, not just in politics but in society as a whole. Moreover, as the years after the peace treaty lengthened, the advocates of neutralism or of a pro-Communist alignment had become increasingly indignant at the continued defense relationship with the United States and the presence in Japan of American bases and large numbers of American military men. Concomitantly, they had become increasingly insistent that Japan establish close relations not just with the free world but with the Communist powers as well. Hatoyama's settlement with the Soviet Union had been designed in part to meet these demands, but Communist China remained the real problem.

Whatever the regime might be that ruled China's vast continental mass, the Japanese people have tended to look on China itself with romanticism and warmth as the source of their civilization—as their Greece and Rome. This attitude has been compounded by a sense of guilt over their wartime misdeeds in China,

plus a corresponding tendency to overlook the un-
pleasant and to lavish praise on accomplishments which
in Japan itself would be considered substandard.

Another factor has been the lure of the hundreds
of millions of theoretically potential customers next
door to Japan—a lure once felt by much more distant
Americans. Japanese businessmen, particularly those
in the less prosperous fields, have constantly kept hop-
ing that deft political maneuvering might somehow
open these supposedly lush new pastures. The Chinese
Communists, however, by their own doctrinaire
obtuseness, did much to destroy the illusion. Seizing
on a minor incident, in which a rightist youth in May
1958 tore down a Chinese Communist flag in Nagasaki, they immediately cut off all trade with Japan
in the hope of exerting a favorable influence on the
election that month. The Communists were instead
the losers both politically and economically. Subsequently, trade crept back; but limited by the Chinese
Communists' lack of foreign exchange or acceptable
trade goods, it has grown only slowly.

Nonetheless, strong desires for the normalization of
relations with continental China (the Japanese maintain full diplomatic and flourishing trade relations with
the Government of the Republic of China on Formosa) remain second only to the opposition to the defense relationship with the United States as the most
bitterly contended issue between the left and the conservatives. This fact was dramatically illustrated when,
in March 1959, Asanuma, the belligerent Secretary
General of the Socialist Party, publicly agreed with the

Chinese Communists that "American imperialism" was the "common enemy" of the Chinese and Japanese peoples.

An incident that seriously exacerbated anti-American feelings had occurred back on March 1, 1954, when fall-out from American nuclear tests at Bikini atoll brought injury and apparently subsequent death to a crew member of a Japanese fishing vessel, the No. 5 *Fukuryu-maru.* The Japanese public reacted with outrage and, with some lack of proportion, linked the incident with the wartime bombings of Hiroshima and Nagasaki as the third nuclear attack on mankind. Annual meetings held at Hiroshima on August 6, the anniversary of the dropping of the first atom bomb, also grew in these years into mammoth protests against nuclear testing by the United States (the activities of the Soviet Union in this regard were conveniently overlooked) and were expanded into general attacks on the United States and Japan's free-world ties.

Meanwhile troubles around American bases were becoming more numerous and intense. Many demonstrations were occasioned by the military accidents, personal incidents or traffic mishaps that almost inevitably occur around large military establishments, and others were the product of labor disputes between the American military authorities and the Japanese workers they hired. The most severe clashes, however, resulted from disputes over land with embattled Japanese farmers, backed by militant leftist demonstrators from the cities. Some disputes were over maneuver or bomb areas, but the worst concerned the extension of runways to accommodate larger and faster jet planes, as in the case of the protracted struggle at the Tachikawa Air Base in the western suburbs of Tokyo, which started in September 1955.

Both the Japanese and American authorities realized that there was need to revise the defense arrangements between the two countries. These, signed the same day in 1951 as the peace treaty, had been the product of a time when Japan was not yet independent. Since that time, many things had changed: Japan had been building up its own defense forces and was gradually returning to a position of full equality with other nations. Thus, in September 1958, the two governments announced their intention to revise the Security Treaty and after protracted negotiations signed the new document on January 19, 1960.

The new Treaty of Mutual Security and Cooperation had many advantages for Japan over the agreement it was to supersede. It and its attendant documents and statements made clear that the United States would seek the agreement of the Japanese government before using its bases in Japan directly for combat elsewhere in Asia, as had happened during the Korean War, or before introducing nuclear weapons into Japan. It also put a limit of ten years on the agreement, after which either party could denounce it. It might have been thought that the Japanese leftists would have welcomed these new and substantial limitations on the Japanese-American defense relationship, but instead they argued that it was worse than the previous treaty in that the Japanese government and people shared in responsibility for it, whereas they had not been responsible for the earlier treaty, which had

been "forced" on Japan before it had regained its independence. The left, therefore, prepared for an all-
out battle to prevent ratification.

Since the Liberal-Democrats held a solid majority
in the Diet, the leftist challenge over the Security
Treaty might have amounted to only one of the many
turbulent but minor incidents in Japan's postwar
history, had it not been for several other coincidental
factors. On May 1, 1960, an American U-2 plane was
downed deep in Soviet territory, and the Kremlin in-
dignantly responded by calling off a planned summit
meeting between President Eisenhower and Khru-
shchev. The Japanese public reacted with sharp
disappointment, and the debate over the defense
alignment with the United States became all the more
bitter.

Still more unfortunate was the proposed visit of
President Eisenhower to Japan, scheduled for June
19, 1960. Probably wishing to have the treaty ratified
by that date, Kishi decided to hold a sudden surprise
vote on ratification in the House of Representatives
in the early morning hours of May 20 so that the treaty
would go into effect 30 days later even if the House
of Councillors failed to act. Since the Socialists had
been trying every possible delaying tactic, including
the boycotting of sessions and the demanding of more
time to debate the issue, both the opposition and the
general public decided that Kishi had "rammed
through" the treaty by un-Constitutional or at least
"undemocratic" methods. Even some of his party deserted him. Two of the faction leaders, who had been
trying to get Kishi to promise to resign the party Presi-

dency, had not been consulted on the vote decision and as a consequence refused to support ratification.

Although Kishi did succeed in clearing the chief legal hurdle to ratification on the night of May 19-20, he had in the process aroused popular indignation to the point of explosion. To the anti-treaty clamor was added an even louder din against Kishi himself and a rising crescendo against the visit of President Eisenhower. Many sincere believers in democracy felt that they must come out into the streets to oppose Kishi for what they believed was "undemocratic" conduct in not permitting the opposition to air its views fully on an important controversial issue. And many people essentially friendly to the United States voiced opposition to the American President's visit, since in their minds it had become entangled with the debate over ratification and therefore seemed to them to constitute outside intervention in domestic politics. The powerful press, which together with television is the chief molder of Japanese public opinion, was almost unanimous in its condemnation of Kishi, further fanning the excitement.

The Communists and other extreme leftist elements quickly seized the opportunity to make up for past losses. Throwing their funds and efforts wholeheartedly into the cause, they did their best to build up the combined anti-treaty, anti-Kishi, anti-visit fervor into a revolutionary upheaval, and large masses of the urban public responded for the first time to these leftist-led causes. The leaders of the Zengakuren, the association of student self-government bodies, who were usually so far left that they regarded Communists as old-fogies, found that their normally more apathetic fellow students were ready to follow them by the thousands in riotous, snake-dancing demonstrations. The members of labor unions, sometimes encouraged by Communist pay, poured forth into the streets, but so also did housewives and shopkeepers, university professors and Christian leaders.

By May 26 the throngs of demonstrators in downtown Tokyo reached about 100,000. When Hagerty, Eisenhower's Press Secretary, arrived on June 10 at Haneda Airport in Tokyo, to make advance preparation for the presidential visit, he was surrounded in his car by Communist workers and students and had to escape by helicopter. But for all their vast numbers and charged emotions, the Japanese demonstrators remained extraordinarily good-tempered and orderly compared to mobs in most other countries. Individual Americans moved about in the streets without fear, little property was destroyed, and injuries, usually occasioned by clashes between the Zengakuren zealots and the police, were relatively few and largely superficial. Only one fatality occurred when, on the night of June 15, during the most massive and violent of the demonstrations, a girl student of Tokyo University was trampled to death in the confusion. But the demonstrations were nonetheless effective in intimidating and paralyzing the government. Humiliated and fearful, it requested President Eisenhower on June 16 to cancel his visit. The action taken on the morning of May 20, however, insured that ratification of the treaty would automatically take effect on June 19, and, once that date was past, the vast disturbance subsided even more rapidly than it had arisen.

During the rioting of May and June, it had seemed to many that Japanese democracy was doomed and that Japan itself was tottering on the brink of chaos. But strangely enough, this most turbulent stretch of water in postwar Japanese politics was followed by an ever lengthening period of calmer sailing—calmer in fact than anything Japan had experienced in many a decade. Japan seemed to be entering on a new phase in its postwar history.

There appear to be many reasons for the quick shift in popular mood that followed the 1960 disturbances. For one thing, the less urbanized parts of Japan had remained quite calm throughout the turmoil. The disturbances had been a phenomenon of the big cities, where leftist attitudes were most concentrated. More important, the Japanese public as a whole had some serious second thoughts. Many who had bitterly opposed what they felt were "undemocratic" actions by Kishi came to realize that violent public demonstrations were not the right corrective. And almost all but the extreme leftists realized that mass rioting was a dangerous way to achieve political decisions. The newspapers, too, appear to have engaged in some serious "self-reflection." In their long history since the 1870's, they had always played the role of public critic against a usually all-powerful government. Not until 1960 did they realize that, with the termination of the occupation in 1952, the situation had changed completely. The government was relatively weak and easily buffeted about by public opinion, which the newspapers did so much to shape. Ever since the 1960 demonstrations, the Japanese press seems to have taken a more balanced and constructive tone in its criticism of public policy.

Most important of all were two related long-range changes within Japan, which had been going on behind the confrontation of conservatives and leftists in the late 1950's and became increasingly apparent after 1960. One was the gradual freeing of the Japanese psyche from the aftermath of the war and occupation; the other, Japan's obvious and tremendous economic success. Prosperity undercut leftist predictions of economic catastrophe, diverted popular attention from the promised panacea of revolution to the enjoyment of immediate pleasures, and poured soothing oil on strife between labor and management. Japan's worst postwar labor dispute at the Miike coal mines in Kyushu was settled on November 1, 1960, when the striking miners were forced to bow to the inevitable rationalization and cutback of coal mining in the face of cheap fuel oil from the Middle East. Increasingly, unions discovered that there was much more to be gained from peaceful bargaining over wage increases, made possible by a burgeoning economy, than from demonstrating in the streets for remote and doctrinaire political objectives.

Another factor in the rapid calming of the situation after the security treaty riots was that Kishi was followed by a man who adapted his policies well to the post-demonstration mood and the changing times. Everyone agreed that Kishi could not continue as

Prime Minister, and the choice as successor went to Ikeda Hayato, another ex-bureaucrat, originally from the Finance Ministry, and a protégé of Yoshida. Ikeda, who became Prime Minister on July 15, 1960, announced that he would take a "low posture," by which he meant he would be more heedful of public opinion and pay more respect to opposition views. He apparently hoped that by avoiding sharp political clashes he could build a broader national consensus. It was to be the strategy of the tortoise rather than the hare. He also adopted with much fanfare a popular, noncontroversial policy of doubling Japanese incomes within ten years. This was not an unrealistic goal, in view of Japan's rapid rate of economic growth, and one well-fitted to Ikeda's own reputation as a highly successful former Minister of Finance.

The general elections which Ikeda held on November 20, 1960, showed that the uproar the preceding spring had done the Liberal-Democratic Party no permanent harm. It emerged with 57.6 per cent of the popular vote, almost exactly the same figure as in 1958, and a small increase in Diet seats to 63.4 per cent. The Communist popular vote remained low at 2.9 per cent, while the Socialists, though showing a clear gain in popular votes from 32.9 to 36.3 per cent, fell off slightly in Diet seats, because of the division of the party that had taken place the previous January.

Strengthened by the results of the election, Ikeda started to pursue a policy of enhancing Japan's international position and emphasizing her equality with the United States. The public naturally found this gratifying.

Already in 1955 Japan had been admitted into the General Agreement on Tariffs and Trade (GATT) and the next year had been accepted into the United Nations. It had also settled its wartime accounts with its neighbors by agreeing to sizable reparations payments, the first to Burma in 1954, then the Philippines in 1956, Indonesia in 1958, and Vietnam in 1959. Ikeda, however, pushed on far beyond this small beginning. In June 1961, despite considerable leftist opposition, he settled Japan's debt of occupation days to the United States (the so-called GARIOA or Government and Relief in Occupied Areas) by agreeing to pay back $490,000,000, or about one-third of the original sum, on much the same terms as an earlier German settlement of a similar debt. The same month, he agreed with President Kennedy in Washington on the formation of a United States–Japan Committee on Trade and Economic Affairs, made up of members of the two cabinets, which held its first annual meeting in Japan the next November. Out of such activities grew what the Japanese public termed a "mood of equality" with the United States, and the close relationship between the two countries came increasingly to be described as a "partnership."

Visiting Europe in the autumn of 1962, Ikeda declared Japan to be one of the "three pillars" of the free world. In the spring of 1963 the Foreign Ministers of both the United Kingdom and France visited Japan for the first time in history and that autumn the President as well as the Foreign Minister of the Federal Republic of Germany. In July 1963 Japan was officially invited to become a full member of the Organization

for Economic Cooperation and Development (OECD)
—the only non-European member, besides the United
States and Canada, of this club of the economically advanced nations.

In October 1961, against strong leftist opposition, Ikeda reopened negotiations for the normalization of relations with South Korea, Japan's nearest
neighbor, promising large-scale grants as well as loans,
though unsettled political conditions in South Korea
made the final conclusion of an agreement a painfully
protracted matter. He also asserted Japan's duty to go
beyond reparations and normal commercial loans in
aiding the developing economies of South Asia. At
home, the government led the public toward a growing realization that military defense was only common
sense in a hostilely divided and heavily armed world,
while the Self-Defense Forces won increasing popular
acceptance.

As a result of all this, Japan's non-Communist
neighbors have begun to look toward her with respect
and hope for economic aid; the people of the West,
and particularly Americans, have come to accept
Japan as one of the leading nations of the free world,
and in the United States there has been a veritable
"boom" for all things Japanese, especially in the fields
of photographic equipment, electronics, architecture,
and interior decorating; and, most important, the
Japanese themselves have begun to feel a long overdue
sense of national pride and self-confidence.

The Communists and Socialists, who had seemed
to gain greatly from the security treaty demonstrations, saw these apparent advances melt away. The

division of the Socialists which had occurred before the demonstrations, was a weakening factor. For some time the right-wing faction had been losing out to the leftists, and finally Nishio, the right-wing leader, unable to tolerate longer the party's fellow-traveling tendencies and its failure to take an unequivocal stand for parliamentary democracy, had bolted and had formed the Democratic Socialist Party on January 24, 1960. While many of the rightist Socialists, including the veteran Christian leader, Kawakami, refused to join Nishio, the Democratic Socialist defection, backed as it was by the Zenro unions, cut seriously into the Socialist vote. Even though the 8.7 per cent of the popular vote won by the Democratic Socialists in the November 1960 elections gained them only 17 seats, it reduced the vote of the main Socialist Party to a mere 27.5 per cent.

Moreover, the Socialists continued to be troubled by policy and leadership disputes. On October 12, 1960, a fanatical rightist youth, in full view of the television cameras of the world, stabbed the leftist leader Asanuma to death. In the midst of these difficulties and in an effort to soothe party differences, the right-wing leader Kawakami was elected Chairman in March 1961. The moderate Secretary General, Eda, however, stirred up great controversy by his advocacy of "structural reform"—by which he meant the achievement of "socialism" by gradual democratic evolution, rather than by revolutionary change—and by his "vision" of a society harmonizing with the high, leveled-up living standards of the United States, the Soviet Union's thoroughgoing social security system, British parliamentary democracy, and Japan's own "peace constitution." Eventually in November 1962 the left wing of the party forced the replacement of Eda by Narita, a more doctrinaire Marxist.

Developments in the outside world seemed almost as injurious to the political philosophy of the extreme left as prosperity at home. The rift between Communist China and the Soviet Union was naturally embarrassing for the Japanese Communists and in some ways was even more upsetting for Communist-leaning Socialists, who tend to sympathize intellectually with the Russians but emotionally with the Chinese. The invasion of India by the Chinese Communists in the autumn of 1962 further embarrassed the left, as did also the insistence of the Chinese Communists on developing their own nuclear capacity. This heightened the division in the popular anti-nuclear-testing movement between the Socialists, who included in their condemnations the Communist countries along with the United States, and the Communists, who would brook no word of criticism of "good" nuclear powers.

All this does not mean that there has been an end to the slow drift of the voters toward the left. The elections for the House of Councillors in July 1962 and the local elections of the spring of 1963 indicated that this trend still continued, despite the obvious drift of Japanese attitudes in the opposite direction.

Another point of interest in these two elections was the strong showing of Soka Gakkai—a militant recent offshoot of the Nichiren Sect of Buddhism—which demonstrated that it exercised disciplined control over a bloc of several million votes. Soka Gakkai has been the most successful of a great number of "new religions" which have prospered during the past century but particularly since the war, obviously meeting certain spiritual and social needs within Japanese society, particularly among the lower classes. Soka Gakkai's successes in these two elections may presage the rise of an important new factor in politics. Many Japanese political analysts, however, feel that it is likely to lose its original religious cohesiveness if it attempts to go more deeply into politics and that therefore its political influence will probably level off.

It is perhaps significant that, in the general election Ikeda called for November 21, 1963, the Soka Gakkai prudently refrained from running candidates. Another even more interesting point revealed by this election was that the shift of voting from the conservative to the leftist side might be slowing down. If one combines the votes and seats won by the Liberal-Democratic Party with those of the independents and minor parties, which are almost all as conservative as the Liberal-Democrats, the decline between 1960 and 1963 for the conservatives was only from 302 to 295 in Diet seats and from 60.8 to 59.6 per cent in popular votes—a rate of annual decline in the latter category of less than half that of earlier years.

Another feature of the November 1963 election was a slight shift in the distribution of the leftist vote and Diet seats. On the right, the Democratic Socialist Party, while losing slightly in popular votes—partly because they ran far fewer candidates than in 1960—

increased their seats from 17 to 23. On the extreme left, the Communists increased their share of the total vote from 2.9 to 4 per cent and their seats from 3 to 5. Between these two, the Socialists, while increasing their popular vote somewhat, in part because of an expanded list of candidates, dropped from 145 to 144 seats. These results suggest the possibility of a gradual polarization of the leftist vote, as it becomes increasingly difficult to straddle the issue between the pro-Communist stand of the extreme left and the staunch support for parliamentary democracy of the moderate left.

Ikeda, who was re-elected for a second two-year term as Party President in July, 1962, had reason to be satisfied not only with his party's victory in the general election of November 1963 but also with the continued smooth political sailing he was encountering. But Japan naturally still faces many serious problems. One of the most dangerous is the continuing division and distrust between large elements within the population, despite the effort to achieve a greater national consensus. As compared with the United States or some of the countries of Western Europe, the cleavages run much deeper in Japan between generations, between occupational groups, and between political parties.

Japan also faces serious economic problems, for all its great and sustained economic growth. As the Japanese realize, they will have to put a much larger part of the nation's resources into housing, roads, and other forms of social overhead than they have in the past. There is also a long way to go in smoothing out the relations between labor and management. Most important, Japan, with its heavy dependence on foreign imports, can develop its domestic economy no more rapidly than it can expand its foreign markets. And since the rest of the world is growing more slowly than Japan, this is not easy to do at the desired rate. The proportion of Japanese exports going to the United States is in some ways unwisely high. The rate of economic growth in most of the less developed countries is so slow that markets there increase very little. Even for those who wish to trade with the Communist countries, their trade practices and poverty have proved discouraging. Only Western Europe seems to hold promise of any rapid expansion of trade.

Japan's most serious problems, however, lie in the area of her political relations with the outside world. Trade with Communist China and the Soviet Union remains more significant as a political than as an economic problem. Japan is only beginning to feel her way toward a new relationship with the less developed countries of Asia as a primary supplier of economic aid and technological guidance. And the defense relationship with the United States, though more generally accepted than some years ago, remains the most divisive issue in Japanese politics.

One particularly difficult aspect of this last problem is presented by the Ryukyu Islands, or Okinawa, as they are commonly called after the largest of the islands. The Ryukyus are inhabited by 900,000 Japanese-speaking people who were controlled by Japan ever since the early seventeenth century and who consider themselves to be Japanese. Conquered by American forces during the war in a costly campaign, the islands were subsequently built up by the United States into a major base of great importance to free-world defense, including that of Japan itself. In the peace treaty of 1952, Japan agreed to support American proposals for the assignment of the islands to the United States as a trusteeship territory under the United Nations. The United States, however, subsequently abandoned this scheme, publicly recognized that Japan had "residual sovereignty" over the islands, and in late 1953 returned to the Japanese the northern sector of the chain. In March 1962 President Kennedy announced a policy of expanding local autonomy for the Okinawans and cooperating more fully with Japan in the promotion of their economic welfare, looking toward the day when world conditions would eventually permit the transfer of the islands back to Japan. This has proved a desirable and realistic policy for both countries, but the Ryukyus still remain a delicate problem.

Yet, while Japan faces many difficult and perplexing problems, its prospects, as one peers into the murky future, certainly give reason for optimism, particularly when compared with the prospects faced by most other nations in the world. Despite the huge population crowded onto their narrow islands, there is no reason to doubt that the Japanese will continue to enjoy rapidly rising standards of living. Despite the great new problems they, like all industrialized peoples, face, there is no reason to doubt that they can continue to deal with these adequately. Despite the turbulence of postwar politics, the Japanese have shown that they possess a relatively stable and effective democratic system, and they can be expected to continue to perfect it. Similarly optimistic statements can be made with confidence only of a handful of other nations in the world.

Perhaps the most hopeful thing about Japan today is its youth, which is well educated, energetic, forward-looking, open-minded, and free of the emotional and psychological burdens of the past. Another very hopeful factor is Japan's vigorous cultural life. There is widespread fear, not only in Japan but in many non-Western countries, that industrialization and other aspects of modernization will blot out their traditional cultures. And in the early stages of industrialization, this has often appeared to be the case. But Japan, which has gone much further in industrialization than any other non-Western country, seems to prove the contrary. To be sure, much of Japan's premodern culture has been sloughed off or drastically changed, but probably no more so than has that of the advanced countries of the West. While vastly enriching its culture by borrowing from the outside world, Japan has found new vitality in traditional traits. Industrialized and modernized Japan shows every promise of remaining a highly distinctive cultural unit in the modern world and at the same time seems to be making an almost disproportionately large contribution, particularly in the field of art, to the common world culture of the second half of the twentieth century.

A major reason for Japan's continuing great cultural distinctiveness is the language and writing system, which cut her off sharply from the rest of the world. This perhaps is a cultural blessing, but it also poses a great problem. Few foreigners are likely to learn to speak or read Japanese, so the Japanese must learn foreign languages; but, because of the distinctiveness of their tongue and the simplicity of the phonetic system, this is no easy task. English is the chosen medium for communication with the outside world, but despite prodigious efforts on the part of millions of students from the seventh grade on into university and about 60,000 full-time English teachers, the results have been meager. As a consequence, the Japanese are handicapped in almost all of their foreign contacts. The voice of the nation is much smaller in the councils of the world than it rightly should be; Japan's potential contribution of skill and know-how to the less developed countries is inhibited; businessmen find themselves at a disadvantage abroad; and the outside world learns far less about Japan than it should.

But despite this language handicap and Japan's other problems, it takes no great daring to predict that Japan will play a rapidly growing role in East Asia and the whole world. As the only major industrialized area outside of Europe and North America and the world's fastest growing economy, Japan obviously has a significant economic contribution to make. Surrounded largely by deficit economic areas, the way it uses its growing economic surplus may prove decisive for the future of that part of the world. Already providing the bases for a major bastion of free-world defense, Japan's economic potential is also likely to become an increasingly important factor in the world balance of power. And most important of all, Japan's brilliant success with a free economy and democratic institutions is almost sure to exert great and possibly decisive influence on the ideological contest in Asia.

If one looks back to 1952, when Japan rewon its independence, and sees how far it has come since then, especially as compared with the other countries of Asia, one can perceive how much greater Japan's relative weight will have become by the 1970's. While the world's attention remains drawn toward the more spectacular events in Southeast Asia and riveted on the unfolding drama of Communist China, as it desperately struggles to reassert the dominant position the vast population of China once held in East Asia, more humdrum and only half-noticed developments in Japan may do more toward shaping the future of that whole part of the world than anything that happens in China or Southeast Asia.

CHRONOLOGY

(The division between years prior to 1868 is according to the lunar calendar.)

660 B.C. Traditional date of accession of first emperor, Jimmu.

c. 1–100 A.D. Invasions of West Japan by Yamato people from Korea.

97–113 Traditional dates of conquests by Yamato Takeru no Mikoto (perhaps to be dated around 230).

200 Traditional date of invasion of Korea by Empress Jingo (perhaps reflecting events around 360).

285 Traditional date of introduction of writing from Korea (perhaps to be corrected to 405).

527 Revolt in Kyushu preventing dispatch of army to protect Japanese holdings in Korea.

552 (or 538) Official introduction of Buddhism from Korea to the Japanese court, where it was supported by the Soga family and opposed by the Mononobe and Nakatomi families.

562 Conquest of the Japanese holdings in Korea by Silla.

587 Destruction of the Mononobe family by Soga Umako.

592–628 Reign of the Empress Suiko.

593–622 Regency of Prince Shotoku, founder of Horyuji and other Buddhist monasteries.

604 Seventeen-article "Constitution" of Prince Shotoku.

607 Dispatch of Ono Imoko on first embassy to Sui dynasty of China.

630 First embassy to T'ang dynasty.

645 Taika *coup d'état* and destruction of Soga Iruka and the

Soga family by Prince Naka no Oe and Nakatomi Kamatari.

663 Defeat of Japanese army in Korea and destruction of ally Paekche by Silla and T'ang.

661–71 Reign of Tenchi, the former Prince Naka no Oe.

669 Granting of surname Fujiwara to Kamatari before his death.

697 Abdication of Empress Jito in favor of fifteen-year-old grandson Mommu.

702 Taiho Law Code.

708 First issuance of copper coinage.

710 Founding of Heijo capital (Nara).

710–84 NARA PERIOD.

712 Compilation of *Kojiki*.

713 Compilation of *Fudoki* (local gazetteers).

718 Yoro revision of law code.

720 Compilation of *Nihon Shoki*.

724–49 Reign of Shomu (d. 756).

729–49 Tempyo year period.

735 Return of Kibi no Mabi from China (went 716).

740 Revolt of Fujiwara Hirotsugu in protest against influence of the monk Gembo.

741 Establishment of Kokubunji (official provincial monasteries).

752 Dedication of Great Buddha (Daibutsu) of Nara.

754 Arrival of Chinese monk Ganjin (Chien-chen) and propagation of Ritsu (Rules) Sect.

c. 759 Compilation of *Man'yoshu*.

764 Defeat and death of Prime Minister, Fujiwara Nakamaro (Emi no Oshikatsu), and his replacement by the monk Dokyo; replacement of Emperor Junnin by Shotoku, the former Empress Koken.

770 Death of Shotoku and exile of Dokyo.

781–806 Reign of Kammu.

784 Move of the capital to Nagaoka.

794 Founding of Heian capital (Kyoto).

794–1185 HEIAN PERIOD.

801 Defeat of the Ainu in northern Honshu by Sakanoue Tamuramaro.

804 Eleventh embassy to T'ang (accompanied by the monks Saicho and Kukai).
805 Introduction of Tendai Sect by Saicho (Dengyo Daishi) with headquarters at Enryakuji on Mt. Hiei.
806 Introduction of Shingon Sect by Kukai (Kobo Daishi).
810 Founding of Kurodo-dokoro (Bureau of Archivists).
816 Founding of Kongobuji on Mt. Koya by Kukai.
838 Twelfth and last embassy to T'ang (accompanied by the monk Ennin).
857–72 Fujiwara Yoshifusa as Prime Minister.
859–77 Jogan year period.
866 Yoshifusa as first Regent not of the imperial family.

866–1160 FUJIWARA PERIOD.
872 Fujiwara Mototsune as Regent.
887 Mototsune as first Chancellor (Kampaku).
889 Granting of surname Taira (Heike) to Takamochi, great-grandson of Emperor Kammu and progenitor of warrior Taira family.
891 Death of Mototsune; Emperor Uda's refusal to appoint a successor and utilization of Sugawara Michizane in attempt to diminish Fujiwara power.
894 Appointment of Michizane as Ambassador to T'ang (embassy subsequently dropped).
901 Removal of Michizane to a post in Kyushu by Fujiwara Tokihira.
901–23 Engi year period.
905 Compilation of *Kokinshu* by Ki no Tsurayuki and others.
930–49 Fujiwara Tadahira as Regent and Chancellor.
939–40 Revolt and execution of Taira Masakado in the Kanto.
941 Execution of Fujiwara Sumitomo, pirate chief in the Inland Sea.
946–67 Reign of Murakami, after 949 without Regent, Chancellor, or Prime Minister.
951 Establishment of Waka-dokoro (Poetry Commission).
961 Granting of surname Minamoto (Genji) to Tsunemoto, grandson of Emperor Seiwa (858–76) and progenitor of warrior Minamoto family.
967 Appointment of Fujiwara Saneyori, reestablishing prac-

tice of appointing Fujiwara Regents, Chancellors, and Prime Ministers.

995–1027 Supremacy of Fujiwara Michinaga.

c. 1002 Writing of *Makura no Soshi* (*Pillow Book*) by Lady Sei Shonagon.

c. 1008–20 Writing of *Genji Monogatari* (*Tale of Genji*) by Lady Murasaki.

1017–68 Fujiwara Yorimichi as Regent and Chancellor.

1051–62 Earlier Nine Years' War: destruction of Abe family of northern Honshu by Minamoto Yoriyoshi.

1053 Construction of Byodoin by Yorimichi.

1068–72 Reign of Go-Sanjo (d. 1073).

1069 Establishment of Kirokujo (Records Office to check the growth of manors).

1072–86 Reign of Shirakawa.

1074 Burning of Onjoji by monks of Enryakuji.

1083–7 Later Three Years' War: destruction of Kiyowara family of northern Honshu by Minamoto Yoshiie.

1086–1129 Establishment by Shirakawa of Insei (rule by a retired emperor).

1107–23 Reign of Toba.

1129–56 Insei of Toba.

1156 Hogen War: destruction of most leading Minamoto, including Tameyoshi, by Taira Kiyomori and Tameyoshi's son, Yoshitomo; exile of retired emperor Sutoku, execution of Minister of the Left Fujiwara Yorinaga, and triumph at court of their rivals, Go-Shirakawa (reigned 1155–8) and Chancellor Fujiwara Tadamichi.

1159–60 Heiji War: destruction of Minamoto Yoshitomo and Fujiwara Nobuyori by Taira Kiyomori (d. 1181) and his son Shigemori (d. 1179).

1160–85 TAIRA PERIOD.

1167 Kiyomori as Prime Minister.

1175 Founding of the Jodo (Pure Land) Sect by Genku (Honen Shonin).

1180–5 War between the Minamoto and Taira (Gempei Wars).

1184 Death in battle of Minamoto Yoshinaka.

1185 Destruction of the Taira and death of the child emperor Antoku in the naval battle of Dannoura (third month).

1185–1333 KAMAKURA PERIOD.

1185 Establishment of Shugo (Constable) and Jito (Steward) system by Minamoto Yoritomo (eleventh month).

1189 Execution in northern Honshu by Fujiwara Yasuhira of Minamoto Yoshitsune on orders of his brother Yoritomo; destruction of Yasuhira by Yoritomo.

1191 Introduction of the Rinzai branch of the Zen Sect from China by Eisai.

1192 Assumption of title of Shogun by Yoritomo.

1199 Death of Yoritomo and assumption of control by his wife Hojo Masako and her father Tokimasa.

1203 Deposition of Shogun Yoriie (murdered 1204) in favor of his brother Sanetomo and assumption of post of Shikken (Shogunal Regent) by Tokimasa.

1205 Elimination of Tokimasa by his daughter and his son Yoshitoki and latter's assumption of post of Shikken.

1206 Compilation of *Shinkokinshu* by the poet Fujiwara Teika and others.

1219 Murder of Sanetomo and end of main Minamoto line.

1221 Shokyu Disturbance: suppression of a revolt in Kyoto against Kamakura inspired by the retired emperor Go-Toba (reigned 1183–98); appointment of two Shogunal governors at Rokuhara in Kyoto (Rokuhara Tandai).

1224–42 Hojo Yasutoki as Shikken.

1224 Founding of Shin (True Pure Land) Sect by Shinran.

1225 Death of Oe Hiromoto, Kyoto scholar who helped organize the Kamakura Shogunate.

1226 Selection of Fujiwara Yoritsune as Shogun.

1227 Introduction of Soto branch of Zen from China by Dogen.

1232 Issuance of *Joei Shikimoku* (Kamakura law code).

1246–56 Hojo Tokiyori (d. 1263) as Shikken.

1252 Selection of an imperial prince as Shogun.

1253 Founding of Lotus or Nichiren Sect by Nichiren.

1268–84 Hojo Tokimune as Shikken.

1274 First Mongol invasion.

1281 Second Mongol invasion.

1318–39 Reign of Go-Daigo.

1331 Revolt and deposition of Go-Daigo.

1333 Desertion to Go-Daigo of Kamakura general, Ashikaga Takauji; capture and destruction of Kamakura by Nitta Yoshisada.

1335 Revolt of Takauji against Go-Daigo.
1336 Enthronement of rival emperor by Takauji; death in battle of Go-Daigo's supporter, Kusunoki Masashige; flight of Go-Daigo to Yoshino.

1336–92 YOSHINO PERIOD (*or* PERIOD OF THE NORTHERN AND SOUTHERN COURTS).
1338 Assumption of title of Shogun by Takauji.

1338–1573 ASHIKAGA (*or* MUROMACHI) PERIOD.
1339 Writing of *Jinno Shotoki* by Kitabatake Chikafusa (d. 1354).
1349–67 Ashikaga Motouji as first Kanto Kanryo.
1358–67 Shogunate of Yoshiakira.
1367–98 Ujimitsu as Kanto Kanryo.
1368–94 Shogunate of Yoshimitsu (d. 1408).
1384 Death of Kan'ami, developer of the *Nō*.
1392 Reunion of northern and southern courts.
1394–1428 Oei year period.
1394–1423 Shogunate of Yoshimochi (d. 1428).
1397 Building of Kinkakuji by Yoshimitsu.
1429–41 Shogunate of Yoshinori.
1439 Suicide of Mochiuji, the Kanto Kanryo since 1410, when besieged by the Shogun's forces, after being denounced by Uesugi Norizane; compilation of *Shinzoku-kokinshu*, last of the twenty-one imperial anthologies of poetry.
1441 Assassination of the Shogun by Akamatsu Mitsusuke.
1444 Death of Zeami, perfector of the *Nō*.
1449 (or 1443)–1473 Shogunate of Yoshimasa (Yoshishige, d. 1490).
1467–77 Wars of Onin.
1473 Deaths of Yamana Sozen and Hosokawa Katsumoto, leaders of the rival factions in Wars of Onin.
1483 Construction of Ginkakuji by Yoshimasa.
1488 Seizure of power in provinces of Kaga and Echizen by members of Shin Sect (*Ikko-ikki*).
1493 Expulsion from Kyoto of Shogun Yoshitane by Hosokawa Masamoto (assassinated 1507) and his replacement the next year by Yoshizumi (Yoshitaka).
1495 Adoption of surname Hojo by Ise Nagauji (Soun), leading daimyo of Kanto (d. 1519).

1499 Death of Rennyo, eighth head of Shin Sect.

1506 Death of the painter monk Sesshu.

1508 Restoration of Yoshitane as Shogun by Ouchi Yoshioki.

1521 Official enthronement of Go-Kashiwabara, postponed since 1500 because of lack of funds; substitution of Yoshiharu as Shogun for Yoshitane forced by Hosokawa Takakuni.

1532–58 Tembun year period.

1538 Establishment of mastery over the Kanto by Hojo Ujitsuna.

1542 (or 1543) Arrival of Portuguese at Tanegashima and introduction of firearms.

1549 Arrival of St. Francis Xavier in Kyushu and start of Christian missionary movement by the Jesuits.

1557 Destruction of Ouchi family by Mori Motonari (d. 1571).

1560 Official enthronement (delayed since 1557) of Ogimachi paid for by Motonari.

1565 Assassination of Yoshiteru (Yoshifuji), Shogun since 1546, by Matsunaga Hisahide.

1568 Seizure of Kyoto by Oda Nobunaga, daimyo of Owari.

1571 Start of Nagasaki as port of foreign trade under patronage of local daimyo, Omura Sumitada (converted to Christianity in 1562); destruction by Nobunaga of military might of Enryakuji.

1573 Death of Takeda Harunobu (Shingen), great warrior of East Japan; imprisonment of last Shogun Yoshiaki by Nobunaga and end of Ashikaga Shogunate.

1573–92 Tensho year period.

1576 Transfer of Nobunaga to his castle at Azuchi on Lake Biwa.

1578 Death of Uesugi Terutora (Kenshin), great opponent of Takeda Shingen; conversion of Otomo Yoshishige (Sorin) of North Kyushu, first great daimyo to become a Christian.

1579 Arrival of Vicar-General Valignano.

1580 Negotiated surrender of the Osaka castle-monastery of Shin Sect to Nobunaga after years of unsuccessful sieges.

1582 Assassination of Nobunaga by Akechi Mitsuhide.

1583 Reconstruction of Osaka castle by Hashiba Hideyoshi, basely born former general of Nobunaga.

1585 Appointment of Hideyoshi as Chancellor.

1586 Appointment of Hideyoshi as Prime Minister and bestowal on him of surname Toyotomi.

1587 Submission of Shimazu family of Satsuma to Hideyoshi; promulgation of decree ordering the expulsion of
Christian missionaries; confiscation of the arms of the
peasantry.

1590 Destruction of Hojo family of Odawara and installa-
tion of Tokugawa Ieyasu in Edo castle as master of the
Kanto.

1592 Hideyoshi's invasion of Korea with Kato Kiyomasa and
Konishi Yukinaga as field commanders; start of missionary activity by Spanish Franciscans.

1593 Truce with Chinese armies in Korea and withdrawal
of Japanese forces to extreme south.

1595 Promulgation of tax laws by Hideyoshi.

1596–1615 Keicho year period.

1597 Resumption of Korean campaign; first executions of
European missionaries and Japanese converts.

1598 Death of Hideyoshi and withdrawal of troops from
Korea.

1600 Victory of Ieyasu at Battle of Sekigahara; arrival of
Will Adams, subsequently adviser to Ieyasu.

1600–1867 TOKUGAWA PERIOD.

1603 Assumption of title of Shogun by Ieyasu.

1605–23 Shogunate of Hidetada (d. 1632).

1606 Completion of reconstruction of Edo castle.

1609 Conquest of Ryukyu Islands by Shimazu Iehisa of Satsuma; establishment of Dutch factory at Hirado; destruction of Portuguese vessel *Nossa Senhora da Graça*
(*Madre de Deus*) in Nagasaki harbor.

1613 Establishment of English factory at Hirado; dispatch of
embassy to Rome by Date Masamune of Sendai.

1614 First siege of Osaka castle by Ieyasu; resumption of
persecution of Christianity.

1615 Second siege and capture of Osaka castle and destruction of Toyotomi family; promulgation of *Buke Shohatto*
(code for military class).

1616 Death of Ieyasu.

1617 Commencement of Nikko mausoleum.

1622–3 Period of greatest Christian martyrdoms.

1623–51 Shogunate of Iemitsu.

1623 Abandonment of Hirado factory by English.

1624–44 Kan'ei year period.

1624 Refusal of further intercourse with Spanish.

1633 Systematization of Wakadoshiyori system.

1634 Systematization of Roju system.

1635 First appointment of Jisha Bugyo and other officers; formalization of *Sankin-kotai* (alternate attendance at Shogunal court) for Tozama daimyo.

1636 Ban on Japanese travel abroad; first issuance of Kan'ei Tsuho coins.

1637–8 Shimabara Rebellion.

1638 Expulsion of Portuguese traders; first appointments of Tairo.

1641 Transfer of Dutch traders from Hirado to Deshima in Nagasaki harbor.

1642 Formalization of *Sankin-kotai* for Fudai daimyo.

1651–80 Shogunate of Ietsuna.

1651 Plot against Shogunate by Yui Shosetsu.

1657 Great Edo fire; commencement of compilation of *Dainihonshi* (*History of Japan*) by Tokugawa Mitsukuni (d. 1700) of Mito; death of Hayashi Razan (Doshun), Shogunal Confucian scholar.

1672 Death of Hoshina Masayuki (Tairo 1651–69).

1680–1709 Shogunate of Tsunayoshi.

1682 Death of Yamazaki Ansai, Shinto scholar.

1684 Assassination of Tairo, Hotta Masatoshi.

1688–1704 Genroku year period.

1691 Death of Confucian scholar Kumazawa Banzan.

1693 Death of novelist Ibara Saikaku.

1694 Death of *haiku* poet Matsuo Basho.

1698 Death of Confucian scholar Kinoshita Jun'an.

1701 Death of Keichu, monk and scholar of early Japanese literature.

1701–03 Chushingura incident ("Forty-Seven Ronin").

1703 Great Kanto earthquake.

1704 Death of Ichikawa Danjuro, first of long line of *Kabuki* actors of this name.

1705 Death of Confucian scholar Ito Jinsai.

1707 Last eruption of Mt. Fuji.

1709–12 Shogunate of Ienobu.

1713–16 Shogunate of Ietsugu.

1714 Death of Confucian scholar Kaibara Ekiken; death of

ukiyo-e painter Hishikawa Moronobu; death of Yanagi-
sawa Yoshiyasu (Yasuaki), *samurai* of 150 koku who became daimyo of Kofu (150,000 *koku*) through Tsunayoshi's favor.

1716–36 Kyoho year period.

1716–45 Shogunate of Yoshimune (d. 1751) of Kii branch of
Tokugawa.

1720 Relaxation of ban on importation of Western books.

1724 Death of Chikamatsu Monzaemon, playwright for
Joruri (puppet) theater.

1725 Death of Arai Hakuseki, scholar and Shogunal advisor
under Yoshimune.

1728 Death of Confucian scholar Ogyu Sorai.

1732–3 Famine in West Japan.

1734 Death of Confucian scholar Muro Kyuso.

1745–60 Shogunate of Ieshige (d. 1761).

1751 Death of Ooka Tadasuke, *samurai* and Shogunal administrator raised to be 10,000 *koku* daimyo.

1758 Punishment of Takenouchi Shikibu for teaching loyal-
ist doctrines to the Kyoto courtiers.

1760–86 Shogunate of Ieharu.

1769 Start of supremacy of Tanuma Okitsugu as a Roju;
death of Shinto scholar Kamo Mabuchi.

1779 Death in prison of botanist Hiraga Gennai.

1779–84 Stay of Titsingh in Japan.

1782 Compilation of *Gunsho Ruiju* (huge collection of early
works) by the blind scholar Hanawa Hokiichi.

1783 Eruption of Mt. Asama.

1784 Famine in North Honshu; assassination of Okitomo,
son of Okitsugu.

1786 Downfall of Okitsugu (d. 1788).

1787–1837 Shogunate of Ienari (d. 1841) of Hitotsubashi
branch of Tokugawa.

1787–93 Supremacy of Matsudaira Sadanobu as a Roju
(d. 1829).

1792 Imprisonment of Hayashi (Rin) Shihei for his imperialist writings; visit of the Russian Laxman to Hokkaido.

1798 Completion of *Kojiki-den* by Shinto scholar Motoori
Norinaga (d. 1801).

1801 Exploration of Sakhalin by Mamiya Rinzo.

1804–18 Bunka year period.

1804 Visit of Russian envoy Rezanov to Nagasaki.

1808 Visit to Nagasaki of British ship *Phaeton*.

1811 Establishment of Translation Bureau for Dutch books.

1813 Levy on Osaka and Edo merchants.

1814 Founding of Kurozumi Sect of Shinto by Kurozumi Munetada.

1818 Death of geographer Ino Tadayoshi (Chukei).

1818–30 Bunsei year period.

1823–9 (1830 in Western calendar) Siebold in Japan.

1825 Death of blockprint artist Utagawa Toyokuni.

1826 Compilation of *Nihon Gaishi* by Rai San'yo.

1830–44 Tempo year period.

1837 Rice riots in Osaka led by Confucian scholar Oshio Heihachiro; visit of American ship *Morrison* to Edo Bay and Nagasaki.

1837–53 Shogunate of Ieyoshi.

1838 Founding of Tenrikyo (Shinto sect) by a woman, Nakayama Miki.

1839 Imprisonment of the student of Dutch medicine, Takano Choei (d. 1850).

1841–3 Reforms of Mizuno Tadakuni (final retirement 1845, d. 1851).

1843 Death of Shinto scholar Hirata Atsutane.

1846 Visit of American Commodore Biddle to Uraga.

1848 Death of novelist Takizawa Bakin.

1849 Visit of American Glynn to Nagasaki; death of woodblock artist Katsushika Hokusai.

1852 Visit of Russians to Shimoda.

1853 Arrival of Commodore Matthew C. Perry at Uraga.

1853–8 Shogunate of Iesada.

1854 Treaty of Kanagawa with United States (March 31).

1856 Establishment of Bansho Torishirabesho (Office for the Study of Barbarian Books); arrival of Consul General Townsend Harris at Shimoda; death of philosopher-economist Ninomiya Sontoku.

1858–60 Ii Naosuke as Tairo.

1858–66 Shogunate of Iemochi.

1858 Commercial treaty with U. S. (July 29); death of woodblock artist Utagawa Hiroshige; founding of future Keio University by Fukuzawa Yukichi.

1859 Start of foreign trading community at Yokohama; execution of Yoshida Shoin, the anti-foreign Choshu scholar.

1860 Assassination of Ii Naosuke by Mito *samurai;* exchange in Washington of treaty ratifications by first embassy to U. S.; death of Tokugawa Nariaki of Mito, head of pro-imperial, anti-foreign faction.

1862 First Japanese embassy in Europe; murder of English-man Richardson at Namamugi near Yokohama by Satsuma *samurai;* relaxation of *Sankin-kotai.*

1863 Visit of Shogun to Kyoto; bombardment of foreign vessels by Choshu forts at Shimonoseki; bombardment of Kagoshima, capital of Satsuma, by British squadron; expulsion of Choshu forces from Kyoto.

1864 Bombardment of Shimonoseki by British, French, Dutch, and American ships.

1865 Imperial ratification of foreign treaties.

1866-7 Shogunate of Yoshinobu (Keiki, d. 1913), son of Nariaki of Mito.

1867 Enthronement of Mutsuhito (Meiji); return of power by Keiki to throne.

1868–1912 MEIJI PERIOD.

1868 Jan. 1, opening of Kobe and Osaka to foreign trade; Jan. 3, resumption of rule by emperor; April 6, emperor's Charter Oath; Nov. 26, establishment of Tokyo (Edo) as new capital.

1869 March 5, return of fiefs by Satsuma, Choshu, Tosa, and Hizen; July, appointment of daimyo as governors of their former fiefs; opening of telegraph line between Tokyo and Yokohama.

1870 Permission for commoners to take surnames.

1871 Start of mail service; Aug. 29, substitution of perfec-tures (*ken*) for fiefs; Sept. 2, establishment of Ministry of Education; Sept. 13, Treaty of Tientsin with China; Nov. 20, departure of Iwakura Mission, including Okubo and Ito, for America and Europe.

1872 Opening of railway between Tokyo and Yokohama.

1873 Jan. 1, adoption of Gregorian calendar in place of lunar calendar; Jan. 10, inauguration of universal military service; July 28, adoption of the new land tax system; Sept. 13, return of Iwakura Mission; Oct. 24, adoption of peaceful policy toward Korea; end of ban on Chris-tianity.

1874 Feb.–April, revolt of Eto Shimpei in Saga; May, victory of expeditionary force in Formosa under Saigo Tsu-gumichi; Oct. 31, Chinese agreement to indemnity for attack in 1871 of Formosans on Ryukyu merchants.

1875 April 14, creation of Genroin; May 7, agreement with Russia over exchange of Sakhalin for Kurile Islands; June 20, convening of Assembly of Prefectural Governors.

1876 Feb. 26, treaty with Korea; March 28, prohibition of carrying of swords by *samurai;* Aug. 5, compulsory commutation of *samurai* pensions; Oct., uprisings in Kumamoto and Hagi (Choshu).

1877 Feb.–Sept., Satsuma Rebellion and death of Saigo Takamori (Sept. 24); May 26, death of Kido Koin; founding of Tokyo University (reorganized 1886 as Tokyo Imperial University).

1878 May 14, assassination of Okubo Toshimichi.

1879 March 20, beginning of elected prefectural assemblies; April 4, incorporation of Okinawa (Ryukyu) as a prefecture.

1880 July 17, promulgation of revised penal code and code of criminal procedure.

1881 Oct. 12, decree promising the convening of a national assembly in 1890; Oct., founding of Jiyuto (Liberal Party) under Itagaki Taisuke and Kaishinto (Reform Party) under Okuma Shigenobu; Oct. 21, Matsukata Masayoshi as Finance Minister and inauguration of retrenchment policy.

1882 Feb. 27, dispatch of Ito Hirobumi to Europe to study constitutional systems; July 23, attack on Japanese consulate in Seoul; Oct. 10, founding of Bank of Japan; founding of Waseda University by Okuma.

1883 April 16, revision of press law; July 20, death of Itakura Tomomi.

1884 July 7, creation of peerage.

1885 April 18, Ito-Li Hung-chang convention at Tientsin concerning Korea; Dec. 22, adoption of cabinet system with Ito as first Premier.

1887 May 1, convening of treaty revision conference by Foreign Minister Inoue Kaoru; Dec. 26, promulgation of Peace Preservation Ordinance.

1888 April 30, Kuroda Kiyotaka succeeds Ito as Premier; April 30, creation of Privy Council (Sumitsuin).

1889 Feb. 11, promulgation of Constitution; Dec. 24, Gen. Yamagata Aritomo as Premier.

1890 July 1, first general election for Diet (convened Nov. 25); Oct. 20, abolition of Genroin; Oct. 30, promulgation of Imperial Rescript on Education.

1891 May 6, Matsukata succeeds Yamagata as Premier.

1892 Aug. 8, Ito again Premier (resigned Aug. 31, 1896).

1894 June 5, uprising in Korea; July 16, Aoki-Kimberley treaty to abolish British extraterritoriality in 1899; Aug. 1, declaration of war on China (Sino-Japanese War); Nov. 22, capture of Port Arthur.

1895 Feb. 12, capture of Wei-hai-wei; April 17, Treaty of Shimonoseki, concluding Sino-Japanese War and ceding Formosa, Pescadores, and Liaotung Peninsula to Japan; Dec. 4, return of Liaotung Peninsula after intervention of Russia, France, and Germany.

1897 March 29, adoption of gold standard.

1898 June 30, Okuma and Itagaki ministry of newly formed Kenseito Party; Nov. 8, Yamagata again Premier.

1899 July 17, coming into effect of revised treaties ending extraterritoriality.

1900 June 17–Aug. 14, participation of Japanese forces in capture of Taku, Tientsin, and Peking after Boxer Uprising; Sept. 13, founding of Seiyukai by Ito; Oct. 19, Ito again Premier.

1901 Feb. 3, death of educator Fukuzawa Yukichi; June 2, Yamagata's political protégé, Gen. Katsura Taro, as Premier.

1902 Jan. 30, signature of Anglo-Japanese Alliance.

1904 Feb. 9, attack on Russian navy; Feb. 10, declaration of war on Russia (Russo-Japanese War); Sept. 4, capture of Liao-yang.

1905 Jan. 1, surrender of Port Arthur; March 10, capture of Mukden; June 27–29, destruction of Russian fleet in Battle of Tsushima; Sept. 5, conclusion of Russo-Japanese War through Treaty of Portsmouth, ceding South Sakhalin to Japan and transferring to her the lease of Liaotung Peninsula; Nov. 17, signature by Ito of treaty of protection with Korea.

1906 Jan. 7, Ito's political protégé, Prince Saionji Kimmochi, as Premier; March 31, announcement of nationalization of railways; Nov. 26, founding of South Manchurian Railway.

1908 Feb. 18, Gentlemen's Agreement on Japanese emigration to U. S.; July 14, Katsura again Premier; Nov., Root-Takahira agreement with U. S.

1909 Oct. 26, assassination in Harbin by a Korean of Ito, recently retired as Resident-General in Korea.

1910 July 4, agreement with Russia on spheres of influence in Manchuria; Aug. 22, annexation of Korea; Sept. 30, creation of Government-General of Korea; Oct. 1, appointment of Gen. Terauchi Masatake as first Governor-General.

1912 July 30, death of Meiji Emperor and succession of his son Yoshihito; Aug. 30, Saionji again Premier (resigned Dec. 21, 1912).

1912–26 TAISHO PERIOD.

1913 Feb. 20, Admiral Yamamoto Gombei as Premier.

1914 April 16, Okuma as Premier; Aug. 23, Japanese declaration of war on Germany in First World War; Nov. 7, capture of Tsingtao.

1915 Jan. 18, presentation of the Twenty-One Demands on China; Sept. 1, death of Inoue.

1916 July 3, Russo-Japanese agreement on spheres on the continent; Aug. 13, clash with Chinese troops at Chengchia-tun; Oct. 9, Gen. Terauchi as Premier; Oct. 10, formation of Kenseikai; Dec. 9, death of novelist Natsume Soseki.

1917 Nov. 2, Lansing-Ishii exchange of notes with U. S.

1918 April 5, landing of Japanese and British forces at Vladivostok; May 16, defensive alliance with China; Sept. 29, Hara Kei (Satoshi) of Seiyukai as Premier.

1919 April, rebellion in Korea.

1920 Jan. 10, conclusion of peace with Germany; creation of Japanese Mandate over former German islands in North Pacific.

1921 March–Sept., trip of Crown Prince Hirohito to Europe; Nov. 4, assassination of Premier Hara; Nov. 12, start of Washington Conference; Nov. 13, Finance Minister Takahashi Korekiyo as Premier; Nov. 25, appointment of Hirohito as Prince Regent.

1922 Jan. 10, death of Okuma; Feb. 1, death of Yamagata; June 12, Admiral Kato Tomosaburo as Premier; Oct. 25, final withdrawal from Vladivostok; Nov. 30, signature of agreement with China for return of Kiaochow (Tsingtao).

1923 Sept. 1, great Tokyo earthquake; Sept. 2, Admiral Yamamoto as Premier.

1924 Jan. 7, Viscount Kiyoura Keigo as Premier; April 16, abrogation of Gentlemen's Agreement by U. S.; June 11, Kato Takaaki as Premier of a Kenseikai-Seiyukai cabinet with Shidehara Kijuro as Foreign Minister.

1925 Jan. 21, signature of Soviet-Japanese Convention in Peking; March 27, dropping of four army divisions; March 30, passage by Diet of universal manhood suffrage bill and peace preservation law.

1926 Jan. 30, Wakatsuki Reijiro of Kenseikai as Premier; Dec. 25, death of Taisho Emperor and accession of Hirohito.

1926– SHOWA PERIOD.

1927 April 20, General Tanaka Giichi of Seiyukai as Premier and his own Foreign Minister; April 21, bank crisis; May–June, armed intervention in Shantung in Chinese civil war; June 1, founding of Minseito.

1928 Feb. 20, first general election under universal manhood suffrage; March 15, mass arrest of Communists; April 10, banning of three "proletarian" parties; May 3–11, fighting at Tsinan; June 4, bombing attack in Manchuria on Chang Tso-lin (d. June 21); June 29, announcement of revised peace preservation law.

1929 July 2, Hamaguchi Osachi of Minseito as Premier with Shidehara as Foreign Minister.

1930 April 22, signature of London Naval Treaty; Nov. 14, wounding of Premier Hamaguchi by an assassin (d. Aug. 26, 1931).

1931 April 14, Wakatsuki of Minseito as Premier; Sept. 18, outbreak of "Manchurian incident;" Dec. 13, Inukai Ki (Tsuyoshi) of Seiyukai as Premier with Gen. Araki Sadao as War Minister; Dec. 14, abandonment of gold standard.

1932 Jan. 28–March 3, Shanghai campaign; Feb. 18, creation of Manchukuo; May 15, assassination of Premier Inukai by young army and navy officers ("5-15 incident"); May 26, Admiral Saito Minoru as Premier; July 24, formation of Shakai Taishuto (Social Mass Party).

1933 Feb. 24, adoption of Lytton Report on Manchuria by League of Nations; March 4, capture of capital of Jehol; May, disciplinary action against liberal professors at Kyoto Imperial University; May 31, Tangku truce; July 14, discovery of plot of the Shimpeitai ("God-Sent Troops"); Sept. 14, Hirota Koki as Foreign Minister.

1934 July 8, Admiral Okada Keisuke as Premier.

1935 March 23, sale of Chinese Eastern Railway by Soviet Union to Manchukuo; July 16, reorganization in army command shifting Gen. Mazaki Jinzaburo and others; Aug. 12, assassination of Gen. Nagata by Lt. Col. Aizawa for his supposed responsibility for army reorganization; Sept. 18, resignation of Professor Minobe Tatsukichi from House of Peers because of "organ theory"; Nov. 24, inauguration of East Hopei Autonomous Regime.

1936 Feb. 20, general elections; Feb. 26, assassination of Finance Minister Takahashi, Keeper of the Privy Seal Admiral Saito, and Inspector of Military Education Gen. Watanabe and attempted assassination of Premier Okada and Prince Saionji by soldiers of First Division ("2-26 incident"); March 9, Hirota as Premier with Gen. Terauchi Juichi as Army Minister; March 10, retirement of Gens. Hayashi, Mazaki, and Araki; May 17, return to active status requirement for Army and Navy Ministers; Nov. 25, Anti-Comintern Pact.

1937 Jan. 29, Gen. Ugaki Kazushige fails to form cabinet because of army opposition; Feb. 2, Gen. Hayashi Senjuro as Premier; April 30, general elections; June 4, Prince Konoe Fumimaro as Premier; July 7, outbreak of war with China; Aug. 8–Nov. 8, Shanghai campaign; Dec. 12, bombing of U. S. gunboat *Panay* on the Yangtse; Dec. 13, capture of Nanking.

1938 March 24, enactment of National Mobilization Law; June 26, Gen. Araki as Minister of Education and Gen. Ugaki as Foreign Minister (resigned Sept. 30); July 12– Aug. 10, battle with Russians at Changkufeng; Oct. 21, capture of Canton; Oct. 27, capture of Hankow area.

1939 Jan. 5, Baron Hiranuma Kiichiro as Premier; Feb. 10, landing on Hainan Island; April 2, fisheries agreement

with Soviet Union; April 28–July, fighting on Manchu-
kuo-Outer Mongolia border; July 27, denunciation of
1911 trade treaty by U. S. (effective in six months);
Aug. 23, German-Soviet non-aggression pact; Aug. 30,
Gen. Abe Nobuyuki as Premier; Sept. 1, outbreak of war
in Europe.

1940 Jan. 16, Admiral Yonai Mitsumasa as Premier; March
30, creation of Puppet Wang Ching-wei regime in Nanking; July 6–Aug. 15, dissolution of the political parties;
July 12, British agreement to close Burma Road for three
months; July 22, Prince Konoe again as Premier with
Matsuoka Yosuke as Foreign Minister and Gen. Tojo
Hideki as Army Minister; Sept. 23, entrance of Japanese troops into French Indo-China; Sept. 26, embargo
by U. S. of scrap shipments; Sept. 27, Tripartite Alliance
with Germany and Italy; Oct. 12, inauguration of Imperial Rule Assistance Association; Nov. 24, death of
Saionji, the last *Genro* (elder statesman).

1941 March 8, start of conversations between Secretary of
State Hull and Ambassador Nomura Kichisaburo; April
13, Soviet-Japanese neutrality pact; May 9, Japanese
sponsored peace treaty between Siam and Indo-China;
June 22, German invasion of Soviet Union; July 18, new
Konoe cabinet with Matsuoka excluded; July 24, Japanese occupation of southern Indo-China; July 26, freez-
ing of Japanese assets in U. S.; Aug. 1, licensing system
for oil shipments to Japan; Oct. 18, Gen. Tojo as Premier; Dec. 7, attack on Pearl Harbor and start of Pacific
War.

1942 Feb. 15, capture of Singapore; March 9, surrender of
Java; April 30, general elections (election of 381 government endorsed candidates out of 644); May 6, surrender of Corregidor; June 3–5, Battle of Midway;
Aug. 7–Feb. 9, 1943, Guadalcanal campaign; Sept. 17–25,
checking of Japanese advance in New Guinea; Nov. 1,
creation of Greater East Asia Ministry.

1943 Jan. 10, enactment of law ending municipal autonomy;
Nov. 1, creation of Munitions Ministry; Nov. 20–23, fall
of Tarawa.

1944 April 22, fall of Hollandia, New Guinea; June 19–
July 9, Saipan campaign; July 18, resignation of Tojo;
Gen. Koiso Kuniaki as Premier with support of Ad-

miral Yonai; Oct. 20, American landing on Leyte; Nov. 24, start of B-29 bombings of Japan.

1945 Feb. 5, fall of Manila; Feb. 19—March 17, Iwojima campaign; March 10 and April 6, great fire bomb raids on Tokyo; April 1—June 23, Okinawa campaign; April 7, Admiral Suzuki Kantaro as Prime Minister; May 8, German surrender; July 26, Potsdam Proclamation; Aug. 6 and 9, atomic bombings of Hiroshima and Nagasaki; Aug. 8, Soviet entrance into the war; Aug. 14, acceptance of terms of Potsdam Proclamation; Aug. 17, Prince Higashikuni as Prime Minister; Aug. 29, issuance to Gen. Douglas MacArthur of *U. S. Initial Post-Surrender Policy for Japan;* Sept. 2, formal surrender received by MacArthur; Oct. 4, "bill of rights" ordering release of political prisoners; Oct. 9, Shidehara Kijuro of Progressive Party as Prime Minister; Oct. 10, release of Communist leaders; Dec. 15, disestablishment of Shinto; Dec. 21, enactment of trade union law; Dec. 27, Moscow Agreement creating Far Eastern Commission and Allied Council for Japan.

1946 Jan. 1, emperor's denial of his own divinity; Jan. 4, first purge directive; April 10, first postwar elections; May 22, Yoshida Shigeru of Liberal Party as Prime Minister; Oct., enactment of land reform law.

1947 Feb. 1, banning of general strike of government employees by MacArthur; April 5, 20, and 25, local and national elections; May 3, new Constitution goes into effect; May 24, Katayama Tetsu of Socialist Party as Prime Minister; Sept. 1, creation of Labor Ministry; Dec. 9, enactment of economic deconcentration law.

1948 March 10, Ashida Hitoshi of Democratic Party as Prime Minister; June 28, Fukui earthquake; Oct. 15, Yoshida again Prime Minister; Dec. 23, execution of Tojo and six other major war criminals.

1949 Jan. 23, general elections and plebiscite on fourteen judges of Supreme Court; April 15, report of Joseph Dodge on budgetary retrenchment; uniform exchange rate of 360 yen to the dollar ordered by MacArthur; May 12, U. S. announcement of end of reparations removals and end of industrial limitations on Oct. 1; Aug. 17, case of railway sabotage.

1950 Feb. 9, authorization of Japanese government to establish overseas agencies; April 6, appointment of John

Foster Dulles as advisor to State Department; June 4, election for half of House of Councillors; June 6, purge of twenty-four members of Central Committee of Communist Party; June 7, purge of staff of Communist newspaper *Akahata* (banned June 26); June 25, invasion of South Korea by North Korea; Aug. 10, promulgation of ordinance creating National Police Reserve; Sept. 14, decision to proceed with preliminary discussions of Japanese peace treaty.

1951 April 11, dismissal of MacArthur; appointment of Gen. Matthew B. Ridgway as SCAP; April 23, local elections; June 20, lifting of purge restrictions on 69,000 persons; Aug. 6, depurging of almost 14,000 more persons, including Hatoyama Ichiro, former head of Liberal Party; Sept. 8, signing of peace treaty with 48 nations and security pact with U. S. at San Francisco; Oct. 24, split of Socialist Party.

1952 Feb. 28, signature of administrative agreement on terms for U. S. bases in Japan; March 28, peace treaty becomes effective; replacement of Gen. Ridgway by Gen. Mark W. Clark as U.N. and U.S. commander in Far East; May 1, anti-American riots in Tokyo; Sept. 18, Soviet Union vetoes Japanese admission to the United Nations; Oct. 1, general elections; Oct. 15, National Police Reserve reorganized as National Security Force.

1953 Feb. 1, start of NHK television broadcasts; March 14, nonconfidence vote in Yoshida and dissolution of Diet; March 18, Hatoyama Ichiro forms separate Liberal Party; April 19, House of Representatives and April 24, House of Councillors elections; May 21, Yoshida forms new Cabinet; July 27, cease-fire agreement in Korea; Aug. 28, start of private television broadcasts; Oct. 21, break-off of Korean-Japanese talks; Nov. 29, Hatoyama and his followers return to Liberal Party; Dec. 24, U. S. agrees to return of Amami group in Ryukyu Islands to Japan.

1954 March 1, fall-out injury to No. 5 *Fukuryu-maru* as result of Bikini nuclear tests; July 1, National Security Force reorganized as Self-Defense Force under Defense Agency; Sept. 27, sinking of Aomori-Hakodate ferry; Nov. 5, peace treaty and reparations agreement signed with Burma; Nov. 24, Hatoyama forms Democratic Party; Dec. 7, resignation of Yoshida Cabinet; Dec. 10, Hatoyama as Prime Minister.

1955 Feb. 27, House of Representatives elections; March 23, local elections; Aug. 6, first Ban the Atom Bomb World Conference held in Hiroshima; Sept. 10, Japan joins GATT (General Agreement on Tariffs and Trade); Sept. 13, start of struggles at Sunakawa over enlargement of Tachikawa Air Base; Oct. 13, reunification of Left and Right Socialists; Nov. 15, founding of Liberal-Democratic Party; Nov. 22, organization of third Hatoyama Cabinet on basis of new party; Dec. 13, Japanese membership in United Nations vetoed by Soviet Union.

1956 April 5, Hatoyama elected first President of Liberal-Democratic Party; April 30, passing of atomic energy laws; May 9, first Japanese-Soviet fisheries agreement; May 9, Philippine reparations agreement; May 19, establishment of Science and Technics Agency; May 21, passing of anti-prostitution law; July 8, House of Councillors elections; Oct. 19, joint statement normalizing relations with Soviet Union; Dec. 12, Japan admitted into the United Nations; Dec. 14, Ishibashi Tanzan elected President of Liberal-Democratic Party; Dec. 20, Hatoyama resigns; Dec. 23, Ishibashi as Prime Minister.

1957 Feb. 23, Prime Minister Ishibashi resigns because of illness; Feb. 25, Kishi Nobusuke as Prime Minister; March 21, Kishi elected President of Liberal-Democratic Party; Dec. 6, signing of Treaty of Commerce with Soviet Union.

1958 Jan. 20, signing of reparations agreement with Indonesia; April 25, dissolution of House of Representatives; May 2, Chinese Communist flag incident in Nagasaki leading to break-off of trade relations with Japan; May 22, House of Representatives election; June 12, Kishi reorganizes Cabinet; Sept. 12, Foreign Minister Fujiyama and Secretary of State Dulles announce agreement to revise security pact.

1959 Jan. 25, Kishi re-elected President of Liberal-Democratic Party; March 9, Asanuma, Secretary General of Socialist Party, makes statement that "American imperialism" is "common enemy" of Communist China and Japan; April 10, the Crown Prince marries a commoner, Miss Shoda Michiko; May 13, reparations agreement with South Vietnam; Aug. 13, agreement for repatriation of Koreans to North Korea.

1960 Jan. 19, signing of Treaty of Mutual Security and Cooperation with United States; Jan. 24, founding of Democratic Socialist Party under leadership of Nishio; May 19-
20, Kishi pushes through ratification of Security Treaty in
House of Representatives; May 26, around 100,000 anti-
treaty demonstrators surround Diet; June 10, Presidential
Press Secretary Hagerty mobbed at Haneda Airport; June
15, giant anti-treaty demonstration in Tokyo, rioting by
Zengakuren, Tokyo University girl student trampled to
death; June 16, cancellation of scheduled visit of President Eisenhower; June 19, automatic ratification of Security Treaty; July 14, Ikeda Hayato elected President
of Liberal-Democratic Party; July 19, Ikeda forms Cabinet; Sept. 5, announcement of plan to double incomes
in ten years; Oct. 12, Chairman Asanuma of Socialist
Party stabbed to death; Oct. 24, dissolution of House of
Representatives; Nov. 1, settlement of Miike coal mine
strike; Nov. 20, general elections.

1961 March 8, Kawakami Jotaro elected chairman of Socialist
Party; June 10, agreement on repayment to United States
of GARIOA debts (economic assistance during occupation period); June 19-30, Ikeda visits United States and
Canada; Oct. 20, reopening for sixth time of negotiations for normalization of relations with South Korea;
Nov. 2-4, first meeting in Hakone of U.S.–Japan Committee on Trade and Economic Affairs.

1962 Jan. 25-31, first U.S.–Japan Cultural Conference; March
19, President Kennedy's statement on U.S.–Japanese cooperation on economic aid to Okinawa; July 17, Ikeda
re-elected President of Liberal-Democratic Party; July 18,
Ikeda reorganizes Cabinet; Nov. 4-25, Ikeda visits Europe;
Nov. 29, Narita replaces Eda as Secretary General of
Socialist Party.

1963 March 28, Lord Home makes first visit of a British
Foreign Secretary to Japan; April 12, Couve de Murville
makes first visit of a French Foreign Minister; April 17,
local elections; July 18, Ikeda reorganizes cabinet; July
26, Japan invited to become full member of OECD (Organization for Economic Cooperation and Development);
Nov. 6, visit of President Luebke and Foreign Minister
Schroeder of Germany; Nov. 21, general elections; Dec.
9, Ikeda reconstitutes cabinet.

BIBLIOGRAPHICAL NOTE

Those for whom this volume is their introduction to Japanese history may wish some guidance in further reading. For a more thorough account of the premodern period, I would recommend first the chapters on Japan in the volume I wrote with Professor John K. Fairbank, *East Asia: The Great Tradition* (Houghton Mifflin, Boston, 1960). (The chapters on China and Korea in this book afford a helpful background for those who can go deeper into the subject, and a companion volume, to be entitled *East Asia: The Modern Transformation* will soon bring the story up to date.) A delightfully written classic on premodern Japanese history is Sir George Sansom's *Japan, A Short Cultural History* (revised edition, Appleton-Century, N. Y., 1944). More detailed accounts by the same author are to be had in *A History of Japan to 1334* and *A History of Japan, 1334-1615* (Stanford University Press, Stanford, 1958 and 1961; a third volume telling the story up to the nineteenth century should be following soon). An invaluable series of translated readings in traditional Japanese history, with appropriate comments, is Tsunoda Ryusaku, William Theodore de Bary, and Donald Keene's *Sources of the Japanese Tradition* (Columbia University Press, N. Y., 1958). Among the many accounts of specific aspects of premodern history, I might mention my own *Ennin's Travels in T'ang China* (Ronald Press, N. Y., 1955); C. R. Boxer, *The Christian Century in Japan, 1549-1650* (University of California Press, Berkeley, 1951); John W. Hall, *Tanuma Okitsugu, 1719-1788: Forerunner of Mod-*

ern Japan (Harvard University Press, Cambridge, 1955); and Thomas C. Smith, *Agrarian Origins of Modern Japan* (Stanford University Press, Stanford, 1959).

In the field of religion the newcomer to Japanese history may find helpful Anesaki Masaharu's *History of Japanese Religion* (Kegan Paul, London, 1930) and William K. Bunce's *Religions in Japan* (Tuttle, Rutland, Vermont, and Tokyo, 1955), while those with particular interest in Zen Buddhism might well start with two of T. D. Suzuki's many volumes, *An Introduction to Zen Buddhism* (Philosophical Library, N. Y., 1949) and *Studies in Zen* (Rider, London, 1955).

I hesitate to suggest specific titles among the many excellent books on Japanese art, but good starting points might be Robert Treat Paine and Alexander Soper, *The Art and Architecture of Japan* (Penguin Books, 1955), Langdon Warner, *The Enduring Art of Japan* (Harvard University Press, Cambridge, 1952; Evergreen Books), and, on the woodblock prints of the Tokugawa Period and their background, James Michener, *The Floating World* (Random House, N. Y., 1954).

For Japanese literature an excellent start would be Donald Keene, *Japanese Literature, An Introduction for Western Readers* (Murray, N. Y., 1953), while a more comprehensive though less readable volume has been published by the Kokusai Bunka Shinkokai under the title *Introduction to Classic Japanese Literature* (Tokyo, 1948). Donald Keene has also provided an excellent *Anthology of Japanese Literature, from the Earliest Era to the Mid-Nineteenth Century* (Grove Press, N. Y., 1955). Japan's greatest classic has, through Arthur Waley's superb translation, become an English classic: *The Tale of Genji* (Allen and Unwin, London; Literary Guild, N. Y., 1935; the first section is also available in Anchor Books). Among more recent translations and detailed studies are Robert H. Brower and Earl Miner, *Japanese Court Poetry* (Stanford University Press, Stanford, 1961); Harold G. Henderson, *An Introduction to Haiku* (Doubleday, N. Y., 1958); Howard Hibbett, *The Floating World in Japanese Fiction* (Oxford University Press, London and N. Y., 1959); William Theodore de Bary, *Five Women Who Loved Love* (Tuttle, Rutland, Vermont, and Tokyo, 1956); Charles Ernst, *The Kabuki Theatre* (Oxford University Press, N. Y., 1956; Evergreen Books); and Donald Keene's two works, *The Battles of Coxinga: Chikamatsu's Puppet Play, Its Background and Im-*

portance (Taylor's Foreign Press, London, 1951) and *Major Plays of Chikamatsu* (Columbia University Press, N. Y., 1961).

For a general view of the past century of Japanese history, there is Richard Storry's brief book, *A History of Modern Japan* (Pelican Books, 1960) and two much fuller volumes, Hugh Borton, *Japan's Modern Century* (Ronald Press, N. Y., 1955) and Chitoshi Yanaga, *Japan Since Perry* (McGraw-Hill, N. Y., 1949). These are backed up on the economic side by a comprehensive volume, William W. Lockwood, *The Economic Development of Japan; Growth and Structural Change 1868-1938* (Princeton University Press, Princeton, 1954) and, on the Meiji period, by a whole series of volumes on special topics translated from the Japanese, such as Kosaka Masaaki (translated and adapted by David Abosch), *Japanese Thought in the Meiji Era* (Pan-Pacific Press, Tokyo, 1958) and Kishimoto Hideo (translated and adapted by John Howes), *Japanese Religion in the Meiji Era* (Obunsha, Tokyo, 1956).

Among the more specialized studies of modern Japanese history which one can recommend with confidence are Albert M. Craig, *Choshu in the Meiji Restoration* (Harvard University Press, Cambridge, 1961); Marius B. Jansen, *Sakamoto Ryoma and the Meiji Restoration* (Princeton University Press, Princeton, 1961); Sir George Sansom, *The Western World and Japan* (Knopf, N. Y., 1950), which treats the Western intellectual and cultural influence on Japan during the nineteenth century; Nobutake Ike, *The Beginnings of Political Democracy in Japan* (Johns Hopkins Press, Baltimore, 1950); Robert Scalapino, *Democracy and the Party Movement in Pre-War Japan* (University of California Press, Berkeley, 1955); Robert Storry, *The Double Patriots* (Chatto and Windus, London, 1957), which tells of the rightist movements of the 1930's; F. C. Jones, *Japan's New Order in East Asia: Its Rise and Fall, 1937-1945* (Oxford University Press, London, 1954); Herbert Feis, *The Road to Pearl Harbor* (Princeton University Press, Princeton, 1950); Robert J. C. Butow's two volumes, *Tojo and the Coming of the War* (Princeton University Press, Princeton, 1961) and *Japan's Decision to Surrender* (Stanford University Press, Stanford, 1954); and J. B. Cohen, *Japan's Economy in War and Reconstruction* (University of Minnesota Press, Minneapolis, 1949).

Of the spate of books on the American occupation, perhaps

the most comprehensive and well balanced is Kazuo Kawai, *Japan's American Interlude* (Chicago University Press, Chicago, 1960), while my own book, *The United States and Japan* (revised edition, Harvard University Press, Cambridge, 1957; Compass Books) offers a fuller account than does this present volume of this phase of Japanese history as well as a broader look at Japanese-American relations. Yoshida Shigeru, *The Yoshida Memoirs* (Houghton Mifflin, Boston, 1962) throws light on an aspect of postwar history, while three somewhat parallel volumes analyze postwar Japanese politics: Chitoshi Yanaga, *Japanese People and Politics* (Wiley, N. Y., 1956); Nobutake Ike, *Japanese Politics: An Introductory Survey* (Knopf, N. Y., 1957); and Ardath W. Burks, *The Government of Japan* (Crowell Company, N. Y., 1961). *Parties and Politics in Contemporary Japan* (University of California Press, Berkeley, 1962) by Robert A. Scalapino and Junnosuke Masumi includes a chapter on the 1960 riots. Ivan Morris, *Nationalism and the Right Wing in Japan* (Oxford University Press, London, 1960) is a specialized study of considerable interest.

In the field of sociology, two works on prewar Japan are worth mentioning: Ruth Benedict, *The Chrysanthemum and the Sword* (Houghton Mifflin, Boston, 1946), which was a pioneer effort to analyze Japanese society and personality, and John F. Embree, *Suyemura: A Japanese Village* (University of Chicago Press, Chicago, 1939; Kegan Paul, London, 1946). On postwar Japan we have Donald Keene, *Living Japan* (Doubleday, N. Y., 1959), which is a pictorial and non-scholarly introduction to contemporary Japan, and such excellent scholarly studies as R. K. Beardsley, J. W. Hall, and R. E. Ward, *Village Japan* (Chicago University Press, Chicago, 1959) and Ronald P. Dore's two books, *City Life in Japan* (University of California Press, Berkeley, 1958) and *Land Reform in Japan* (Oxford University Press, London, 1959).

Since the end of the war a series of fine translations of the works of contemporary Japanese authors has appeared. Among the best of these are those published by Alfred A. Knopf of New York. These include Jiro Osaragi, *Homecoming* (Brewster Horwitz, 1954); Junichiro Tanizaki, *Some Prefer Nettles* and *The Makioka Sisters;* and Yasunari Kawabata, *Snow Country* and *Thousand Cranes* (all translated by

Edward G. Seidensticker, 1955, 1957, 1956 and 1959); Yukio Mishima, *The Sound of Waves* (Meredith Weatherby, 1956); Shohei Ooka, *Fires on the Plain;* and Yukio Mishima, *The Temple of the Golden Pavilion* (both translated by Ivan Morris, 1957 and 1959); and Junichiro Tanizaki, *The Key* and *Seven Japanese Tales* (both translated by Howard Hibbett, 1961 and 1963).

INDEX

[*Numerals in italics refer to maps.* Names that appear only in the "Chronology" are not included.]

PRINTER'S NOTE

This book was set on the Linotype in Janson, a recutting made direct from type cast in matrices made by Anton Janson some time between 1660 and 1687. This type is an excellent example of the influential and singularly sturdy Dutch types that prevailed in England prior to Caslon. It was from the Dutch types that Caslon developed his own incomparable designs.

The book was printed and bound by The Haddon Craftsmen, Inc., Scranton, Pennsylvania.